"This extraordinarily important book could not be better timed, nor could it have a more credible author. Haroon Ullah has been, and remains, a key figure in disputing the cyber/information sphere, and waging digital conflict with those who would traffic in terror, disinformation, and hatred. It was my honor to serve with him in this struggle, one in which he will be recognized as a leader for years to come. Ullah has done us all a great service in writing this marvelously researched and splendidly written book." John R. Allen, General, U.S. Marine Corps (Ret.), Former Special Presidential Envoy to the Global Coalition to Counter ISIL

"As we come upon nearly a decade of intense protests and revolutions across the Middle East, social media has demonstrated its enormous potential to mobilize citizens and challenge regimes. In this important new book, Haroon Ullah provides a comprehensive analysis of the interplay between political rebels and cyber communities—and how they will reshape the world's most turbulent region." Parag Khanna, author of *Connectography*

"Through research, deep knowledge and one-of-a-kind experience, Haroon Ullah brings to life the fight for hearts and minds with digital and social media as a proxy. In a world that is more connected than ever before, *Digital World War* examines how information, tools, and platforms are remaking the Muslim world. Everyone should read this book." Jonathan Perelman, former VP at Buzzfeed Studios, Director of Digital at ICM Partners

"Haroon Ullah's visceral first-person story takes us across enemy lines on the emerging digital battlefield." Nova Spivack, co-founder and CEO, Bottlenose

"Haroon Ullah has had a front-row seat to radical Islam's rise in South Asia and the Middle East—and to how social media has increasingly shaped political landscapes in these regions. The result is a must-read book, challenging stereotypes about how Islamist and extremist movements both use, and are fueled by, social media. Ullah argues that a more nuanced understanding of the dynamic environment in which these groups and their opponents operate would provide the West with greater opportunity to navigate an ever-changing online and political terrain."—Kenneth R. Weinstein, President and CEO, Hudson Institute

"Haroon Ullah's book is a must-read for anyone who wants to understand the future of public diplomacy. The digital war going on right now for the hearts and minds of young people throughout the Muslim world is the single most critical battle for global peace."—Marc B. Nathanson, entrepreneur, investor, and philanthropist, former Chair of the US Broadcasting Board of Governors

"We've badly needed someone to make sense of the countervailing forces of repression and revolt unleashed by Web 2.0 in Islamic countries. Thank goodness Ullah has done it. Few have his policy chops and expertise; fewer still can match his eloquence. The result is an absorbing account of the war of digital words being waged in Muslim Asia and Africa and

what it portends for the region and the world."—Will McCants, author of *The ISIS Apocalypse* and Director of the Brookings Institution project on US Relations with the Islamic World

"Haroon Ullah has written a unique book, offering a panoramic view of 'digital warriors' across the Muslim world. Rather than focusing on young English-speaking liberals, Ullah shows us a dizzying and fascinating world where Islamist groups are fusing religion and cutting-edge technology to pursue their goals. Everyone who thought they knew about social media's role in revolt and rebellion should read Ullah's account." Shadi Hamid, Senior Fellow, Brookings Institution and author of *Islamic Exceptionalism: How the Struggle Over Islam is Reshaping the World*

"In view of recent events, *Digital World War* makes an unquestionably timely and valuable contribution. The geographical breadth of the author's discussion is matched by his analysis of a wide variety of online platforms and techniques employed by many different Islamist organizations (both moderate and extremist) in their efforts to recruit followers and disseminate their messages. The overall picture of a cyber-savvy community of discourse whose adept use of social media is inherently radicalizing is an ominous one." James Jankowski, author of *Egypt: A Short History*

"*Digital World War* unfolds like a novel, haunting and gripping. This is the new *Homeland* TV series." Ahmos Hassan, CEO of Chariot Management

"One of the best books this year. Haroon Ullah is a visionary and master storyteller. He has given us a roadmap to win this war." Ben Silverman, CEO of Propagate, former co-chairman of NBC Entertainment and Universal Studios

"Haroon Ullah is one of those rare persons that sees patterns on the information and intelligence battlefield and what's at stake for our children's generation." Steve Petruso, retired senior intelligence officer

DIGITAL WORLD WAR

DIGITAL
WORLD
WAR

ISLAMISTS, EXTREMISTS, AND THE
FIGHT FOR CYBER SUPREMACY

HAROON K. ULLAH

YALE UNIVERSITY PRESS
NEW HAVEN AND LONDON

Copyright © 2017 Haroon K. Ullah

For information about this and other Yale University Press publications, please contact:
US Office: sales.press@yale.edu   yalebooks.com
Europe Office: sales@yaleup.co.uk   yalebooks.co.uk

Typeset in Adobe Caslon Pro by IDSUK (DataConnection) Ltd
Printed in the United States of America

Library of Congress Control Number: 2017948472

ISBN 978-0-300-23110-6

A catalogue record for this book is available from the British Library.

10 9 8 7 6 5 4 3 2 1

To my brother Muneer Ullah,
who taught me how to love and learn
(1990–2015)

CONTENTS

INTRODUCTION

The Medium is the Message

IT WAS ANOTHER of those gruesome online videos put
out by extremists that, with weary repugnance, the
world has come to expect. Yet this was not simply your
run-of-the-mill display of wanton bloodshed captured on
a terrorist's shaky, low-definition cell phone: this was a
high-end production, shot in super-HD on state-of-the-
art cameras, and showed a considerable level of skill in
digital manipulation. It depicted Salman Taseer, the
governor of Punjab, speaking at a public event in Lahore,
footage that was intercut with shockingly realistic
computer-generated pictures of him in the process of
being beheaded by a black-cloaked figure wielding a
gleaming broadsword. This was a "virtual" beheading,
designed by skilled propagandists in the digital realm, and
shared on the social media forums 4chan and Playit.pk
(Pakistan's answer to the banned YouTube) to reach and

mobilize a niche, targeted audience. This online video marked Taseer for death.

It was in January 2011 when that virtual threat became a reality. Taseer was leaving the Kohsar market in Islamabad to meet a friend for lunch when a member of his own security team stepped forward with a machine gun and fired a volley at him from ten feet away. Taseer was struck twenty-six times and died on the spot.

Living a few blocks from Kohsar market at the time, I knew the apparently safe, middle-class area in Islamabad well. I could feel the change that had come over Pakistan in recent years: tragic assassinations had become more common; government dominance did not seem as strong. It was also all too clear why Taseer had been targeted. A prominent politician, a supporter of the 1960s democratization campaign, and a trusted advisor to Benazir Bhutto during her two terms as prime minister, Taseer was also a successful businessman, and throughout his career had been outspoken in his belief that democracy and pluralism are inseparable and that all religious minorities should be allowed to vote in general elections—opinions antithetical to the positions taken by hardline Islamic fundamentalists. Recently Taseer had particularly outraged them by criticizing Pakistan's strict blasphemy laws as unjust and indefensible, arguing that they were being abused by extremists and that Islamic law should not supplant the laws of the state.

Taseer was no stranger to the fact that his beliefs and views put him in danger, most notably from al-Qaeda and the Taliban: he had received numerous death threats over the years, even served time in prison, and his son was then still being held as a hostage in an extremist camp in Pakistan. And political assassinations were nothing new. But this time, something different was afoot. Living in the region at the time, I could see how the internet and digital technology were fundamentally altering the terrain of politics. Non-state actors were launching new offensives on government, with a different set of tactics, ammunition, and insurgency—a digital war on a digital battlefield.

So it was that, long before his gruesome murder, Salman Taseer was enmeshed as an enemy combatant in an online battle across various social media platforms as his avatar was targeted with cyber weapons. Short audio clips of his speeches were taken out of context, cut, packaged, and shared by "key influencers" on Facebook and Twitter. Websites and blogs were dedicated to smearing him and others who were deemed to have "crossed the line." Geolocation software tracked his movements in real time. Some extremists employed bots to retweet inflammatory content against him. And, in a few cases, TV networks carried some of the coverage reported online as "breaking news." Fake news had gone multimedia.

And the digital war didn't end with Taseer's death. As shocking as the assassination was, the aftermath was even

more so. When the perpetrator, Malik Mumtaz Hussain Qadri, a member of the "moderate" Sufi organization Ahle Sunnat Wal Jamaat, arrived at court several days after the murder, he was met by cheering crowds who showered him with flowers. Much of the adulation was being stoked online, as fanboys hailed Qadri as a hero on websites and blogs; Qadri became the most popular trending topic on Twitter in the region. In the following weeks, religious confessional political parties used social media to mobilize marches of up to 40,000 people, honoring Qadri's "heroic" action and celebrating Taseer's death. Even more disconcerting, moderate political leaders remained silent, issuing bland statements acknowledging Taseer's passing, but not speaking out against the mass rallies in support of vigilante Islamism, afraid of their comments going viral and their families being attacked and threatened; indeed, the provincial court judge who found Qadri guilty of murder was forced to flee the country after his home address was posted online. Extremist groups successfully pressured the government to suspend the case against Qadri indefinitely. Finally, after years of delays, Mumtaz Qadri was convicted of murder and hanged in February 2016. But he continued to be a hero to many, online and offline. Long before extremists struck in the well-to-do area of Islamabad— and long afterward—they jubilantly celebrated their victory in digital territory.

* * *

A second video, released in 2015. The screen literally hops with upbeat pop music as an attractive, Middle Eastern teenager sits in his room, thinking about what he wants out of life: nice clothes, cool friends, a "hipster" lifestyle— things that maybe seem far off amid all the chaos and turmoil of the Middle East. But the video also makes clear that true happiness isn't really anchored in the physical world; there's also the spiritual side, with or without religion. The slick, unremittingly positive video encourages its viewers to always foster peace and goodwill toward men in all walks of life, and offers the promise of a better future for the young than their fathers have known.

The video runs to only seventy seconds, but presents a powerful narrative of hope and positive thinking. Within days of its release it had gone viral across the Middle East; within weeks it had grabbed 14 million views, making YouTube stars of the original actors. Immediately, young people across the region reposted the video and various versions of it on social media, editing their own version on the Snap app, and creating and uploading GIFs on Telegram, WhatsApp, and Signal, along with scores of other messaging apps. It was a counterblast to the huge amount of extremist video content proliferating online. As one young man in Cairo commented on the Facebook posting of the video, "This is why ISIS, al-Qa'ida and Taliban should be afraid. The Resistance strikes back!"

It wasn't long before the video caught the notice of others who looked to use it for their own ends. In Amman, a group of Jordanian college students formed an online group inspired by the video, and made copies of it with their own branding inserted. In Fez, Morocco, a group of students decided to put together a sixty-second-film festival to encourage the production of videos on the theme of tolerance and unity. In the Egyptian capital, the video and its knock-offs were reposted and repurposed as memes by civil society groups (including those affiliated with the ousted Muslim Brotherhood) and various community coalitions to rally more recruits and raise funds. Distributing such videos with their own name and logo inserted at beginning and end, the groups were thumbing their nose at the establishment, propounding the idea that the status quo was doing all it could to keep the younger generation down, in its place. On the Telegram app, several channels remain devoted to new ideas for media productions based on the viral film.

But where did the original video come from? Who was reaching out and communicating a message of hope to so many millions?

In 2016, researching this video led me to Jeddah, Saudi Arabia's second largest city. It was near the holiest city in Islam that I stumbled upon what might be called a "social media incubator" by the name of UTURN, a production company tucked away in a small, nondescript

office building on the outskirts of the city. This tech savvy group, or alliance, was responsible for the video and much other media content that had created a huge buzz across the region.[1] Though young Saudis (and Gulf youth in general) were among the earliest and savviest of digital consumers, with some data suggesting they constitute the largest viewership of YouTube videos per capita in the world (over 5.5 hours a day), it was still hard to believe that many of the enormous ripple effects across the digital landscape were emanating from this unassuming studio in Jeddah.

As I visited with UTURN's chief executive officer, a young man named Kaswara, he pulled back the curtain of his hidden empire. He kindly showed me around the facility which housed lots of "green rooms" where highly creative tech artists were developing unique content. The whole place was bustling with laptop-wielding young men and women in loose flowing thobes. The UTURN staff view themselves as a grassroots resistance team working against militant jihadist groups and caliphate wannabes. Kaswara explained that they maintained a 24/7 eye on terror groups using a sophisticated monitoring dashboard with all the bells and whistles—some of the best Big Data counter-extremist analytical tools I have ever seen.

Kaswara and a senior associate showed me a horrific, frame-by-frame breakdown of the iconic ISIS video of the downed Jordanian fighter pilot being burned to death in a steel cage. The clip was meant to scare and terrorize, which

it certainly did, sending shivers of horror across the globe as it went viral in February 2015. The extremists released the video in multiple versions, suitable for distribution across various platforms—one three minutes long, and a longer, movie-like version, scarcely watchable for its visceral ghastliness.

UTURN didn't look away. Instead it distributed the appalling video to their key subscribers and content creators to help show the young and the righteous the level of evil they were up against. In so doing, they empowered anyone with a mobile phone to take part in the movement for a better world. Nothing illustrates this battle for superiority on the digital battlefield more than the work and activity at UTURN.

* * *

Huge advances in digital technology have led to seismic rebellions that have swept across the Muslim world in recent years, risings led by Islamists who more often than not have used social media and associated networking technology to harass and defeat regimes—corrupt, secular, or both—at the ballot box. Social media has enabled these digital rebels to wage guerrilla warfare on their own terms and without the need for massive budgets— heralding, quite literally, the "weaponization of information." From recruitment, mobilization, and organizing gatherings to donations, digital apps, censorship evasion,

image protection, hacking, and unlikely alliances between governments and private sector conglomerates, the ability to exploit social media is a game-changer of enormous importance.

It comes as no surprise that in many Muslim-majority nations there is a conspicuous official distrust of the internet. Muslim governments claim that social media "causes unrest." Turkey's ruler has called Twitter a "menace"—which it certainly is, to those in power, if enough citizens are unhappy. If it used to be the case that, in these heavily censored regimes, "Big Brother is watching you," these days it is Little Brother who is doing the watching and the rulers who are afraid. With 125 million of the 381 million living in the Middle East and North Africa connected to the internet, and with populations of which, on average, around 60 per cent are under thirty years old, many in these countries (over 53 million) are actively engaged with social media technology and recognize its power to oppose the establishment. As was proved most forcefully by the peer-to-peer Arab Spring revolts in 2010–12—in which social media played a crucial role—the old guard in many Muslim countries is being challenged, even pushed aside, often rather unceremoniously. As a message on social networks during the 2011 Egypt revolution stated, "If your government shuts down your internet, it's time to shut down your government."

One of the catalysts for much of the radical upheaval in the Middle East and South Asia during the last few years—

what has been stoking the fires of "freedom" at the grass-roots level—has been the empowering of ordinary, often disenfranchised citizens via their smartphones and laptops. Rather than needing deep pockets and years of work to organize and mobilize enough bodies to threaten a sitting government, now it takes only a few hours and a $20 per month internet connection to start a revolution. The enrichment of the information environment brought about by social media—from the increased ability to evade government censorship, to the advent of "citizen reporting" and a plethora of news and views, to exposés as well as increasingly sophisticated propaganda wars—has itself been emboldening. "As the communications landscape gets denser, more complex, and more participatory," writes Clay Shirky, "the networked population is gaining greater access to information, more opportunities to engage in public speech, and an enhanced ability to undertake collective action."[2] Though a number of studies have—rightly—challenged the idea that recent political revolts can be defined as direct and sole products of social media,[3] the accessibility of these constantly evolving platforms has created a new outlet for public expression and global communication. Certainly, revolutions do not occur because of Twitter or Facebook, but their role in providing a meaningful outlet for public disenfranchisement should not be overlooked.

Data gathered and developed over the last few years indicate that Muslim social networking is a major causal

factor in the exponential increase of new voters in the Islamic world. Citizens view social media as a kind of "edutainment," a new phenomenon in the political arena, and one that is helping to convince young people everywhere that taking part in politics is not just for their parents' generation. Now ordinary citizens are able to "click-and-play" their way to political power—whether that is as conspicuous, democratic voters, or as elusive forces using virtual private networks and identity- and location-concealing apps in order to operate with more freedom than ever before. Social media, then, provides not only a useful means for the spreading of information or the promotion of a particular message—though those are clearly important components. The technology itself is effecting change. In this way, the 1960s media guru Marshall McLuhan's most-cited dictum, "The medium is the message," reverberates throughout the Muslim-majority world today.

Yet, as pervasive as Twitterstorms, grainy mobile phone video footage of electoral fraud, or YouTube coverage of street riots have been in (more traditional) Western media, they are hardly the whole story. What most Western observers fail to fully realize is that much of the Islamic world's upheaval can be traced directly to the tactics employed by many and varied groups who are uniquely skilled at using social media to achieve their own ends. Though we may be sadly all too familiar with the Hollywood sheen of barbaric ISIS videos and images, many other

extremists, as well as more moderate Islamist groups, are harnessing the power of social media. In every country in which they have a presence, the Islamists have proven more adept at using social media than established governments, and indeed almost all other politically active forces, crippling ruling parties first in the court of public opinion and then on election day. These groups' younger cadres took up digital technology with more facility than the legions of complacent, and often older, government bureaucrats and authorities, who summarily failed to perceive the need, or to muster the capacity, for online campaigns that might gain support and reinforce loyalty. This tardiness proved damaging and many governments are still playing catch-up. In the meantime, these upstarts are changing the way millions of people live and choose their leaders.

Digital World War looks closely at what happens when the Islamists' and extremists' social media activity moves from harassment—the modern-day versions of James Scott's "weapons of the weak"[4]—to become a serious threat to sitting governments. This asymmetrical warfare has led to nothing short of a redrawing of the political map and the emergence of new political actors capturing prominent roles in and out of power.

In analyzing the range of social media behavior in the Islamic world, in this book I use the terms "Islamists" and "extremists"—for the sake of convenience—to differentiate between different types of organizations. While all

organizations purportedly based on Islam agree that Islamic tenets should inform governance, they vary tremendously in how strictly they interpret religious laws and how significant they believe government's role in enforcing those laws should be: the distinction between the groups thus concerns the various organizations' public positions on state enforcement of religious mores, not party members' personal adherence to religious law or practices.[5] In one corner, then, "extremists" include fundamentalist groups committed to using violence to impose their version of religious law and build a theocratic state. "Extremism" indicates engagement in a very specific set of behaviors that arguably pose a threat to democracy.[6] Less radical are the Islamists. These parties are "Muslim" in that they believe that Islamic teachings should inform public policy, and they support calls for civil enforcement of some religious laws. But they do not always look to the Koran for specific policy prescriptions, promote a literal interpretation of religious texts, or support major political or economic reforms derived from a fundamentalist view of the Koran. In terms of their use of social media, we could say that, simply put, most media-wise Islamist parties attempt to make a "mass market" play with an eye to compete and win in the mainstream political arena. For many of the extremists, on the other hand, it is not a matter of electoral revolution: they are geared toward attracting niche audiences (foreign fighters) and fueling local fears in order to leverage security payments.

This schema, however, is certainly not meant to suggest that there are strict, permanent, or even obvious demarcations between the organizations that fall under each category; in fact, the opposite is the case. Throughout this book I see Islamic-based organizations existing on a spectrum, ranging from an insistence on the necessity of the Muslim world being governed by religious law, to the belief that religious authority has no place in governance. On this sharia–secularism continuum, extremists would be placed at the sharia end, with Islamists located nearer to the middle. This notion of a continuum bears some resemblance to Ishtiaq Ahmed's conception of four ideological orientations among public audiences, which range from "a sacred state excluding human will" to "a secular state excluding divine will."[7] The spectrum I propose is, of course, not a straightforward disaggregation of distinct groups. For instance, the fact that Islamist parties share roughly similar conceptions of the role that sharia should play in govern-ance should not obscure the significant differences in their political programs, their different interpretations of what sharia entails, or the contested nature of the term "sharia" itself.[8] That helps to explain the surprising fact that Islamist parties occupying much the same space on the continuum are as likely to disagree with one another as they are with groups to their right or left. Parties that are close on the continuum will often compete more fiercely

with each other than with their supposed ideological opponents.

Furthermore, as I shall show, religion-based political parties and extremist groups frequently move back and forth along this spectrum in order to gain political advantage. Organizations locked in a close electoral race will often make surprising ideological shifts as they angle for votes. The party's original position on the spectrum constrains its options for ideological maneuvering, but it does not dictate them. Even if Islamist parties hold to their theological underpinnings, their leaders are not singularly (or even primarily) committed to pursuing a purely ideological agenda: like all political parties and groups, Islamic-based organizations want to exert power and influence. So we see a form of politics that talks sharia law to attract the mosque-going masses, while backing carefully selected democratic norms that appeal to the more secular voter. Islamist political parties operate back and forth along this fluid continuum—ranging from support for an outright religious theocracy to urging a more moderate, more outward-looking government with secular trappings. It is a clever way of talking out of both sides of their mouths—and a definite vote-winner. Social media charts this process, and also facilitates it.

This reality has been overlooked in the literature on Islamic-based organizations and social media, because most current scholarship makes the false assumption that

such groups are primarily or solely interested in over-throwing regimes. So too, more generally, the monolithic view of Islamists as, in toto, part of the failed opposition in the Arab revolution, misconstrues the nature and intentions of organizations on the continuum. In addition to challenging the misperception that Islamists and extremists are homogeneous and universally extreme, then, my research also upends the assumption that the policies, particularly those of the extremists, are fixed and immu-table. Quite the contrary: Islamist organizations shift along the spectrum according to the changing political environment and organizational incentives over time. A central finding of this book is that Islamist organizations become more extreme or more moderate in order, simply, to maintain political viability. Social media is the setting for and the means by which these organizations establish their currency and appeal.

The Hornets' Nest

The power of religious social media networking was uniquely demonstrated in 2012 when riots broke out all over the Muslim world in reaction to a low-budget amateurish video that insulted the Prophet Muhammad. This global upheaval was not a word-of-mouth affair, but was generated and coordinated through Islamist social media outlets. The same was true in 2011 when a

confrontational Christian pastor in Florida carried out a public burning of the Koran. Again, social media was full of outrage and calls for jihad, resulting in riots in Afghanistan in which many were killed and wounded. In 2005 a Danish newspaper printed a group of cartoons offensively depicting Muhammad. Radical leaders used the insulting illustrations as the mechanism to spur mobilization, resulting in violent protests and two assassination attempts. The recent terrorist attacks in London and Paris were ultimately linked with internet and social media activity, specifically extremist groups radicalizing young people online with the threat of a civilizational war.

In each case, social media was used to stir up the hornets' nest—to spread the news, and then to goad the incensed community into action. Though traditional media (TV and radio) were quick to pick up on these news stories and express their own outrage, it was the Islamists' use of social media, specifically through calls for jihad, organizing protests, and so on, which sustained the heightened emotions. Without Facebook, Twitter, and other internet venues stoking the anger of millions, it is unlikely that any of these "outrage events" would have caught the attention of a global audience. Social media provides the ability to recruit new members for the Islamic cause, and to recruit them en masse, rather than winning acolytes one at a time.

Islamists and extremists are adept at the double-barreled strategy of blending religious conservatism with

twenty-first-century consumer technology. Twitter memes, Facebook posts, Instagram selfies, and YouTube videos effectively promote ISIS' radical vision of an Islamic utopia. ISIS fighters tweet photos of their dead comrades with ghoulish rictus grins alongside messages such as, "We have seen many martyrs smiling when they meet with their God, but we haven't seen a smile this wide. What did he see to make this beautiful smile? Oh God, grant us martyrdom."⁹ One of ISIS' most popular religious leaders, Ahmad Musa Jibril, tweeted to over 30,000 followers that "I just learned of a great brother & his death in Syria! They informed me he loved the Tawhid classes YA ALLAH accept Abu Layth and grant him ferdous [Paradise]."¹⁰

Various Islamist and extremist groups use social media as a "watchdog," overseeing traditional values as well as protecting specific groups' territory. Although groups might share the same basic religious beliefs, infighting, factionalism, and conspicuous one-upmanship are all too common. Organizations try to outdo each other in playing the "God card": one Islamist party will post its latest sermon on Facebook, only to be countered by a rival party posting a sermon even more full of hellfire and venom. Groups openly compete to attract the most "likes" and work hard at maintaining a holier-than-thou image. Their all-important "brand," often focused on their leaders, frequently becomes the target of social media attacks. One group will obtain a camera-phone clip of an adversary

drinking alcohol at a private event, and immediately upload it to various social networks with comments of outrage and shock. In response, the maligned party will put up a video of its rivals at a party where they were being over-friendly with women—a clip that may have been held back for months for just such a retaliation. This is equivalent to the "negative ads" run during US elections which, though maligned, have proved to be effective. Thus, a senior Pakistani religious leader was recently publicly shamed and totally discredited when a video on YouTube caught him swearing heatedly at a conference held at a mosque. The clip went viral and for weeks was one of the most viewed on social media sites in Pakistan. The cleric's career was jeopardized and his party lost a certain amount of core supporters—all thanks to social media. In these contests for theological virtue, the level of hypocrisy knows no bounds.

Islamist and extremist political contenders regularly use innovative social media platforms to subvert the image and credibility of those they want to depose—whether using flat-out lies, disinformation, the plain truth, or useful half-truths. Their web strategies include wide dissemination of facts (and propaganda) on government and military corruption, exposure of the ruling party's inability to deliver basic goods and services, the neglect of certain ethnic regions and minorities, even out-and-out gossip about the ill-gotten gains and "diseased inclinations" of individual

politicians and elites. And they are more than capable of outmaneuvering any crackdowns. The leading Islamist parties can often go toe-to-toe with the authorities with so-called "smart power." By collecting information—text messages, social media posts, and real-time reports from their network of on-location "spotters"—they can quickly assess the tactical situation wherever riot police and crowd control units are operating. This "hotspot mapping" allows the Islamists to efficiently deploy ground forces and countermeasures where they are most needed to confront the threat, or simply to outmaneuver it.

Islamist groups are expert mobilizers. A Muslim Brotherhood spokesman assured me shortly after it had taken power in Egypt in 2012 that the party "knew we could outwit [the government] on the social media circuit." He continued: "You see, for us fighting a dictator was hard to do. President Mubarak had the police and the army to back him. We used social media as a way to level the playing field, to bring our supporters into a single camp large enough to stand against Mubarak's henchmen. Social media for us was a voice that could not be silenced." Using sites like Twitter and Facebook, Islamists can rapidly organize and launch street protests of nearly any size, as well as synchronize "flash mobs" and other guerrilla actions, all with the operational security provided by encryption and password-protected platforms. As the Western press has reported for years, most (or, at least, many) Islamist

parties have links to hard-edged extremist organizations, such as al-Qaeda, Lashkar-e-Taiba, and Sipah e Sahaba. The Islamists are capable not only of defending themselves; they can mount offensive operations of their own through proxies or alliances of convenience, as has been seen over the last few years. "You must remember one thing," an Islamist politician told me over tea in Lahore's Anarkali bazaar. "We of the faithful have much experience with guns and violence. More so than certain governments. We have literally thousands of party members who have much trigger time fighting with guerrilla groups. They remain armed to this day and stand ready to render service."

Not all attacks have to be so personal. Sometimes Islamist insurgents will go for the jugular, acting as a cyber hit-squad by hacking into "secure" computer networks maintained by government, military, and corporate entities. Much mischief has been done by the theft of classified information, correspondence, and trade secrets. WikiLeaks was the trailblazer with its release of secret government documents, but the Islamists also know how to hang out each other's dirty laundry. Indeed, they think nothing of making up damaging stories about their adversaries. Nor are they shy about planting malicious scripts and tricked-out viruses that can sabotage websites and networks.

Digital World War reveals that social media mobilization does not necessarily yield moderation; it does, however,

lead to pragmatism. In fact, Islamic political organizations frequently engage in political strategies that require them to condone actions—including the use of extra-electoral means (violence) and the formation of coalitions with militant and secular organizations—which are opposed to their own platforms. We need to take more seriously various Islamic groups' interests in winning "the arena" as well as reaching a niche audience if we are to understand their nature and intentions. It is only by way of this, too, that we can properly understand what drives ordinary people into the arms of religion-based groups. Whereas the literature largely mischaracterizes their motivations, assuming them to be founded in economic deprivation or some sort of generalized Islamic militancy, examining social media evidence suggests volunteers make much more sophisticated and specific calculations about their self-interest. Recognizing that Islamic organizations are as tethered to practical political considerations as any other organization has huge implications for our understanding of what drives political extremism and how to create incentives for moderation via social media.

The Downside

The Islamists have not had it all their own way, either online or offline. In recent years, the disclosure of the alleged US National Security Agency's wide-angle

collection of all phone and net traffic records shows how concerned governments are with public communications channels. Muslim-majority regimes are no less eager than their Western counterparts to monitor extremist groups, especially within the social media sphere, the most visible landscape of Islamist politics. Many governments have launched digital counter-campaigns, shutting down Islamist and extremist groups' accounts, monitoring their activities, and proactively contacting private sector social media companies to block or censor content. And a range of "hard power" force has been brought to bear against various Islamist parties, factions, and individuals, including everything from covert surveillance and "moles" planted inside groups, to police intimidation, assassination, and even military action. Yet there is really little that authorities can do about controlling the internet. When one site goes down, another inevitably springs up, and it is no simple matter to block access for long periods, let alone permanently.

Neither are the new social networking technologies themselves without their limitations and drawbacks. At the most basic level, the penetration of social media is only as broad and deep as the internet coverage, which still leaves much to be desired across large swaths of rural and poverty-stricken areas. Network signal coverage in outlying areas is unreliable, rural residents cannot always afford the cost of an internet-capable computer or cell phone, and in any case

tend to be less sophisticated users of web services. This has posed a particular problem for the Islamists' political program since these regions not only make up a significant part of most Muslim-majority nations, they are often where the key constituencies of conservative religious voters live. The situation has been rapidly transforming over the last few years, however, with an exponential growth in the use of text messaging and the improving coverage of mobile hotspots and cell towers, giving rise to the growth in text campaigning and a sense that once largely disaffected and agrarian-based voters now have a way to express themselves—and be impressed. Now that groups have realized the rural voter must be addressed to capture popular support, those reaching out to them have an early competitive advantage.

Another limitation of the technology is fundraising. It is still difficult to raise money on the web in Muslim nations; most of their financial systems are not as simple and secure as in the West; and services such as PayPal and Google Money are unavailable. In the Arab world, campaign financing is still a matter of cash in hand. Digital media cannot yet manage such transactions effectively, but it seems clear that this is only a matter of time—and, when the time comes, the Islamists will be given a major boost.

Despite its pervasive reach, social media cannot perform the all-important ground game. Vitally, the electronic

realm cannot produce viable political candidates out of thin air. Political ability is a matter of the human presence, the candidate's personality, public-speaking style, level of charisma, and ability to draw voters. Even the candidate's height plays a psychological part. Social media can certainly amplify and exploit these traits (in fact, social media has in many cases impacted the kinds of candidate who come forward, are selected, and potentially succeed), but it cannot create them. Furthermore, candidates still need to appear before large crowds and address matters of "substance," such as a pressing single issue or a vital party position. This is basic to building esprit de corps and mobilizing voters— which must be done in person, not just on the internet.

And religious confessional parties still depend heavily on volunteers to do the old-fashioned legwork. A campaign can hype a party on social network platforms, but these can only boost and disseminate the message: the core campaign must still have a traditional ground force at work. So we also see Islamist groups using social media to bolster traditional campaign strategies. Given the Islamists' and extremists' long history of organized opposition in the region, from hard-hitting propaganda to hard-nosed street protests, it was perhaps natural that they would seize upon any technology that would enable them to carry on the work of opposition in their tried-and-tested manner. So the Muslim Brotherhood kept its original social media campaigns tightly linked to recruitment channels in

operation since the 1980s, ultimately putting it in power in Egypt. In Pakistan, too, the Tehreek-e-Insaf (PTI) party worked social media heavily in the run-up to the 2013 elections in order to reach out to a wider audience with its press releases and announcements, posting more of these on Twitter than all of the other political parties combined. Often Islamists use their social media output to attract and manipulate traditional TV, radio, print, and web coverage, erecting a powerful multilevel platform that punches above its weight. Social media alone cannot claim to have entirely transformed the landscape, though it has certainly forged many new and exciting paths.

No Promised Land

Digital World War takes a clear-eyed look at the much-touted dawn of democracy which was to have ridden into the Islamic world astride the social media phenomenon. Certainly, digital developments are giving a voice and a power to many. Social media strategies are also swelling the ranks of voting constituencies and driving mobilization come election time—as well as exposing fraud and intimidation. Yet the sense that social media in and of itself promotes pluralistic values is shortsighted. One thing is certain: no new form of grassroots, interpersonal means of communicating will automatically lead to more freedom, or to any freedom for that matter. Social media activity

does not offer a panacea, or a promise that Islamists will become more open-minded, more transparent, and more democratic, once they are voted into office. Witness the downfall of the double-talking Muslim Brotherhood in Egypt, with hundreds now on death row and many imprisoned indefinitely, including the deposed president. Given this, there is nothing to indicate that even the most digitally literate Islamists will embrace liberal democracy— especially when it comes to issues like minority rights, religious tolerance, and freedom of the press. (It will never be acceptable to criticize the Prophet.) Indeed, social media is used to stir up intolerance as much as pluralism, defensive nationalism as much as a global outlook, religious conservatism as much as pluralistic value systems.

Even if states cannot control content and the potentially subversive coordination and contact made through open platforms, they still control the infrastructure, and have the power and audacity to use social media against its users. Digital surveillance has increased since the Arab Spring. "Big Brother isn't watching anymore . . . Now, he is remembering the past perfectly and he is making connections between people and events in ways that even [George] Orwell couldn't have imagined."[11] Of course, this ignores the fact that these revolutions occurred and drew global attention because citizens themselves were acting as a surveillance state by capturing improper actions and violations. Such mirroring of tactics, with the force enabler of

transnational online connectivity, reflects infractions to a global arbiter audience, forcing governments to be receptive to the opinion of their people, and ensuring the "revolutionary promise that new media will transfer control to viewers and consumers."

The findings in this book also counter the so-called "net delusion" theory (Chapter 3), which holds that the World Wide Web actually makes us less free, less democratic, and more paranoid. Such a sweeping thesis covers so much territory that there will naturally be some truth to it. But research has shown time and again that social media networks have been an enormous boon to opposition activists, empowering those who previously had no voice beyond their own four walls. Social media has consistently pulled in hordes of new voices and first-time political participators, and, while it may not be an open door to progressive ideas, and might even be a dangerous development for the West, there is little "delusion" in the eyes of the suddenly empowered.

The changes wrought and exploited by social media will have both a positive and negative impact on the West's war on terror. In this fast-paced environment, the Islamists are being increasingly forced into more moderate stances with regard to geopolitical and foreign policy issues. Old enemies can become new allies overnight, and vice versa. The young Islamists of the web are rewiring the rules of the game.

* * *

Digital World War is based on a unique data set and a large number of interviews with political elites, focus groups, and organizational and social media leaders and supporters across the Muslim-majority world, including in Egypt, Tunisia, Pakistan, UAE, Malaysia, Indonesia, Kosovo, Afghanistan, and Turkey, as well as primary and secondary archival and published sources and open source material. The weft to this warp is a close analysis of social media usage, online engagement, hacking metrics, local and national election results, survey results, and voter behavior experiments. This book is therefore one of the first to apply both qualitative and quantitative analysis to the ways in which Islamists and extremists are engaging with social media.

The first chapter charts in detail the development and usage of the main "information weapons" wielded by Islamists and extremists—the platforms themselves, existing and specifically developed, and how such groups manipulate them to achieve their particular aims.

Chapter 2 examines how Islamists and extremists reach out to, recruit, and mobilize followers. From brand-building, audience disaggregation, content molding, and the "gamification" of online participation, social media enables and encourages these practices, behaviors, and ethos.

Wars waged online between hackers, governments, extremists, and even established political parties, are the focus of Chapter 3. I examine the different weapons wielded by these frontline forces and their wider political effects, as

force-multipliers for change, or playing into the hands of repressive regimes. Social media usage in the Islamic world throws into question the pessimism of Evgeny Morozov and his "net delusion" theory concerning the technology's power to affect real-world behavior—though whether it is for good or ill remains an open question.

Chapter 4 uses the tools of social media to scrutinize its role in revolutions, comparing the outcome of outrages before and after the advent of digital technology, and quantifying its effects and value.

Private and public sector involvement via social media in the Middle East, North Africa, and South and Central Asia is the topic of Chapter 5. I look at the ways in which (often Western) multinationals square up against Islamist principles, and how ostensibly internet-phobic Islamist regimes and groups have embraced social media's ability to connect with their constituencies.

The funding of Islamist and extremist groups is the subject of Chapter 6, and particularly the ways in which charitable donating, transnational cooperation, and international organizations have been implicated in Islamist and extremist activity. Social media acts as facilitator, frame, and battlefield for civic and charitable causes, and their exploitation.

Chapter 7 looks at the new internationalism in the Muslim world that is fostered by social media. Islamists and extremists influence each other and are influenced by

much that is happening outside the region, as well as themselves being key influencers on the international stage, including in mainstream media. One crucial effect of social media's information flows is the online recruitment of Western youth to the extremist cause, a topic currently worrying many countries in the West.

The book concludes with a discussion of the implications of building a new understanding of Islamists' and extremists' engagement with social media. Oversimplified and uninformed depictions of Islamist politics have negatively affected international policy, resulting in the mismanagement or total neglect of potentially vital relationships. Awareness of the broader context, history, and motivations underlying the way these groups use social media could vastly improve diplomats', and the West's, ability to navigate the ever-changing and often bewildering online terrain. More specifically, understanding that Islamists and extremists are motivated as much by online branding as by righteousness should impact relations with Muslim-world allies and antagonists, and potentially open new opportunities for diplomacy and intervention.

Given recent events in Iraq, Syria, Libya, Tunisia, Pakistan, and Egypt, and across the Middle East, Europe, and the US, the strong likelihood is that greater engagement with social media will only increase the political power of Islamists in future. In order to engage these

organizations in a productive dialogue—as we must—it is imperative that we in the West understand how this technology is being used to usher millions toward either end of the politico-religious spectrum, and everywhere in between.

ONE

THE WEAPONIZATION OF INFORMATION

K HALID WAS A baby-faced fifteen-year-old from Beirut.[1] His father ran a fruit stand in nearby Najmeh Square, while his mother earned a few pounds from her sewing crafts. Though not dirt poor, the family of eight barely scraped by and Khalid had to fend for himself from an early age. One thing that drove Khalid was his love for computers and software. He was eight when he was taken to his first internet café. Learning code came easy and he was prolific on social media by age twelve. He earned extra money working as a waiter at the local coffee and hookah house. But he was fascinated by the digital community he had become part of, something that had never happened in his own hometown neighborhood.

At a net café, he came across certain online forums and chat rooms run by Hezbollah, one of the most active groups in the space. Khalid eventually jumped in with a

few questions and comments of his own. Then he started receiving daily SMS messages from online recruiters who talked of an impending revolution in Lebanon, predictions they bolstered with brief history lectures. He soon became fascinated with this more expansive worldview, which dwarfed his own small existence. For the first time in his young life, he began to feel a camaraderie toward the whole group, the sense of being part of something greater than himself.

It was not long before Khalid took to regularly visiting the local Hezbollah chapter. Offering his by now considerable tech skills, he began helping the group build a host of websites and educational portals. Khalid's ability to write code and construct useful algorithms, as well as his deep knowledge of hacking, made him a welcome and valuable addition to their digital staff. Before long, Khalid ended up as one of the first members of what Hezbollah began to call its "E-militia team." Their task was to recruit new members and to deploy advanced online methodologies—that is, high-grade encryption and cyber hacking—against their opponents, mainly state actors. In little more than a decade, the radicals had established a transnational, social media revolution, one devoid of conventional borders.

* * *

It has taken little more than a decade for social media to become the indispensable tool for legions of activists

inside and outside the Islamist political establishment. It is no less important for the tens of millions of generally disaffected people across the Muslim world who may or may not have a religious or political agenda. Access to social media technologies offers a means for anyone to express their opinion—yet it also provides a number of platforms for those opinions to be shaped and swayed. Islamists and extremists were among the first to recognize this, and are adept at employing the new information weapons to full—and sometimes lethal—effect.

This is not merely a case of spreading propaganda (the "classic" definition of the weaponization of information); rather, the various ways in which information is disseminated are themselves part of the war. And if social media is a smoking gun, Islamists and extremists are proving to be the most expert at loading the bullets. Having been underground for years, they are the ones who are now able to use the various platforms to wage war on the information battlefield. For the more pragmatic Islamists, the aim is to bolster their mass-market appeal; for the extremists it is rather to capture a niche audience and stoke the fears of the infidel. Different social media platforms are like different weapons, each with pros and cons, some more suited to one group than another, but all are wielded with pinpoint accuracy and deployed with acute force.

Where It All Started, and Why

The Islamists' entry into cyberspace was inevitable. In a sense, it was nothing new: the Islamists already enjoyed a long-established history of skillfully using the latest technologies in reaching out to the public at the time the new social media interfaces surfaced.

From the 1970s through the 1990s, Muslim clerics (or "imams") spread their sharia ranting and vitriolic demands by way of audiocassette recordings—state-of-the-art stuff in the boombox and Walkman era. (See Chapter 4 for the use of cassette tapes in Iran.) Tapes were the perfect medium for spreading the Islamist message: they were readily available (and smugglable) in almost all urban markets, easily transported from one place to another, and relatively inexpensive, able to be sold in small kiosk-type stores in bazaars or in the back of pharmacies on every street corner. Dissemination was done secretively, furtively, under fictitious names, as most of these tapes contained anti-government messages and exhortations and outright calls for rebellion, which could lead to a stretch in prison or even a death sentence. Some eight-track videos were also produced (such as those by Jamaat-e-Islami founder Maulana Maududi), but few people had VCRs in order to watch them. Using tapes was a slow, word-of-mouth way to gain attention and support, totally reliant on them being passed from hand to hand. Except for personal

contact at mosques and rallies, the Islamists had no effective way of tracking or quantifying their audience, and no real method for marketing their cause or getting in touch with the great mass of potential followers. It was all very catch-as-catch-can, quite amateurish, and only as effective as the messenger on the ground.

Nevertheless, these evasive, innovative tactics were necessary. Governments were wary of anything that might "incite a population" and wanted to make sure nationalism and allegiance to the flag reigned paramount. However, by the end of the twentieth century, Middle Eastern governments had begun to lose their traditional iron-fisted control over Arabic-language television and radio. It was shocking to behold: the long-running state monopoly on basic information had come to an end. This new freedom of the press (at least in TV broadcasting) had been propelled by the success of the CNN-style, Gulf-controlled Al Jazeera news service, founded in 1996. And in its wake came an exponential rise in TV channels across the region. In most Middle Eastern and South Asian countries, there were two or three state-run channels, offered as part of the terrestrial network that most offices could tap into. Satellite TV allowed for the expansion of new licenses for channels on a variety of subjects, from morning religious prayers to sermons, talk shows on religion, documentaries, soap operas, and so on. Many countries had over a hundred channels available via satellite.

Satellite TV made it possible to bypass state-run networks altogether. New groups were able to broadcast messages and programs to countries in which they were banned. The Muslim Brotherhood, for instance, set up shop in Qatar and broadcast its channel to the rest of the Middle East, regularly featuring videos and clips. Satellite TV feeds were relatively easy to pick up. These were powerful tools for politicking, indeed for the Islamist cause and activism as a whole. Ambitious imams wasted no time in retooling their propaganda efforts from the old-fashioned audio- and videotape distribution system to full-blown mass-media penetration. This put the Islamist political parties in touch with everyone, and more or less beyond the roughshod reach of spies, police, and censors. Here was a major shift in tactics, which did not go unnoticed in the West, and which caused plenty of conster-nation within official circles in the Middle East. The government ax could still fall, and did, but it was now almost counterproductive to get tough with the Islamic crusaders when they had access to their own media, enabling them to generate hours of negative publicity and anti-regime propaganda on news and opinion programs. And as the 2000s wore on, the increasing prevalence of mobile phones encouraged the interaction of viewers with TV shows (texting questions, polling answers, giving feed-back, stating likes and dislikes), allowing several key players to enter the scene.

Hold Shift

Not everyone could afford the license application, studio space, equipment, and start-up costs of launching a TV channel, however. The first to make the transition to internet-based media, generating content, and achieving some momentum, were Salafi-leaning groups in Pakistan, Jordan, and the Gulf. It all started in the early 2000s with Jamaat TV. These groups could use the internet cheaply, evade police detection of their location, and disseminate content much more quickly than via television. If TV coverage was a great boon to Islamists, airtime was also limited. The internet, however, was unlimited, offering a vision of inexorable, righteous expansion under the name of Allah: the new Islamic caliphate.

The Islamists seized and continue to seize upon new and established internet platforms in order to launch and extend their media presence and campaigns, and to consolidate their power base and influence—some of which have ultimately toppled governments. The Islamists have also embraced the ability to create an online alternative reality, a click-through utopia to capture internet users. Thus the Muslim Brotherhood paints pictures of communities without corruption, enjoying the robust provision of social services and good governance. Extremist groups like ISIS put out glossy digital magazines (such as *Dabiq*, now called *Ramiyah*) whose layouts eerily echo *Time*, with lifestyle articles and

advice for families, as well as idealistic portrayals of the restoration of the Islamic caliphate, news stories glorifying its deadly attacks, and even advertisements (albeit for Western and Chinese hostages it has taken). The intention is to portray a place where any believer could come and live, get married, and raise children—a kind of "Club Med for Muslims." Clearly, Islamists and extremists see and position themselves as brands, reaching out to, and in a sense creating, their consumer through the power of social media. The impact of visually "showing" the narrative using religious symbols cannot be overstated.

Whether it is extremists urging civilizational war, electoral offensives by Islamist parties, or imams preaching moderation, there is an acute understanding of how best to stoke the social networking machine. Civil society leaders have long recognized the need for a steady presence in the social media arena and the games they can play there, the threats they can monitor, the troublemakers they can head off or even nail. Many Islamists plan their campaigns carefully. The precise media-mix is calibrated to a group's identity and ambitions, with varying levels of impact and authority. Of course, it is not merely a matter of establishing a Facebook page or a Twitter profile, and there is an exponentially expanding universe of links and clicks, uploads and downloads, messages sent and received, places to go, things to see, contacts to be made, information to digest, opinions to hear, and feedback to give. Neither is it a case of

outlining the handful of major players who make an impact; all too often the digital warriors rise up from nowhere, flourish mightily, and then disappear without warning. It is quite impossible to know all that is operational at any one given time. The rest of this chapter therefore can only consider a sample of the more important and established sites and apps being used in the struggle for Islamic "branding" supremacy. The various ways in which these "information weapons" have been deployed by Islamists and extremists will play out through the rest of the book.

I Say Jump: Twitter

Twitter came online in 2006, and first made its mark on the Islamic world during the 2009 Green Revolution in Iran. Twitter was used for the geolocation and organization of liberal Islamists and opposition groups. Some made use of it as a coordinating mechanism to launch denial-of-service (DoS) attacks against the Iranian establishment. Recognizing how important it was, the Iranian government temporarily blocked the site but could not maintain the jam for long.

Twitter's power lies in the efficient sharing of information and links in 140 characters or less, but also the ability to organize rapid on-the-ground mobilization, flash mobs and coordinated demonstrations. A participant in the 2011 Tahrir Square protests wrote, "When I arrived [home], the Twitter hash #jan25 lit up. Someone said that earlier tweets

had been deliberately planted as decoys to mislead authorities. Now, in dozens of real locations throughout the city, protesters had begun to mobilize. I ran out the door and took the subway back to Tahrir Square."[2] Twitter's speed, versatility, and encouragement of intense but pithy give-and-take also make it one of the most widely used digital platforms for Islamists in power as well as in opposition, for both secular and religious ends: Malaysian Prime Minister Najib Razak has more than 3.6 million followers, for instance; as of August 2017, the Sunni Islamist militia Jabhat al-Nusra had over 300,000 followers on affiliated sites;[3] and @ikhwanweb, the Muslim Brotherhood's English-language account, had 145,000. In Saudi Arabia, according to *The Economist*, in 2017 "four of the top ten most-followed Twitter accounts [were] those of clerics."[4] Number 1 is Mohammed al-Arefe, with over 17 million Twitter followers, making his the most-followed account in the entirety of the Middle East. This religious cleric is a key influencer sympathetic to ISIS, cited by many ISIS defectors as the reason they joined the rogue extremist group.

Many Twitter users accept tweets as being "the truth" and this grants the platform huge popularity and power. Tweets are the quickest and most direct way to articulate a message, as well as to pinpoint locations in real time (particularly useful during fast-moving events, police attacks, or occasions when tear gas is being deployed). Hashtags enable instant searchability and content coherence, and a simple

"hashtag campaign," when followers are asked to tweet certain hashtags at particular times of the day so that they start trending, can significantly boost profile and participation. A hashtag might garner a thousand appearances within a few hours; hot-button issues have been known to amass 100,000 tweets an hour, with tweets and retweets driving the excitement or outrage. Hashtags also give both Islamists and extremists a direct line to their audience's concerns. Even ISIS has been known to conduct focus-group research via Twitter, for instance when proposing a "rebrand"—a name-change to focus on the rebirth of an Islamic caliphate. The acrimonious response meant they abandoned the idea.[5]

Twitter has also been a choice platform for Islamists and extremists because, until recently (2014–15), it has been reluctant to issue takedowns or restrict access. Twitter's noninterventionist approach was lauded by free internet usage groups but also criticized by several governments and security-based NGOs. It was the tragic case of James Foley, the journalist whose 2014 execution by ISIS went viral as video and film stills were shared by thousands, especially on Twitter, which led the company to assume a more hardline stance on images and objectionable content, taking down 10,000 extremist accounts in March 2015. Many extremist groups now use Twitter understanding that their accounts will get shut down, but knowing that with a simple letter or symbol change in their handle they can be back online within twenty minutes. One of the most notorious is the al-Shabaab

press office's English-language Twitter account, originally set up in 2011, which continually posts extremist content, is continually blocked, and continually regenerates under slightly different usernames. During al-Shabaab's attack on a Kenyan shopping mall in 2013, for instance, the group live-tweeted the attack's progress despite Twitter's best efforts to stop them. The group sprang up as @HSM_PressOffice, @HSMPress, and other names during the course of the incident, successfully spreading terror and justifying its actions to a global audience.[6] Dealing with Twitter extremists requires something of a "whack-a-mole" approach.

Extremist groups do not simply sit back and wait for their followers to tweet and retweet content: they go out and create, inflate, and control the message themselves. ISIS effectively "gamed" Twitter with its official Arabic-language Twitter app, "The Dawn of Glad Tidings" (or simply "Dawn"), which was unveiled on Google Play in April 2014 (and removed that June). It was downloaded over 10,000 times. Not only does it help users stay informed with ISIS-related news, keep track of their daily prayers, and access short sayings or scriptural references encouraging religious war.[7] Downloading the application actually allows tweets (quotations, links, and images)—content that is scripted by ISIS' social media crack squad—to be posted to its users' accounts directly and almost concurrently, though sufficiently spaced to evade Twitter's spam algorithms. This has allowed for tweet blitzes that can reach into the tens of thousands per day, swarming the

Twittersphere with intimidating updates from the front line, the ground gained, and the atrocities committed, and making certain images—such as those accompanying the meme "Baghdad we are coming!" including the 2014 Photoshopped picture of a jihadi gazing upon the ISIS flag fluttering from the top of Baghdad's Palestine Hotel (long favored by Western media personnel)—among the top results for several searches.[8] ISIS also uses more conventional Twitter strategies, such as organizing hashtag campaigns, and tapping into the @ActiveHashtags stream (a popular Arabic Twitter account that tweets the top trending terms of each day), ensuring its content is available, and palpable, on the platform. Despite a number of shutdowns and account removals, ISIS is winning the extremist Twitter war hands down, registering in February 2017 more than 12,000 mentions of its hashtags per day, far more than the 2,500–5,000 referring to the al-Nusra group.

Seeing the Light: YouTube

With now over 1.5 billion active users a month, a great number of them young,[9] the video-sharing global phenomenon YouTube is probably the second most important social media platform for Islamic groups in the Middle East and South Asia. It was one of their early big-hitters, bursting onto the Islamic scene the year after its 2005 founding when Jamaat-e-Islami in Pakistan began

uploading *nasheed* (traditional songs), which at that time were not being played on Pakistani TV. This content was seen as a source of inspiration for believers, the videos featuring photos of the most breathtaking views of Pakistan, and often being played in barber shops and cafés.

Not only does YouTube serve the old function of distributor of film and video content—minus the inconvenient and often repressive production executives—enabling easy uploading of clips as well as full-length videos often hours in length, particularly if they are sermons or religious preaching. YouTube has also become so influential that most regimes in the Muslim-majority world themselves go to the site for intelligence and counter-propaganda campaigns (always neatly packed with disinformation). YouTube gives both Islamists and extremists the ability to visually impart their narrative, toy with their audience's emotions, and spread their propaganda. The platform's strict DoS regulations usually mean extremist content, such as videos depicting extreme violence and bloodshed, or those advocating such action, is swiftly taken down. And so Islamists have been able to make more straightforward use of the site, though still not always safely: Tarak Mekki, the host of "One Thousand and One Nights," a popular weekly YouTube podcast in Tunisia, attacked President Zine El-Abidine Ben Ali's regime in a series of comic sketches. This led to exile in Canada,

although, after the 2011 Tunisian revolution (also known as the Jasmine Revolution), he was treated to a triumphant return by his fans.[10]

Extremist groups actively post content that, while not overtly violent (and thus avoiding the website's "flagging" system), depicts their enemies' horrible acts to elicit sympathy and outrage. The YouTube pages of the al-Nusra Front and the Free Syrian Army ("FSAHelp") have also featured instructional videos on the proper use and maintenance of firearms, stealth tactics, and hand-to-hand combat—a questionable, but still viable, dissemination of educational material.[11]

Furthermore, as YouTube stores content on its own servers, it greatly facilitates the uploading of videos taken on mobile phones (which have very limited storage space), making it hugely popular with Islamist groups who rely on this technology.[12] In fact, phone users account for almost 50 per cent of total YouTube consumption, another reason why this video-sharing platform is particularly popular.

Peer Pressure: Facebook

Facebook is the behemoth of social networking sites, with over 2 billion active monthly users worldwide. Over 3.5 billion "likes" are generated every day and 1.32 billion people log on every twenty-four hours. Because it is a fully fledged multimedia platform where material of

any length and any kind (be that text, pictures, videos, PDFs, links, feedback, or comments) can be posted, it has played a major part in seismic events across the Muslim-majority world. For instance, it came to be at the center of the anti-government online action in Tunisia during the country's 2011 Jasmine Revolution, with visceral images and words grabbing hearts and minds across the country and around the globe. Various Islamist groups (such as Ennahda) used Facebook to rally potential volunteers, recruit district-level workers, and spread awareness on government repression of the movement. Over 20,000 posts were put on Facebook in a two-month period focused on the organization of Jasmine movement teams. Islamists also posted details and mobile phone footage of demonstrations and injuries to protestors, sending an undeniable message that ordinary people were willing to participate in rallies against the establishment. Islamists are especially drawn to Facebook because its size and fame helps generate TV, newspaper, and web coverage, and the platform's hybrid media axis is giving Islamist political parties and actors a significant boost in recognition and popularity.

Although Facebook proved to be an extremely effective forum for organizing activities and actively engaging numerous people during the Arab Spring, many more radical groups are wary of its inbuilt propensity to connect people, places, and times. Its facial recognition technology

and monitoring techniques have made some groups cautious about operating an official Facebook account. So, although the platform can be critical to driving extremists' messages home and having them acted upon, a large number of terrorist groups' Facebook pages are actually operated by supporters or individuals who want to identify with the organization, such as the al-Battar Media Foundation and Nukhbat al-I'lam al-Jihadi.[13] As a result of Facebook's strict authentication process and a vigilant 24/7 anti-extremist message team, the social media network has tended to act more as a platform for extremists to connect with like-minded sympathizers rather than facilitating active recruitment and propaganda dissemination.

The New Newspapers: Blogs

Paid readership of print newspapers has been declining for some time. Newspaper penetration has only ever reached around 20 per cent in Muslim-majority countries, although papers and other print media were often passed around among communities and among families, perhaps belying point-of-sale calculations. Blogs and online newspapers have, however, come into their own in recent years, especially among young people who are using their smartphones to access the daily news and latest editorials in more immediate and less censored ways. These are the

forums for journalism that often cannot survive in print anymore.

Egyptian journalist and writer Ahmed Naji's blog, updated almost daily, documented life during the overthrow of President Hosni Mubarak. While many sites were banned or found it difficult to get up-to-date information, Naji provided incisive commentary. His site garnered thousands of hits a day and often became a key source for TV, radio, and international reporting on Egypt. Similarly influential was the online independent Egyptian newspaper *Mada Masr*, set up in the wake of *Egypt Independent*'s demise, then shut down by the authorities in 2013 after it was critical of the country's Supreme Council. *Mada Masr* thrives on being home to "a different kind of journalism," especially important in times of crisis and in Egypt where, since the military coup, there is renewed pressure on journalists to toe the party line.

With the right skills, blogs and websites can host any content, and with enough cash they can come into being quickly and persist for a long time. They can simultaneously attract a great deal of attention—being linked to from different platforms, and picked up by other more traditional media worldwide—as well as fly under the radar of regime watchdogs. That makes them an attractive, if more complicated, option for Islamists and extremists. For the latter, interaction—when the visitor can comment or directly contact the blogger—perhaps makes for the telling difference in winning over the niche audience. For

Islamic policymakers, the ability to track traffic and page views delivers incredibly valuable data.

Rolling News: Tumblr

This interactive microblogging site has become increasingly popular with different Islamist and extremist groups for their high-powered recruitment campaigns. Tumblr's power lies in its customization: its users can easily create a unique viewing experience for themselves, posting images, links, and notes on their page, and choosing which other blogs to follow which pepper the dashboard with what they have posted, constantly feeding new stories. It makes a true feast for the eyes, with wall-to-wall color and interest and the famous near-continuous scrolling. It is also very easy to search for specific subjects and have the screen populated by enticing images, perfect for religious-oriented outreach to specific audiences. The notoriously savage ISIS terror group used to frequently use Tumblr text and video postings to show the "exciting" and "adventurous" life of jihadists participating in the Iraq/Syria conflicts. Tumblr was the extremists' dream: straightforward to use, visually rich, password protected, and encryption friendly. It is not surprising that Tumblr postings are known to be responsible for inspiring many young people to "lone wolf" acts of terror carried out around the world, from Islamabad to London, Copenhagen to Sydney, New York to Texas.

Seek and Ye Shall Find: Ask.fm

"You've got questions, we've got answers." So went the old Radio Shack slogan—now updated for the twenty-first century by Ask.fm, a website where anyone can create a (cloaked) profile and send questions to other anonymous users for them to reply to. It is an electronic hotbed of extremist recruitment (though not exclusively so), providing a way for groups to reach a niche captive audience of one, as well as countless others who might be viewing the thread. It is an especially valuable tool for targeting young Westerners who naturally have many queries about how different life is in the Muslim world. Sometimes questions can be more contentious, such as those once posed to the Jordanian Muslim Brotherhood group: "Do you want to overthrow the government?" and "How is it Islamic to criticize other Muslims in the political process?"

The questions and answers frequently become more detailed, and exclusive. Often the interrogatives have to do with living standards for mujahideen fighters or ISIS members ("Are the bugs a problem?" or "Can I buy a smartphone there?"),[14] or how one can go about joining the various conflicts going on in the Muslim world. As with almost all Islamic recruitment and PR campaigns, the focus is less on religious doctrine and more on how jihad is "cool," the cutting-edge of modern Islam. The extremists

THE WEAPONIZATION OF INFORMATION

make outlandish promises, with all the high-pressure sincerity of a used-car salesperson; yet, for the impressionable young, such promises are taken on faith. Recruiters become guides and mentors, following up with private individual communications in which they can be (or seem to be) direct and candid. Step by step, the target is brought around to enlisting in the religious cause.

Ask.fm became particularly notorious in the West for its apparently laissez-faire attitude to cyber bullying, which tragically led to some young people taking their own lives. The site, which was originally almost entirely unmoderated and had no tracking or reporting systems in place—clearly a boon for propaganda-touting extremists as well as bullies—now has a raft of reporting and blocking features. There is, now, a limit to extremist content. When an extended conversation goes over the line, that particular account is banned—but not before the Islamists have interacted with a wide audience and made new contacts, many of whom will already be "converted."

Snap to Kik-Start: Messaging Apps and SMS

Mobile phones have become ubiquitous across the Middle East and South Asia, as across the rest of the world. The region is also seeing a massive growth in the use of smartphones, particularly in the 15–34 age bracket (which accounts for about three-quarters of the total users), with

the sales and penetration level hovering around 57 per cent today.[15] This means that messaging, by way of either simple SMS or web-based programs, is still an important component of the Islamists' and extremists' social media strategies.

Text messaging is the most basic and straightforward means of electronic communication, with the added advantage of not requiring an internet connection or web-enabled phone. Several studies have also shown that Islamists and extremists use text messaging because it is the most personal and appropriate way to interact with someone, especially of the opposite sex; women can get bombarded with twenty to twenty-five texts per day from extremists encouraging them to come to Syria as foreign fighters or to become wives of the believers. Extremists will also text information about occasions when the West has insulted Islam, intending to incite and enrage their followers. Islamists, by contrast, use texting more sensitively and regularly. They will send, for example, daily *hadith* sayings extolling the virtue of dedicating time and service in the path of God, which also provide subtle hints about duty to the organization. Instant alerts and texts about breaking news also serve the purpose of creating broader awareness. However, whereas the Islamists' use of text messaging seems to garner a good response and take-up rate, the tactical use of text messages by extremists—as recent tracking of high-volume text messaging traffic by anti-extremist NGOs and human rights groups indicates—has actually met with limited success.

Instant messaging enables direct and personal contact with just one person or a whole address book full of contacts. Islamists have been known to acquire bulk lots of phone numbers within targeted areas from spammers and hackers (yet another way that the sharing of information on the internet can benefit these groups). And Islamists and extremists are highly attuned to how established and new instant messaging apps can be used to maximize outreach and recruitment, including WhatsApp, WeChat, Telegram, Threma, LINE, Viber, and Hookt. Always seeking personal contact to make the sale, Islamic recruiters are quick with their requests to "Kik me" (a phrase originating with the Canadian messaging app Kik, and meaning "Send me a private message") across various forums, chat rooms, blogs, and other social media platforms.

Programs such as WhatsApp (very popular in Turkey, Pakistan, and North and East Africa) are often used by extremist groups because their end-to-end encryption ensures a much higher degree of security and privacy. WhatsApp is known to have been used to pull in and radicalize a number of young men who have travelled to Syria, Iraq, Afghanistan, and Pakistan. As a result, security officials in major nations—including China, Saudi Arabia, Russia, and the US—have expressed deep concerns about these instant messaging apps. They are now seen as a locus for terrorist "grooming" of the impressionable and susceptible. Steps have been taken to monitor and

infiltrate a number of these sites, though with uncertain success to date.

In the wake of the game-changing NSA leaks by Edward Snowden in 2013, and the resulting increase in internet surveillance, a considerable amount of instant messaging traffic has gone over to encrypted or self-destructing messaging apps. For example, photos sent via Snapchat can reach any number of designated recipients, but disappear within seconds—frequently before the server even knows they were there. Wickr, Telegram, and certain extremist-owned messaging apps utilize highly sophisticated military-grade encryption protocols that allow for truly undecipherable communications.

These quick-fire apps are effective, too. Some data suggest that Snapchat achieves a higher engagement per piece of social media than other platforms. Its unique linear storytelling appeals to young millennials, leading key influencer clerics like Mohammed al-Arefe to issue "Snapfatwas" of eight-second religious decrees. And there are now several dozen similar apps (in different languages) aimed at potential recruits. For Islamists and extremists, apps are a great way to design and build a sense of community.

E-Graffiti: JustPaste.it

JustPaste.it is a favorite of Islamists and extremists though it operates from, of all places, Poland: it is a true labor of

love, run by one Mariusz Żurawek, a young entrepreneur holding degrees in informatics and econometrics, who works "out of his bedroom" (shades of the Google founders in their garage), and has amassed an impressive 2.5 million unique users a month since starting the site in 2013. The extremely simplified format allows users to attach text, images, and videos to an anonymous page, creating a "note" that anyone can see. The site does not require registration, it provides password and encryption protection, there is no internal search feature, and the lone administrator does no real "managing" of the site—hence its anonymous users can flout all rules and upload anything they like, including illegal pornography, stolen financial data, details of drugs for purchase, and other underground links and services. The site is a secure haven for extremist material, and within the last couple of years JustPaste.it has become a particular favorite of terror groups like ISIS and the Taliban.

Partly, JustPaste.it's standing as a must-use medium in the Islamic world lies in the fact that it works well with right-to-left scripts like Arabic, and, since there are no ads or pop-ups, the site runs smoothly even with a slow connection, giving it an edge in the Middle East where the internet tends to be sluggish. But, more importantly, the site's multimedia capability gives the extremists a platform for posting write-ups, images, videos, and links to breaking news: minute-by-minute battle reports, for instance, which always include images of gruesome death and wanton

destruction, and graphic images of beheadings by ISIS fighters. So horrific are some of the pictures that the site is issued with takedown notices on a regular basis. If the request comes from law enforcement agencies (Interpol, the UK Metropolitan Police's anti-terrorism unit, Pakistan's ISI), the offending material is removed—albeit slowly, or sometimes not at all. However, the original poster, or anyone else for that matter, can simply repaste the deleted material in a new note. It really is like electronic graffiti: a scandalous way to rub your message in the face of the establishment, leave it for all to see, and get away with it.

JustPaste.it has also inspired legions of other text-paste sites, often low-budget, highly obscure, and hard to find. They are mostly used for messaging followers, whether a call to street demonstrations or simply to arrange a meeting, and once the information has been sent and received it is deleted. It is a fast run-and-gun system, completely anonymous, easier to use than most blogs, and nowhere near as heavily patrolled by content monitors as the big names. These are the websites that often continue to carry links to videos that were removed from the closely managed social media giants.

Extremist Close-Up: Instagram

Now with more than 700 million active users, the picture- and video-sharing site Instagram is a major player in the social media field, popular among Islamists and extremists

(who numbered among some of the platform's earliest users) for its ability to humanize otherwise faceless or forbidding groups, to facilitate image-building campaigns, and to glorify selfie-loving extremists. An iconic Instagram photo depicts old weapons (a gun, a knife) alongside a mobile phone with Instagram pulled up on its screen. The message is clear: this is the new weapon of choice. And it has proved to be a more effective way of targeting young people.

Extremists are undoubtedly the Instagram experts. They post memorial montages of suicide martyrs that look more like family photo albums, showing the upbeat young men in casual, even intimate scenes, with no indication of the bloodthirsty acts for which they gave up their lives. Extremists tout their guns, beaming, in countless photos. Not all the extremists' videos are warm and fuzzy, however. Footage depicts young boys in mujahideen uniforms, firing shoulder-launched missiles, gunning prisoners, or involved in vicious attacks (those they win), or beheadings and other grotesque executions. The images are meant to goad susceptible Muslims into action, and frighten everyone else.

The globally ubiquitous Instagram also raises the real possibility of Westerners "stumbling upon" content that celebrates more extreme religious thinking—something that extremist groups are fully aware of, and exploit. The hashtag function on Instagram allows users to sift the material easily and bring up a smorgasbord of related images, as on Twitter. In fact, many photos are posted on both sites concurrently,

with Twitter links updating Instagram. Although Twitter content managers have become increasingly aggressive in removing extremist material and banning those who post it, Instagram managers have been criticized for the slowness of their clampdowns. And, because pictures are often tougher to monitor than words, arty photos by Islamists and extremists often stay up on Instagram for longer than the authorities would like. They are subtle and often layered with meaning, and they really speak to a particular, and young, audience.

The Twenty-First-Century Minaret: SoundCloud

Designed as a way for musicians to share and promote their tracks, the audio-distribution service SoundCloud has over 177 million unique monthly listeners and today hosts far more than musical talent. For extremists, it is a good place to post audio sermons and religious speeches. The voice is often that of a famed cleric from the past, although most of SoundCloud's talks and lectures are by the newer and more violently strident leaders, such as the American-Yemeni militant imam Anwar al-Awlaki, killed by an American drone in 2011. Islamists will post political rally videos and broadcast public service messages about their campaigns; for example, Anwar Ibrahim's People's Justice Party (PKR) in Malaysia used SoundCloud to publicize one of his lectures at a campaign rally, and it went viral. SoundCloud provides a

great way to share audio content quickly and in high quality. It also offers yet another opportunity for young people to find extremist material, as many high-profile social media outlets (like Twitter and Facebook) post links to it. In October 2014, an ISIS radio service began broadcasting out of Mosul, spreading the call to jihad via pop tunes, anthems, and battle songs. Listeners are referred to SoundCloud for more of the same material, which can lead to direct recruitment contact. To date, SoundCloud moderators have been slow to remove most of the extremist content, even though it violates the site's terms of use agreement.

Extremists have also used SoundCloud to upload scandalous audio to embarrass political leaders and expose corruption in high places. In early 2014, a series of intercepted phone calls were posted to the site, making public very private conversations between the then Turkish prime minister, Recep Tayyip Erdoğan, local politicians, and business elites discussing a bribery scheme. The Turkish government promptly blocked access to SoundCloud; only when the material had been deleted was the ban lifted. However, untold thousands had already copied the clandestine recordings.

The New Town Hall: Reddit

The massive interactive discussion forum and entertainment/news website Reddit acts as a rambunctious town

hall for all comers. The site consists of bulletin-board posts submitted by registered users, divided into hundreds of categories and subcategories (called "subreddits"), and voted up or down by users in order to push the "best" material to the top. It means that many if not all of the posts are read by someone (hence the punning wordplay of the name: "read it"), almost guaranteeing at least a modicum of exposure. But here is a platform that, in many ways, is countering the spread of toxic rhetoric—not through delimitation but through further dissemination and dilution. This is one site where the Islamists have been slow to gain a firm foothold and face informed criticism.

Many Reddit account holders, especially the active posters, are from Western countries, and are well-informed and engaged in current affairs, policy matters, and global events. Whenever a post or comment takes on an extremist tone, users jump in with counterarguments attacking and deconstructing the radical argument, often with witty putdowns. Reddit is in the vanguard, along with a few other websites, in pushing back against extremist propaganda. However, one recent counterexample is the foreign fighter whom the extremist group Jabhat al-Nusra had sign up on Reddit to answer questions on living in Syria. The foreign fighter had an excellent command of English (he was probably from the UK) and did a robust job of answering both simple and complex questions, covering marriage, what to pack, daily life, the availability of Nutella,

how the group members kept clean, and so forth. These answers were read by thousands and provided an easygoing, humorous, and very much romanticized view of fighting abroad, making the chat a useful recruiting tool.

In the late 1990s, there were only twelve known websites used by extremist groups for recruitment and radicalization efforts. Today, there are over 10,000 extremist websites and forums—and this does not include the social media sites. This extraordinary growth tells its own story of the vital importance of online activity to extremists. And it is by way of such sites and social media networks, which draw a greater level of active engagement, that we can see both extremists' and Islamists' recruitment and mobilization prowess most explicitly.

TWO

JUST WATCH ME

SEVENTEEN-YEAR-OLD Waris was walking across the main campus of his university in Lahore when he got a message on Signal, his preferred end-to-end encryption app for messaging.[1] One of his good friends, Abdul, had sent him a link to a secure video, "New Revolution," and the access password. It was a fifteen-minute clip that looked like a trailer for a new video game. An extremist leader spoke firmly and with unearthly passion: "We must fight the enemy. If we don't protect our community, who will? Are you ready to heed Our Leader, to do *your* duty?" The clip ended with a call to meet for an action strategy.

This local extremist group, Lashkar-e-Taiba (LeT) had been active on campus since tensions with India had increased and the disturbances in Afghanistan and Pakistan's northern tribal regions had intensified. Waris had grown up in a wealthy family in Karachi, with servants, imported cars,

the best food. His father was a staunch believer in the democratization of Pakistan, though Waris had never paid much attention to politics, or to religion. But he had become sick of the news popping up on his mobile phone about nuclear India's domination and how crime-ridden Karachi was merely an afterthought in the global economy. Waris sent a quick Signal message to Abdul: "I'm in." The rich kids he'd hung out with all of his life were only interested in cars, girls, partying and getting high. Waris was ready to say goodbye to all that.

Two months later, after an intense period of online indoctrination and individual recruitment messaging on Signal, the two friends were gathered with a hundred others in a LeT camp in a remote valley far from the city. They shared a tent and, after a hard day in the training fields, would attend lectures on political and religious issues. Waris turned out to be pretty sharp with an AK-47, while Abdul performed well with a captured American M230 Bravo pod-mounted machine gun. They even had an armored Humvee to practice run-and-gun drills on. Weeks were spent on learning how to construct various types of improvised explosive devices and their most effective deployment. The physical training was tough, but the food was decent, served to the young recruits in a large tent used as a mess hall. Such closeness fostered a solid esprit de corps.

* * *

Social media is a crucial tool for both Islamists and extremists to engage potential recruits in their (very different) causes. The aim is to attract onlookers with powerfully "watchable" material, potent branding, and irresistible PR campaigns, and then to transform passive observers into active participants by galvanizing them into action—be that retweeting a photo, partaking in a protest, voting in elections, or joining the mujahideen. The ways in which Islamists and extremists use social media platforms transform casual connections, drive campaigns, deliver new recruits, and can help shape revolutions.

This chapter examines Islamists' and extremists' digital strategies of mobilization. The tactics rely heavily on the targeting of particular segments of their audience, finessing their "brand" and thereby manipulating the way they are perceived by the public at large, making hay when the sun of Western outrage shines, and rallying sophisticated teams to blitz the spectrum of social media platforms in the hope of "going viral" and reaching even greater audiences. Whereas Islamist parties are out to fortify their constituencies and reach key swing voters, extremists use social media to glorify their adherents and sway disaffected youth who may be sitting on the fence. The central factor for both groups is, obviously, religion—which, it transpires, gives them a significant edge on their nonreligious cohorts—and a polarizing moral narrative molded on "good" versus "evil." Both Islamists and

extremists use social media to bolster this stark frame of reference.

Seeing Clearly

The seismic power of the visual image was never demonstrated more forcefully than in Tunisia in 2010. Street vendor Mohamed Bouazizi set himself on fire and burned himself to death in a public protest over a bogus $200 fine imposed by the local government. Mobile phone videos of the local protests were posted online, quickly rocking the country, and then the wider Arab world. Although Tunisian state-run media ignored the tragedy, the country's Islamic opposition led the charge. As Bouazizi lay dying in hospital, videos of protesters clashing with police were shared on Facebook and YouTube, and rapidly went viral. Soon blogs and postings were filled with abuse, scorn, and hatred for President Ben Ali and his "hoodlum" regime. As news of the "burning man" spread around the world there came calls for Ben Ali to resign. The influential Al Jazeera network ran reports about Bouazizi's plight. In quick succession, other mainstream and international broadcast outlets picked up the story. This was the beginning of the end for secular rule in Tunisia, and in rapid order the end of dictatorships in neighboring Libya and Egypt.

In a sense, the Islamist movement Ennahda had been gifted extraordinary, attention-grabbing images—but it

also knew what to do with them. Ennahda and several other opposition groups used the videos to create memes, posts, and tweets extolling Bouazizi's sacrifice, lamenting the state's arrogance and absolute disregard for one of its ordinary citizens, and expressing anger at the current state of Tunisia. Ennahda was able to leverage a number of memes and posts, one of which had great resonance throughout the Arabic community: "This is our time." Once anger had flared, Ennahda quickly started calling for peaceful protests in the city squares, advertising the time and place on several social media platforms. Its loyal computer whiz-kids and others skilled in web evasion managed to navigate around government firewalls and the official bans of social media sites like YouTube in order to keep the fire burning.

Changing Perceptions

Islamist groups of both political and extremist persuasions are turning to social media and websites in order to craft their image. Influencing external perceptions is crucial to both, but it is certainly more obvious—because the stakes are far higher—with extremist groups such as ISIS, the Taliban, and Hamas. The ways that they use social media make clear that they want to change the way people think about them—that is, they are using the technologies to contour their image—one crucial reason being to encourage potential recruits to relate to them, and then join them. The

goal may also be simply to receive more positive coverage in the media.

This was certainly the case when a Pakistani stand-up comedian, Sami Shah, accidentally got into a Twitter conversation with the Taliban in 2013. Shah tweeted a remark about the Taliban's media tactics, saying, according to his own account, "The Taliban's complaints about TV are a lot like when old people whine about how nothing good is on." Ehsanullah Ehsan, at the time an official Taliban spokesperson, responded to the tweet, saying, "Yes, but our old people have exothermic reactions." Shah, who believed Ehsan's account was fake, wrote back, and the two entered into a prolonged exchange of gags which continued until a journalist interjected to point out to Shah that he was "trading fart jokes with the Taliban." Shah broke off the conversation.

The exchange was a PR win for the Taliban. Though as an organization it had been incensed by Shah's original jest, Ehsan had defused its potential force with wit. Many Twitter users appreciated the comedic value of the exchange, retweeting Ehsan's jokes alongside comments such as "I thought the Taliban were monsters, but they actually have a sense of humor." Shah's discomfort was testament to the potential power of the exchange. He told me in 2014: "Comedy was humanizing [the Taliban] and I didn't want to be a part of such a humanization. I prefer my monsters to remain monsters."[2] Ehsan had singlehandedly sculpted a

new, very "normal" face for the Taliban, achieving a more youthful, human appearance for the group, and one that had mass appeal. Ironically, Ehsan subsequently quit the TTP and laid bare its broken ideology: "they started using social media to mislead young people. They used wrong interpretations of Islam to share messages on social media and shared propaganda through which they caught these youngsters in their trap. I want to especially tell youngsters who use social media to not get caught in the wrong propaganda of these people."[3] The Taliban quickly labeled Ehsan one of the new infidels.

The most sophisticated of the extremist groups in using social media is undoubtedly ISIS. It is clear that online branding is exceptionally important to the group—as is branding in general, if its Mosul gift shop selling flags, T-shirts, and memorabilia in 2015 is anything to go by.[4] The group has worked hard to shape and temper its image. In social media posts aimed at young people, references to religious victory are limited to raised-finger emojis, promises of paradise, and celebration of the martyred. The stream of photos and videos depicting its reign of terror appear alongside other content touting the lighter, more ordinary or indeed more glamorous aspects of living a "pure" life. These are certainly influenced, and more often than not generated, by the many foreign fighters who have gone to join the group. They tweet about their relaxed daily lives: a European ISIS fighter described on his Kik account "a normal-life day:

washing clothes, cleaning the house, training, buying stuff" in between fighting, while others mention animals they have seen and what their Syrian breakfast was like.[5]

These social media users make clear to potential Western recruits that familiar pleasures—pizza, swimming, girls— can still be enjoyed alongside the Muslim lifestyle, which, peppered with emoticons and internet slang, sounds fun: "Lol there's plenty of sisters her [sic]. Marriage is always on the go. We all want to get married here ☺."[6] Memes deliberately make a play for the MTV and YouTube generation: the meme "Pimp My Ride ... Jihadi style" accompanied photos of battered, bombed, and mud-caked cars. Hundreds of photos and videos of lavish mansions, crystal-clear pools, Humvees, and guns extol the apparent luxury and wealth of the "gangsta" ISIS lifestyle. One unofficial video shows mujahideen "drifting" a Soviet-era armored personnel carrier around a town center accompanied by pop music. While this Twitter approach may seem rather banal and harmless, it can have a powerful, normalizing impression on those following the daily lives of ISIS foreign fighters.

Interestingly, this kind of footage is lapped up by nations in South and Central Asia (SCA), despite those conservative, Muslim-majority countries' otherwise often poor response to social media displays of wealth and immodesty, and despite the region's very low penetration of Western social media sites (Russian versions are preferred) and usage compared with the Middle East and

North Africa (MENA). (The relatively poor moderation of those Russian sites actually makes tangible the influence of extreme Islamist—and Russian soft-power—recruitment in the Caucasus and Central Asia, a region in a precarious political state and with not a small history of extremism.) ISIS' social media strategy is proving successful, backed up by the competitive monthly salaries of between $300 and $2,000 it can offer, well above much of SCA's per capita income and particularly attractive to the young people throughout the region unable to find gainful employment.[7] (The wage is perhaps less enticing to those in the affluent West—hence all those Hummers.)

ISIS also seems to want to show its softer side. No doubt with one eye on the viral videos of cats that dominate the internet and particularly delight Western audiences, photos of ISIS fighters playing with kittens appeared in summer 2014 under the Twitter handle @ISILCats.[8] Several of the users' photos also showed children being given cats by the fighters, and a video depicts ISIS combatants handing out ice creams.[9] This is a markedly different story than the usual reports of ISIS having brutally killed or recruited children during its murderous rampage through Iraq and Syria, and is aimed to demonstrate the group's more compassionate side and to appeal to local populations living in occupied territories. These images, alongside the spate of photos in 2014 showing ISIS fighters holding jars of Nutella in occupied areas of Syria and Iraq,[10] were a

deliberate strategy to make the so-called Islamic State appear friendlier and more familiar to Westerners. It seems all these memes were pre-planned and organized in online forums and then rolled out on social networks. ISIS' hope is that some viewers might be encouraged to stop sitting on the fence and join the fight against the infidels.

That encouragement also extends to women. Remarkably for such a vicious organization dominated by young male fighters, ISIS has been a forerunner in crafting a female-friendly image and specifically targeting women with propaganda. Presenting the conservative, maternal role expected of women joining the ISIS cause has been the work of the Zora Foundation, an ISIS media arm.[11] A colorful, animated YouTube video released in 2014 depicts a sewing machine, a first aid kit, and cooking appliances, and gives advice to women in Arabic on how they can contribute to ISIS' insurgency through performing maternal and domestic tasks rather than as active participants.[12] Interestingly, the video also includes a guide to make and edit slideshows—encouraging and prolonging the creation of online propaganda. Charlie Winter, a noted researcher on violent online extremism, confirmed the novelty of such visual outreach: "There will probably be forums doing similar things online, but this is the first time I've come across an actual media organization giving guidance to women on their role."[13] Accordingly, the Zora Foundation has built up a following on Facebook and Twitter, and regularly posts lifestyle tips

and recipes for "between-battle snacks." Although the West is particularly concerned with the recruitment of its girls and women, the Zora Foundation's Arabic-language messages seem intended also to attract Middle-Eastern women living in ISIS-controlled areas.[14]

Though it is belied by the Zora Foundation's Arabic focus and crude clipart, the very professionalism of ISIS' visual and multilingual output is also a strong contributor to honing its image, particularly in the West.[15] The group's videos, thought to be produced by the organization's propaganda arm, the al-I'tisam Media Foundation, under its Western media division, the al-Hayat Media Center, evidence a close familiarity with sophisticated marketing and PR techniques. For instance, *There Is No Life Without Jihad* is a film specifically designed to recruit young Westerners, presented in English by a British former medical student and a young Australian who reference popular video games, proselytize about social degeneration, and wax poetic about the fulfillment found in pursuing an "untainted" life. They are surrounded by other ISIS fighters, in a lush green setting with swaying palm trees in the background—not the dry and dusty battlegrounds many expect.[16] Like all ISIS films, it is carefully choreographed, captured by multiple cameras in high definition, and features near-professional editing and music—a deliberately far cry from the shaky camcorder videos released in the past. It all contributes to a "Hollywoodization" of

fighting for ISIS—a glamorous dream, but one not so very hard to imagine.

The Muslim Brotherhood also uses recruitment videos to cement a particular image in viewers' minds. One that went viral on YouTube lays out the group's grievances against the Egyptian regime and political establishment. It features a preacher discussing the lack of social services, with a succession of shots of rundown neighborhoods, closed bread shops, and overcrowded hospitals. The voiceover then describes the social services work the Brotherhood sponsors, showing its schools, preventative health care, and social work. The video was particularly effective because it showed something most people knew (but didn't see), and portrayed the Brotherhood as social heroes. (See also Chapter 6.) Social media provides an easy platform for the circulation of visualizations of social ills— queues outside government buildings, a lack of electricity, interactions with incompetent government officials, and so on. This authentic, crowdsourced "candid camera" material is extremely influential, and readily sharable.

The Brotherhood (*Ikhwan* in Arabic) also used its websites Ikhwanweb and Ikhwanonline both to improve its public image and spread its messages to the masses. Its central concern is to persuade the public that it is a non-violent victim of government oppression, and to do so it often works through front organizations that at first glance appear to be independent.[17] The Brotherhood has varying

levels of presence on Facebook (the most popular social network in Egypt),[18] but its more innovative image-honing is conducted on its official pages, particularly that managed by the group's political wing, the Freedom and Justice Party, which is mostly focused on outreach and messaging. Not only does the Brotherhood boast a dedicated team of social media entrepreneurs who create and administer websites, it also enjoys the skills and dedication of a loosely organized clutch of young Brotherhood initiates who promote whatever image the group desires across the web. This "E-militia" is formidable.

Posing as ordinary, rational members of the public, members of the E-militia will interject when conversations on Facebook and Twitter seem to be suggesting that the Brotherhood is otherwise, steering the dialog in new Brotherhood-friendly directions. To all appearances they are bona fide discussants simply putting forward a different point of view that anyone might share. One of the few ways their true affiliation can be detected is when identical answers are accidentally posted concurrently in threads—answers that are basically cut-and-paste jobs, crafted and approved from on high. The E-militia will post messages supportive of the Brotherhood while disclaiming formal affiliation by saying—as a Facebook meme of Hassan al-Banna, the founder of the Muslim Brotherhood, which circulated during the 2012 presidential run-offs, humorously put it—"I'm not from the Brotherhood. I disagree

with them on a lot of issues but I respect them."[19] Net-savvy Egyptians quickly sniffed out such ploys. But more sophisticated tactics and campaigns have the potential to change the narrative surrounding the period of Brotherhood rule.

PTI's most colorful campaigner, Imran Khan, also displayed a keen sense of the importance of image when he was campaigning for office. When a serious fall from the speaker's platform four days before the 2013 elections landed him in hospital for some weeks, Khan updated Facebook frequently and kept himself in the public eye, milking maximum sympathy from his accident—to the extent that some on social media accused him of faking the severity of the injury. More recently the former cricket star has strived to align himself with the ideas of hope and a forward trajectory, and to document these in real terms. If this sounds like an Obama-esque image, it is—even down to the clever tagline, "Yes we Khan."

In a country whose prime minister had to step down because of corruption charges and whose government looks increasingly out of touch with the common person, Khan has made himself approachable and human. He has engaged in a highly publicized social media strategy of "inform and invite," in which he has ensured that online Pakistanis are notified about every aspect of his digital campaign, and has even allowed them to inform his thinking on a variety of subjects via a Google+ Hangout live Q&A session. In contrast to the usual overly formal

and aloof candidates, many who watched Khan were attracted by his down-to-earth folksy style and his ability to explain concepts clearly and free of jargon. It was a direct, intimate way to see both Khan and his considerable fan base—stoking the "concert" effect, where you cheer because everyone else is cheering. So when Khan invites his newly minted social media followers to his marches and speeches, hundreds of thousands show up. Propelled by his social media celebrity status, Imran Khan easily won his seat in the National Assembly in 2013, and his party now leads a large northern province. While the word "engagement" might be just a buzzword, the case of Imran Khan shows that voters want to be included in the political process. They want to be heard and talked to as if the candidate were a friend.

The intention behind much of this social media usage is to establish a coherent identity—a brand behind which supporters can amass, be that as friend or foe. If the PTI represents the former, ISIS has largely built its social media campaigns around being the latter—the scourge of all infidels, with terror at the heart of its strategy. Its attention to its brand is clear. The organization's flag, the Black Standard, which harks back to the caliphate that ISIS imitates, appears everywhere. In the recruitment video mentioned above, precise directorial attention had been paid to the placement of flag and speaker. The opening shot, with the camera positioned on the ground, shows the

speaker following the other mujahideen along a path; he is carrying the flag in a way that drapes the black cloth over him, and fills the screen as the camera pans upward. For the rest of the film the Black Standard sways in the breeze behind the speaker in the center of the frame, focusing attention on the continuity between the individual jihadist and ISIS. This is so effective that many other little-known extremist groups have jumped on the video-branding bandwagon. The Salafist militia group Ansar al-Shariah burst onto the scene in 2013 via YouTube videos of its members taking over communities and riding into ungoverned areas across Libya—its own black flag flying high. This helped brand it immediately as a coherent force attempting to revolutionize the northern areas. Its Arabic-language videos were aimed not at Westerners but at the Libyan diaspora and expatriates who had fled the Qaddafi regime, in the hopes that some might come back as foreign fighters or aid its resistance movement—which was how its social media positioned the group.

Know Your Enemy

One of the key components of developing a digital strategy is determining who your audience is, and which segmentation is most crucial to attract and inform. Although it is often touted that social media's power lies in the ability to reach a broader audience than ever before, it is actually the

more specific, narrow viewership that is often sought, especially by extremist groups.

Peter Neumann, director of the International Centre for the Study of Radicalisation and Political Violence, believes that "ISIS understands very well that in order for an act of terrorism to be effective, it needs to actually terrorize people . . . The act of communication that follows the act of violence is almost as important as the act of violence itself."[20] ISIS is well known for its aggressive public relations campaigns featuring atrocity videos and explicit messages that stress a call to action. Though the products are different, the pitch is consistent: God commands his true followers to a holy war. Such films display an acute understanding of how to milk maximum terror and awe out of videos that fly (just) below the regulatory radar. Thus, the carefully stage-managed execution of James Foley in 2014 "capture[d] the full horror of the crime without explicitly showing the exact moment when the captive [was] decapitated—thereby staying within the social media guidelines that ban the dissemination of acts of extreme violence."[21] Films released by ISIS' al-Hayat Media Center in support of domestic terrorism have also more specifically targeted certain Western audiences,[22] though with the recent Coalition advances they are now appearing less frequently. Al-Hayat released two separate videos in 2014 featuring foreign fighters who sought to convince sympathetic Muslims to conduct domestic terrorist acts in their home countries of

France and Canada.[23] ISIS ensures that its videos—particularly those depicting beheadings—prominently feature international converts, especially those hailing from the West, such as the notorious "Jihadi John" (now known to have been the Kuwaiti-born British national Mohammed Emwazi, finally confirmed dead in January 2016 after a 2015 drone strike), and the Frenchman Maxime Hauchard.

Like ISIS, the militant al-Qaeda-affiliated group al-Shabaab also trades in a potent combination of fear, atrocity, and glossy PR to spread its message, expertly identifying its core market (disaffected urban males aged 15–25, anti-government, former madrassa student, and so on). Al-Shabaab was particularly smart in recruiting from the Somalian diaspora, skillfully targeting the numerous second-generation Somali-Americans, a number of whom were living in Minnesota, whom the group knew to be disillusioned and not fully integrated. The online strategy to woo these young men involved powerful YouTube videos led by well-spoken Westerners, which look like mini TED talks. One featured a Somali (with a good American accent) using inspiring rhetoric and funny anecdotes to extol the virtues of fighting for his grandfather's land and bringing an end to the suffering—which the West had created. Over 150 young men ended up setting off for Somalia to join the group (many of whom were, however, stopped at the airport by law enforcement authorities).

Social media is itself extremely useful in disaggregating populations in order to finesse online campaigning. A 2016 Rand study revealed how sophisticated some extremists' social media usage is. Profiles will be pored over in order to learn how best to target susceptible individuals or groups, based on certain defining factors (such as religion, race, ethnicity, and even location)—a technique known as "narrowcasting." Webpages, videos, images, and information can thereby be tailored to appeal to a specific group or individual. The young are often in the crosshairs. And the terrorists intensely scrutinize these websites and precisely calibrate their responses to "the way a pedophile might look at those sites to potentially groom would-be victims."[24]

Islamist groups are also using advanced metrics and tools to examine their engagement and analyze which campaign messages resonate with key audiences. Traditionally, this entailed on-the-ground research conducted house-to-house, neighborhood by neighborhood—and that does still go on. However, rather than relying solely on grassroots supporters pounding the pavements, the shrewder groups are now complementing that information with data drawn from crowdsourcing and hotspot-mapping social media programs, allowing them to tabulate opinions and sentiments on a street-by-street basis. Similar to Pew Research Center polls and Nielsen ratings, online analyses of hard data help to quantify patterns of sentiment and statistical views on key issues. Enhanced search engine optimization

(SEO) tools comb blogs, chat rooms, Twitter feeds, Facebook posts, YouTube comments, and Google queries for keywords. A wide range of Islamist political entities can then use these metrics to help them decide upon a range of strategies, from where best to invest advertising dollars to get more clickthroughs and views, to what line an entire political campaign should take.

The flipside of creating an image is being reactive to the demands and desires of an audience—and, in a sense, creating that desire. From the earliest years of social media, and in contrast to secular parties and certainly to ruling governments, Islamist forces have been acutely receptive to their audience. The clips of sermons and lectures issued by the Islamists in the early days were essentially mini outreach programs or encapsulated some other form of feedback based on audience concerns. These quickly morphed into thousands of Islamist-sponsored blogs and Q&A forums where citizens could interact with each other online, drawing unprecedented numbers of interested participants and eventually supporters. Incumbent governments offered nothing comparable, because this sort of citizen is not exactly desirable from a ruling party's standpoint: there would be too many questions they didn't want asked, let alone answered.

Islamists and extremists are using sophisticated online strategies to reach and react to their audience—getting what they want by giving the people what they want. Al-Shabaab has gone much further than jihadi videos. It made a major

online play for the attention of the establishment via its English-language Twitter account, and not only by tactically updating the precise locations and movements of various engagements (see Chapter 1). @HSMPress has also set itself up as a press organization and a legitimate source of knowledge—a news feed that explicitly decries journalists whom it feels have a biased view of what is "really" going on in Somalia. Under its numerous Twitter handles, the HSM Press Office charges journalists "to verify and double-check their sources instead of regurgitating unreliable accounts often from subjective media" and even warns its followers not to expect impartial reports from the "Kafir media" about the mujahideen.[25] It engages in overly obvious fact-checking and rides high on whistle-blowing. The irony of an extremist organization touting itself as the lone voice of objectivity is not lost on the West. But it is an extremely effective strategy, despite the frequent suspensions of its various Twitter accounts. By establishing itself as the source—sometimes the only source—of the "truth" that the good citizens of Somalia deserve and desperately need, al-Shabaab achieves a legitimacy it could not otherwise dream of.

Religious civic groups also connect with more militant groups—even religious political parties that use extra-electoral means—to leverage legitimacy, and because the latter can provide security, which is a limited good. For example, pro-Palestinian Twitter feeds—such as @PalinfoAR, @felesteenonline, @qudstvsat, and @alresalahpress—often

perform outreach on behalf of Hamas, using the hashtag #Hamas, and publish information relevant to the organization. In turn, these civic groups have the ability and flexibility to create and amplify awareness of Hamas across a wide spectrum. Hamas' strategy here is to cultivate its "fanboys" and grassroots base. And the group has found considerable success across its social media platforms, receiving 140,000 mentions a month, while #Hamas appeared over 30,000 times.

Round-the-Clock Recruitment

Hezbollah's E-militia is a 24/7 dedicated team of twenty-five to thirty online operators who are producing, generating, and reposting content that promotes the group's campaign ideas. Hezbollah's social media HQ is a room filled with computers, servers, and large-screen TVs, all monitoring data—a command center for cyber warfare, though its operations are primarily geared toward recruitment. Lacking the kind of coordinated force enjoyed by the Muslim Brotherhood, Hezbollah's team tactically befriend susceptible groups, seeing in them potential members of the organization, establishing trust before beginning to spread the organization's message. This is much like its offline tactics: social media simply gives Hezbollah a broader audience of potential friends. And the tactics are working: the group's Twitter handle, @almanarnews, had 8,000 followers in 2012, and now has over 470,000.

Groups such as al-Shabaab and Boko Haram also rely on "fanboys" to amplify, repost, and retweet content. Between 600 and 700 loyal grassroots supporters are tasked with spreading content organically within two to four hours of an initial posting on YouTube—through manipulating the number of views, reposting, tagging, linking, generating chatter on other platforms, and so on. In Lebanon, Hamas, which has a sophisticated social media team, will often post the URL of its YouTube videos on a variety of Arabic-language blogs, daily newspaper comments sections, and American University of Beirut student pages as well as user-generated chat rooms and web forums. It is a laborious but necessary task if Islamist propaganda—which so often violates established social media platforms' terms of service—is to evade removal, but also achieve penetration.

These sorts of platform limitations are one reason why many Islamist organizations operate across a number of social media platforms concurrently. Increasing clamp-downs by Facebook, Twitter, and YouTube are pushing Islamist groups further afield to the margins of the web, and they are using decentralized and less popular social media networks such as Diaspora and Friendica to spread propaganda.[26] These sorts of sites, functioning with open-source software and existing on private servers, make third-party oversight more difficult but do not deliver on the audience front.[27] Extremist groups like ISIS tend to use them as jumping-off boards, developing content

before repurposing it elsewhere. Either way, the variety of approach contributes to the overall impression of determined and concerted campaigning.

Groups that stick to the main networks hit them all hard. While some sites will obviously appeal more to certain audience segments than others—Ask.fm and Facebook are used to reach a younger audience, for instance—a lot of the time the across-the-board bombardment is geared simply to grab and then retain the attention of social media users wherever they can be snagged. ISIS' multipronged approach using Twitter, Facebook, and Instagram not only increases the likelihood of material being seen (either searched for or stumbled upon), but creates a feedback loop that can ensnare social media users, and gives adherents even more incentive to remain active online. And the content is coming twenty-four hours a day—often documenting in real time what those twenty-four hours have held and will hold in store for mujahideen fighters, as with the popular series "Mujatweets" (popularized with the Twitter hashtag #mujatweets) launched by ISIS' al-Hayat Media Center in 2014.

It's Catching

The golden ticket for online Islamist and extremist groups is to "go viral." Karine Nahon and Jeff Hemsley define this as being "where many people simultaneously forward a specific

information item, over a short period of time, within their own social networks, and where the message spreads ... to different, often distant networks," until the content has reached a widespread audience and is no longer shared.[28] There is, then, no explicit threshold that defines viral content. "Going viral" is more a process than it is a particular "moment."

Islamists and extremists employ a number of strategies to encourage the "virality" of their content. First and foremost, they are expert manipulators of SEO and the use of popular search terms and key phrases. Almost all parties know how to optimize YouTube video descriptions to make their videos as discoverable as possible. The Parti Islam Se-Malaysia (PAS) in Malaysia will often paste a list of politically loaded terms—"revolution," "change agents," "oppression," "dictatorship," "struggle," "tomorrow is today"—underneath its videos, a fundamentally effective SEO tactic which helps to broaden their audience. A more aggressive strategy used by some groups is to deploy keywords and phrases that are related to current events, but completely unrelated to the actual content of their posts, in order to artificially generate user interest and hits, such as, in 2014, ISIS' use of #worldcup.[29]

More sophisticatedly, religious organizations, extreme and liberal, which have long used soccer camps and other youth groups to mix fun and play with serious religious rhetoric, have today shifted this tactic to the web. Some organizations might host a server for a popular video game

or promote youth publications. LeT used comic books to get their message across, and, although ISIS has not yet got around to actually creating a playable version, its 2014 *Grand Theft Auto*-style shoot 'em up trailer—so innovative it garnered international media coverage—points to what might be possible. The cleverly constructed PR strategy of smuggling extremist subject matter in "cool and entertaining" content has become so prevalent that we are now almost inured to it.

Incentivizing online engagement is a critical strategy for extremists—and one that the counterterrorism community has been slow to catch on to. This includes the "gamification" of online discussion forums and websites—that is, the encouragement of online users to compete with each other to gain status-based rewards. Virtually every hardline Islamist web forum now uses a points-based game system. Users can compete for badges, access to higher levels, more "reputation," and sometimes even physical prizes. Websites might reward those who post most often or with most extreme or fundamentalist content, and who might then gain, on sites such as the leading extremist forums al-Fida and Shumukh al-Islam, the revered status of "Mujaheed."[30] More "rep" points can mean anything from a differently colored name, to a longer e-signature, or access to more information, and even becoming a site administrator.

Anwar al-Awlaki, an extraordinarily influential US-born religious extremist who was one of the leaders of the

al-Qaeda affiliate in Yemen until his death by a drone strike in 2011, played the gamification game expertly both online and off. He urged those in his online forums to increase their participation, and also jocularly assigned grisly tasks to readers of the notorious English-language magazine *Inspire*, such as "make a Bomb in the Kitchen of Your Mom" and "pull off Mumbai [attack] near Whitehouse till martyrdom."[31] Most crucially, al-Awlaki realized that he himself was a prize to be won: messages and videos from him were traded like baseball cards, and personal emails from him (or what were deemed to be so) could make the difference between acts of terror remaining at the level of discussion or becoming real. Al-Awlaki was known to have encouraged a number of extremists (allegedly, the shooter at Fort Hood in 2009, and the 2010 Times Square bomber) into real-life attacks, though there is little research into gamification's specific role in the translation from the online world to reality. Whatever the connection, the game-related aspects of competition and reward do motivate people to return to such sites and to stay there for longer, prolonging their exposure to extremist ideology.

Click to Mobilize

Islamist political parties are also keen to attract and motivate followers to take action—that is, to vote. I witnessed

the crucial elections of 2013 in both Malaysia and Pakistan, and in both cases social media played a key role.

As befits a system often described as "electoral authoritarianism," the Malaysian electoral campaigns offered a veritable showcase of governmental scrutiny, scaremongering, and crackdowns, and the opposition's fleet-footed non-mainstream media tactics that ultimately helped to secure them victory. Against the ruling coalition Barisan Nasional's menacing, but rather desperate, reports (published in conventional news outlets) of "experts" warning readers that they were living in a "bubble" that was "devoid of reality" if they spent too much time online,[32] opposition forces proved how effective online mobilization could be. So, while the UMNO and its pet news outlets (such as the laughably pro-government *New Straits Times*)[33] predictably badgered and hectored, painting the opposition as a bunch of untrustworthy hooligans whose campaign slogans were slanderous at best, and could possibly ignite an ethnic civil war, the opposition groups reached out through alternative online channels to a youthful demographic they knew could change the course of the election.

The opposition's successes in the past two elections (the upcoming election in 2018 will be significant) were accompanied by, and perhaps even dependent on, the explosion of alternative media outlets. In the historic 2008 elections, Malaysian voters could access a wider variety of news sources than ever before, including indigenous online

newspapers like Malaysiakini.com, global news sources such as Al Jazeera, and numerous blogs from across the political spectrum,[34] including that of the former prime minister Dr. Mahathir Mohamad (who himself blogged about UMNO's iron grip on the country's media and free speech a few months later).[35] The government's online presence was rudimentary. But still, internet media during the 2008 elections was top-down, unidirectional, very much Web 1.0. It was not until the 2013 general election that Malaysian political parties began to recognize social media as a game-changer. In fact, Prime Minister Najib Razak declared it Malaysia's "first social media election"[36] and even said he would pick UMNO candidates for parliament based on the strength of their social media presence[37]—a clear statement about what he deemed to be a vote-winner.

Social media was crucial to attract and convince the millions of new voters who were under the age of forty, most of whom (90 per cent, according to one study) preferred it over newspapers or even television as a news source.[38] The platforms were also seeing an explosion in user numbers, with 2 million using Twitter (up from 3,000 in 2008) and more than 13 million on Facebook (up from 800,000 in 2008).[39] Crucial to the strategy was to genuinely interact with voters, who wanted to hear from their politicians not via formal speeches or pre-scripted television ads, but through direct and (seemingly) unmediated contact over the internet. Thus, whereas the then prime

minister and chair of UMNO, Najib Razak, simply used Twitter to update his 1.7 million followers on government initiatives and economic growth, retweeting from a few select feeds, the opposition leader Anwar Ibrahim followed almost 15,000 accounts on Twitter (in contrast to Razak's 129) and used his far more frequent tweets (which gave the impression of being self-penned) to interact with other users, including his wife and daughter, who are also politicians. Despite having less than a quarter of Razak's followers (only 400,000), Ibrahim won the Twitter war.

Another crucial strand was the tone of social media interactions. Ibrahim's party, PKR, scored a hit with an August 2013 Facebook post featuring a Photoshopped version of the poster for the hit 2011 movie *KL Gangster*, replacing the faces of the movie's stars with those of UMNO leaders. It received nearly 800 "likes"—a number no post on UMNO's more staid and predictable Facebook page ever came close to. Even naughtier was the DAP's parody of the globally ubiquitous "Gangnam Style" music video, titled "Ubah Rocket Style" (*ubah* is Malaysian for "change": it references the Pakatan Rakyat party's GE13 campaign slogan). The video, shot on location all over Malaysia, touches on a number of serious social issues (such as the rising cost of living, business scandals, environmental concerns, and military armament) as it follows DAP mascot Ubah the hornbill as he fights corruption and crime.[40] It has been viewed over 530,000 times on YouTube alone—a moderate hitter

compared to other videos on the DAP YouTube channel, one of which has been played over 800,000 times.[41] No videos on UMNO's YouTube channel come anywhere close to that figure, and many fall far below it.[42]

Bizarrely, the spiritual leader of PAS and undisputed political king of Malaysian Facebook, the late Nik Abdul Aziz Nik Mat, did not make much effort in capitalizing on the attention of the 1.8 million who "liked" his page (700,000 more than Prime Minister Razak). Nik Aziz's posts were regularly the most liked, most commented on, and most shared of any Malaysian political figure. One post from September 9, 2013, discussing his efforts to combat corruption in the state of Kelantan, which has been governed by PAS since 1990, was liked more than 13,000 times, shared by nearly 2,000, and received more than 500 comments. It had no flashy graphics, and its subject matter and style were serious (and a little dull)—but that did not matter. The PAS knew that its constituency was older, conservative Malaysians living in rural districts—exactly the group least likely to be web-savvy, or even to have internet access.

However, noting the Arab Spring's demonstration of the power of social media, and political campaigns across the MENA and SCA regions, the PAS has established a strong online presence since the elections in 2011. With opposition parties attempting to portray the PAS as a dangerous, extremist Islamic group, it is downplaying its religious identity. The PAS has shifted attention away from

the racial and ethnic problems perpetually focused on by other parties, and which the Malaysian public is growing tired of, to the corruption and authoritarianism of Malaysia, and to economic issues—a central reason for unrest among younger populations.[43] Its Turun ("Bring Down") campaign hosted many small rallies in local communities of every state, which culminated in a large protest in Kuala Lumpur. A great deal of the party's resources is put into achieving direct interaction with individuals, often from the poor and the middle class. The PAS now has considerable presence on five or more social media platforms, including Twitter, Instagram, and WhatsApp as well as Facebook, and it is a great facilitator of online discussions, even if it does tend to the emotive rather than remaining issue-driven.[44]

These strategies for mobilizing mass support were all learned from other political campaigns, and particularly emulated Egypt's Muslim Brotherhood and Pakistan's Imran Khan. I was in Pakistan for the run-up to the 2013 national elections and observed at first-hand the extent of that mobilization. Imran Khan and his PTI party ran their campaign on an anti-corruption platform and the core message was how they would clean up the establishment. The media-savvy PTI's digital strategy was built on a series of before-and-after photos of Pakistan, showing the old (signs of corruption and abuse) and the new (PTI's work in communities, visions of a better future). This culminated in a YouTube montage depicting a number of

blatant voting irregularities at polling stations alongside photos of booths in PTI strongholds. The contrast between corruption and legitimacy could not have been stronger, and resonated with a population one of whose major complaints was the lack of transparency in past elections. With a governance system incapable of monitoring election corruption, PTI used this visual material to launch a campaign to encourage ordinary people to report any electoral irregularities. And they came through in force: within a day the clips were appearing on primetime TV throughout Pakistan. PTI had successfully crowdsourced election monitoring. The national outrage was immediate. As a consequence, for the first time in its history the Election Commission nullified returns in eight fraud-prone districts and ordered a revote. The video proof of election deceit was a powerful boost for Islamist candidates in the 2013 election. In more than one way, social media mobilization had won the Islamists votes.

Righteous Defenders

Muslim communities pre-date the establishment of any modern state. For the majority of citizens within the Islamic world, their faith identity can supersede support for any political party or party line and even outdistance the loyalty they have for their native land. It is certainly no secret that most voters who are drawn to religious

confessional parties give their support out of adherence to Islamic principles. Thus, with this religious-driven support behind them, Islamic parties have a distinct advantage in battling nearly every secular ruling party or government of almost any nation—and social media has become the main instrument of change, the key enabler.

Islamists and extremists know that the seismic political effects they desire and often achieve do not always have purely political roots. Islam plays a crucial part. And so politicians of every stripe (secular or religious) vie over gaining the support of imams—key influencers who are enormously popular on borderless social media. Imams, unsurprisingly given the patronage networks, usually support religious parties. One imam in Nigeria, however, made a stand against it all. He spoke out against the use of social media campaigning by political parties in the run-up to the country's March 2015 elections, condemning the practice of disseminating propaganda while gathering information on voters, and calling on the youth of Nigeria to take to social media to challenge their politicians' electioneering. He also accused politicians of recruiting, even bribing, other local imams to include political language in their sermons, in person and over social media, and was outraged that imams were giving their support to "the highest bidder." It appears to have been a lucrative business.

Whether it is downplayed or put front and center, barely referenced or saturates outreach messages, Islamists'

and extremists' campaigns often draw on their status as defenders of their faith, or at least of their people's identity. This zealous mobilization is most often seen in times of crisis, such as when Islam is felt to have been insulted— often by events that have happened overseas, and which only come to exert the pressure they do because of social media. (See also Chapter 4.) One such outrage was committed on March 20, 2011, when Florida pastor Terry Jones put the Koran "on trial." He found it guilty of harboring a "dangerous religion" and burned a single copy. Islamists and extremists immediately seized upon this otherwise isolated stunt, committed by a maverick figure, which had been largely ignored by US and other international media (though Islamists claimed falsely that Jones enjoyed popular support in the United States).

Non-mainstream and online Islamist-dominated news sources were crucial in mobilizing action around this event. The UK online newspaper *Asian Image*, which caters to Britain's South Asian community, first reported the story, having previously featured news of Jones' plans to burn a copy of the Koran.[45] Online articles like this are easily shared, and there is clear data to show how effective they can be. Pakistani media had also given extensive coverage to Jones' earlier intentions,[46] but the Punjab Assembly beat the media to it, issuing a statement condemning Jones less than forty-eight hours after the burning took place. Many got the story directly from the internet. Religious

leaders almost immediately began to call for action. An Urdu-language newspaper controlled by the Islamist party Jamaat-e-Islami wrote on March 23, "The Muslim world should take serious notice of the filthy act of the US pastors. They should not only protest the incident, but also demand punishment for the cursed pastors. It should be remembered that this act too is a part of the crusade war." The first protests took place in Pakistan on March 23, only a day after the news had broken, and were led by representatives of extremist groups and right-wing political parties.[47] On March 25, 2011, the first Friday after the Koran-burning took place, thousands of Pakistanis throughout the Sindh province joined protests that had been organized by the local head of Jamaat-e-Islami.[48]

News of the Koran-burning took a little more time to fully penetrate Afghanistan. The then President Hamid Karzai made a televised statement on the evening of March 24, calling on the United States to prosecute Jones, and made another speech about it on March 31. The Koran-burning was discussed on television on March 27, yet, according to BBC World Monitoring, it was far from the most important news item that day. The much more violent protests in Afghanistan were therefore entirely unexpected. On April 1, 2011, a demonstration over the burning of the Koran escalated into a riot, and a mob stormed the United Nations building in the northern city of Mazar-i-Sharif, killing seven UN employees and five Afghans. Although

there had been some "traditional" media coverage of the Koran-burning in the Afghan press, the real fan to the flames had been the three mullahs at the Blue Mosque who had devoted their Friday sermons to the incident and urged their congregants to begin protesting for Jones' arrest.[49] Protests also took place in other parts of Afghanistan as word of both the burning and the unrest spread via online networks and word of mouth. High-profile condemnations of Jones' actions by the US president, among others, did not calm the violent demonstrations, which continued for two days. Hezbollah placed a bounty on Jones' head. Later, Iran's foreign minister called Jones "evil and an apostate,"[50] further contributing to the anger surrounding the pastor's actions.

The situation was exacerbated when, on February 22, 2012, US soldiers stationed at the airbase in Bagram, Afghanistan, burned several copies of the Koran, apparently by accident. Afghan workers there noticed the charred books and notified an Afghan commander. The country's media seized on the incident, again enflaming a population already sensitive to and primed by the Koran-burning coverage the previous year. The airbase was besieged for days, and deadly riots sprang up across the country. There was extensive reporting on the incidents and the protests on Afghanistan's most popular independent broadcast outlets, including Dari-language 1TV and broadcast outlets based in the Kandahar province, which may have incited protests in southern Afghanistan, the Taliban's traditional stronghold.

It is important to note that reactions in the mainstream media were mixed. Some, including prominent political figures, propounded an anti-US stance; 1TV quoted Afghan MP Mullah Tarakhel as chanting "Death to America, long live Islam," while another member of parliament, Abdul Sattar Khawasi, claimed that "we will make a decision, we will ask them to declare jihad against America." But many other media outlets urged restraint, and featured apologies by US and International Security Assistance Force officials. Even President Karzai, while he condemned the incident, refrained from the anti-US rhetoric he sometimes employed. Nevertheless, the outrage and violence went on—precisely because of the mobilization of Islamists and extremists.

Many recognized at the time and subsequently that the furor over and actions against the burnings were the work of Islamist and extremist organizations. Kandahar ex-member of parliament Yunus Fakoor said radical religious groups were pouring oil on the fire for their own purposes: "This is not a defense of faith. They are exploiting the religious feelings of people."[51] Islamist political parties seized on these events as opportunities to advance their cause—as a way to recruit financial supporters, volunteers, and votes. They also played themselves off against their governments, whom they chastised and condemned for not taking a stronger stance against those whom they viewed as "defamers of Islam." The extremists' strategy lay in playing up reports (both true and false) about the

Koran-burning in order to stir up the innate emotions surrounding the holy book to incite a sense of outrage, even of hatred—to agitate a reaction that would conscript and drive warriors to jihad. There were also political points to be scored. That same day, the Taliban stated on its "Voice of Jihad" website that 6,000 protesters in Jalalabad in Nangarhar province had chanted "Death to America," "Death to the puppet government," and "Long live the Taliban"—and so were clearly in favor of the Taliban's return to power. It claimed that the US military's Koran-burning increased its popular support.

However, for many Afghans who took part in these 2012 riots, it was not about supporting a particular organization, but a matter of principle—a case of mobilizing against "the enemies of our soil, our honor, our country, and our religion," as one protester told pro-government Kabul News TV on February 21. Islamist groups not only rally supporters but also encourage and in some sense co-opt their constituents' moral judgments by mobilizing around the rhetoric of justice and "right and wrong." Social media offers the potential for greater numbers of citizens to be exposed to, and gravitate toward, Islamist and extremist messages of the struggle between "good" and "evil."

Key for both Islamists' and extremists' defense of Islam is an anti-West stance that is founded on the legacy of imperialism as much as on the West's more recent forays into Iraq, its support for Israel, or a fundamental clash of

value systems. Churchill himself had written a manual for dealing with the tribal regions separating Pakistan and Afghanistan, with undertones of bringing "civilization" to the tribal peoples. The Koran-burnings were seen as yet another instance of white imperialists—Christian and/or Western military—interfering in the region. Islamist organizations' strategy of associating present-day American soldiers with the British occupation of Afghanistan a hundred years earlier resonated with many.

ISIS is the most prevalent manipulator of this anti-West rhetoric. Alongside more abstract concepts like honor and duty, or assurances of the financial gains to be had from military service, or the "coolness" and excitement offered by a military lifestyle, ISIS recruitment videos turn to history. One YouTube video entitled "The End of Sykes–Picot" is presented in fluent English by a Chilean man, Abu Safiya, who wields an impressive knowledge of the Sykes–Picot Agreement and of the workings of the current American government. ISIS' social media campaign also focuses on current controversies in the Western world—inequality, seemingly widespread depression, and so forth—and then highlights how its converts have overcome the deficiencies of the modern world through jihad. The European converts so prominently featured in its videos draw on many of the grievances about military advancement and intervention in the Middle East, and emphasize governance and fighting against imperialism. Digital strategies work best when they

play upon inbuilt identity grievances like those surrounding the perceived imperialist motives of foreign powers. And Islamists and extremists are able to draw on this rhetoric in a way in which other political organizations do not, or cannot.

Unlike secular parties, the Islamists can call on religious iconography and traditions to entice members into the fold. "God is on our side," they claim. In their campaign rallies, they can say that a vote for their cause is a vote for God. As many Jamaat-e-Islami rallies would put it, "God was campaigning for them." A vote for them would not only lead to a good outcome in this world but also in the afterlife.

Getting people to believe their messages of morality and justice is, of course, a two-pronged boon for Islamist parties. Not only do they spread the word of God, but they spread their own words too. Campaigns based on their own "goodness" (religious and otherwise) paint their opponents as "evil," and with the full force of faith. Social media allows Islamist parties to increase their audience, and also to influence it, as other political movements are not able to. This is one of the key goals of digital engagement. Using social media to mobilize followers to their cause, spread messages, and, in some cases, to make prescriptive statements on moral and religious principles, Islamist and extremist groups have expanded their presence online. It is, for many groups, a position of real power—which they are increasingly wielding directly against their enemies, using the digital strategies that served them so well in the past.

THREE

GUERRILLA WEBFARE

"YOU SHOULD HAVE seen the explosion!" exclaimed Salman, a seventeen-year-old Taliban foot soldier.[1] It was August 2015, and he had just assisted in blowing up two NATO armored cars on the "White Road" in Afghanistan, having hacked NATO's systems to ascertain its soldiers' location and movements. After two difficult years of training in code and software development, especially encryption detection programs, this poor farmer's son had become adept at using technologies developed on the other side of the world. Information itself had become weaponized.

Salman had meticulously planned the attack using new software stolen from the British military which had allowed him to break into NATO command's main computer system. It was a simple matter to ascertain planned routes and track movements of response forces. What's more, Salman was able to plant viruses in the mainframe

computer which disabled NATO field operations for more than a week.

Using geolocation information gleaned from the hack, Salman's team hid an IED along a curve in the road, which was detonated as the armored cars drove over the spot. "We had guns set up on both sides of the road," Salman explained. "When some of the bastards tried to get out of the burning wreckage, we cut 'em down." The attackers salvaged some gear, including a laser pistol-sight and a handheld computer. This was how they proved a mission had been successful—by bringing back the enemy's belongings, not just pictures of the dead.

Salman also employed his cyber skills to help weed out those disloyal to the cause. One time, it was suspected that a Western spy was operating within the Taliban. This mole was gathering information about plans and strategies, then passing it on to his CIA handler. Salman was put on the case. He quickly discovered the traitor's identity and bugged his computer, tracking all of his online activities. Some days later, a Taliban gunman followed the spy to a train station in Islamabad, where he was gunned down in a men's room.

* * *

Information has become weaponized in more than one way. Many Islamist and extremist groups now use their digital expertise to hit their opponents, be they governments or competitors, where it hurts: online. Having mobilized a

digital support system, they can cripple their adversaries. This chapter lays out the tactics, strategies, and unintended consequences of a multitude of cyber-attacks, information wars, and faceless guerrilla "webfare."

Prepping the Soil

Having visited Malaysia a number of times, during the 2013 presidential elections I saw how central to the political struggle social media had become. Any country whose prime minister tweets to more than 3.7 million followers, 'grams to 50,000, blogs on his personal website, and has received more than 4.8 million likes on Facebook (when the Indonesian premier musters a paltry 700,000 despite having a population ten times the size), obviously takes social media very seriously indeed.[2] Perhaps even more impressive is that the main opposition leader, Anwar Ibrahim, is also prolific online, boasting over a million Twitter followers and maintaining a high level of engagement despite his politicized incarceration. In 2013, I interviewed candidates, aides, managers, and campaign workers. It became clear that social media was an important weapon in their twenty-first-century arsenal—and that it had changed the tactics of the battle.

It has also transformed the experience of ordinary Malaysians. One young Islamist has spoken about social media sites like Facebook and Twitter offering "a secure place we can inhabit without fear or censorship. In fact,

social media is our weapon and a place where we can all engage in discussion and take on pro-government forces without worrying about tear gas or a police beating. It is our virtual army ... Without social media, we'd be back in the Stone Age."[3] The weapons of resistance may be new, but the history of using such tools is a long one.

Islamists were early adopters of social media and cyber warfare due to historic restrictions placed on them by the authorities. For instance, in many countries (such as Saudi Arabia and Egypt), Islamists were not permitted to congregate in public; their public meetings were banned or members would be arrested. "Meeting" online was a good workaround, and they came to the internet with a close knowledge of covert operations. So too, for the more militarily minded of the groups, the acquisition of physical weapons was difficult and very risky, especially for new recruits: cyber warfare offered different ways to get back at their oppressive governments. The Islamists' previous underground status had already led to their embrace of technology (such as audio cassettes—see Chapter 4) in order to spread their message and avoid detection. Subsequent generations, emanating from the middle classes and educated to university level, have the capacity to migrate these tactics online, as well as often the more specialized skills in technical computing and software development to mount very real and serious attacks.

Cyber Pearl Harbor

The cyber realm has today become an operational domain in the military sense, just as air, land, and sea are. Cyber-attacks really do mean war. Since 2012, the US has been warning of—and recognizing its vulnerability to—a "cyber Pearl Harbor," a devastating bolt from the blue that could change the whole course and outcome of the war currently being fought to protect American online security.[4] Governments, intelligence officials, and policymakers nowadays all recognize this new threat, which, like physical attacks, could disable communications systems, power plants, electricity transmission systems, and so on, and might demand a counteroffensive or even pre-emptive strikes.

It is clear to many that a significant proportion of such strikes are emanating from the Middle East and South Asia. Indeed, that warning of another "cyber Pearl Harbor" came from the then US Defense Secretary Leon Panetta in a speech made in October 2012 in the wake of two ruinous cyber-attacks. That summer saw the most destructive online offensive on the business sector thus far when the "Shamoon" virus infected almost 30,000 computers at Saudi Arabia's state oil company, Saudi Aramco, collecting information on the firm's refining capabilities via a keystroke logging system, and then disabling the infected machines.[5] The religious hackers identified themselves as the Cutting Sword of

Justice (there is some evidence that the attack was carried out by Iranian militias upset about sectarian rivalries developing in Saudi Arabia), and left their calling card on each affected computer: an image of the American flag on fire. That September, too, the US was hit directly: a distributed denial-of-service (DDoS) attack denied customers access to the websites of nine US banks, including the Bank of America, Wells Fargo, and JP Morgan Chase, for several days. The Islamic hacktivist group Izz ad-Din al-Qassam Cyber Fighters, a group with links to the military wing of Hamas, claimed responsibility.

There have, of course, been many more cyber-attacks on Western governments and major companies emanating from all over the world—China, Russia, and North Korea being most recently in the crosshairs of the US administration.[6] Yet, although the law is trying to catch up with the new crime (even in defining what it is), and judicial cases and sanctions are under way in international courts, there have so far been no instances of direct military response to cyber threats. Thus, although it is not necessarily the case that governments will always respond to cyber-attacks in cyberspace, for now the difficulty of ascertaining attribution and location, and fixing a definition of a serious cyber-attack in international law, means that opposition groups and rogue states view this type of warfare as an opportunity to inflict serious damage with little real consequence.

New Battle Formations

A range of actors—authoritarian states, pro-government sympathizers, anti-government protestors, hackers, intelligence services—go head-to-head on the information battleground. Cyber-attacks enable everything from the quashing of dissent and the furthering of political motives to the takedown of websites and infraction of online security networks—with very public outcomes.

This chapter outlines the key cyber threats—including DDoS attacks, malware, hacking, and surveillance—and examines who is using them, against whom, for what purpose, and to what effect. Each has potentially devastating results, be that Islamists and extremists exacting leverage on governments and international actors, or governments protecting themselves by closing down on their opponents and populations at large. Rivals are squaring up against each other wielding the same digital weapons.

The Online AK-47: DDoS

Easy to use and the most common weapon wielded by Islamists and extremists against sitting governments, denial of service is the AK-47 of the cyber war. DDoS attacks have the addition of being "distributed," in that they originate from many different sources rather than just

one. These e-assaults target websites or networks, flooding them with server requests or visits and overloading their capacity, thus preventing users from accessing them. In a sense they function similarly to physical protests insofar as they block access to a desired "location" on the internet, bring attention to the site, and spread a group's narrative.[7] While visiting Malaysia's federal administrative capital, Putrajaya, to monitor the run-up to the 2013 elections, I witnessed an Islamist hacker squad temporarily knock out the official website of the ruling UMNO party. This DDoS attack served as an embarrassing event for this one-party state which had been in power ever since obtaining independence. A group of advanced bloggers were further able to hack into the website and download personal information on UMNO party members. A young blogger who participated in the takedown proudly bragged: "We are doing all we can to create noise and confusion for the establishment! They are the enemy. For years they have kept us under their thumb. Now we are hitting back and it's going to hurt." DDoS attacks are a means of flaunting the empowerment of the previously disempowered in the faces of the ruling powers.

This was nowhere more prevalently seen than during the Egyptian Revolution of 2011. Islamists aligned themselves with (and in some cases contracted out to) Anonymous and Telecomix—loose conglomerations of hacktivists and hacker communities holding a variety of libertarian ideals,

but very much dedicated to the freedom of information—against the Mubarak government. Anonymous crashed the networks of the Egyptian Ministry of Information and the website of the then-ruling National Democratic Party with its DDoS attacks on their interdepartmental computer lines.[8] These included highly confidential data transfer sites dealing with accounting records, equipment purchasing, and offshore financial transactions. An angered Mubarak struck back by blocking internet servers and arresting a number of bloggers, but it did not stop the attacks. The Muslim Brotherhood simply came up with workarounds to bypass "impenetrable" firewalls.

Telecomix—another network of libertarian activists, which came together in protest against European surveillance laws—weighed in on the Egyptian efforts to "shut off the internet."[9] The group assisted in reestablishing the connection via dial-up modems in Europe, then faxed the dial-up numbers to every publicly available fax number in Egypt, effectively outmaneuvering the government's blackout. The Muslim Brotherhood was therefore able to continue coordinating mass rallies and building on the agitation and momentum around Tahrir Square. While it is unlikely that Anonymous or Telecomix were motivated by any affiliation with Islamist groups or were in the pay of radical organizations—though Islamists have been and are members of these types of groups, given their technical expertise in the field—the Islamists had been successful in establishing an online

coalition to augment their own program, which at its heart was also a freedom of speech project.

The Brotherhood's own DDoS strategy was multi-faceted. The Brotherhood had a dedicated team of coders, social media managers, and engineers working on the web. After Twitter was blocked by pro-Mubarak security forces, Google coded a "speak-to-Tweet" platform and, with help, disseminated phone numbers to the protesters, allowing access to the website and continued contact with the outside world.[10] Similarly, Facebook recoded its website to allow users to livestream videos to its servers to ensure a constant flow of information to Western media outlets. Conversely, Vodafone and France Telecom—the largest mobile carriers in Egypt at the time—complied with official orders to shut off cell service to the Egyptian public, allowing only government agents access to cell networks. The companies even disseminated pro-Mubarak text messages and compiled lists of dissenting Egyptians. (Once it became clear that Mubarak had been defeated, Vodafone released advertisements in the West claiming that it had been instrumental in toppling the regime—a change of face that disgusted many who had been involved in the struggle.)[11] Still, the DDoS workarounds established in support of the resistance eventually played into the political hands of the Brotherhood, who took power. One senior cleric told me, "Once we realized the dictator Mubarak could not stop us issuing orders to our supporters, and more importantly

once he realized it, it was clear his regime was going to die. It just died a little faster than we had expected."

The Islamists' DDoS strategies have been directed against extremists as well as governments. In June 2014, Anonymous received technical support from engineers affiliated with Islamists via the Egyptian and Jordanian Brotherhood. They began planning and implementing Operation #NO2ISIS, which involved large DDoS attacks against ISIS websites and social media accounts, as well as attacks against governments which openly supported the group, in order to disrupt communication and recruitment channels, as well as potentially stymying cash flows and political power.[12] These came in response to pro-ISIS groups having taken control of an Anonymous Twitter account, @theanonmessage, and posted violent and shocking images. Anonymous specifically targeted the Saudi government, which the group considers to be a major supporter of both ISIS and religious extremism in general. These digital attacks were attempts to take down Saudi servers and the main websites dedicated to financial transactions.

Extremist groups generally favor first-mover proactive attacks in order to maximize fear and surprise. But they too are growing to be more sophisticated in their DDoS strikes. The so-called Operation Ababil was launched in the autumn of 2012 by the Izz ad-Din al-Qassam Cyber Fighters, apparently originating from Iran, who claimed to be acting in protest at a YouTube video made in the West

which mocked the Prophet Muhammad, called *Innocence of Muslims* (see Chapter 4). The group promised to continue the assault until the film was taken down.[13] Their goal was to at least threaten Western centers of power and show that rebel groups could use the cyber world to level the playing field. Their DDoS campaign targeted American financial institutions. Each new "phase" of high-powered DDoS attack shifted targets and grew in complexity and sophistication, from the "traditional" means of flooding sites with network traffic, to more focused directing of their packets to where most of the banks' online business is conducted, and precursory "probing" of sites with four-to-six-minute bursts of requests to see if they faltered— and then returning days later to the ones that had showed weakness. The evolution of the group's strategy was, it said, in response to the banking institutions' improving ability to fend them off with new DDoS mitigation strategies which had been developed in the "quiet periods" between the months-long blitzes. There is a real sense that hackers and hacked are locked in a battle of wits, which doesn't look like stopping any time soon.[14]

The New Navy SEALs: Hacking

Easy to plan and execute, DDoS attacks are by and large carried out by low-materiel actors against the big boys— conglomerates, companies, and states (unless the state

actor wants to pin an attack on another group). Hacking, by contrast, requires high levels of expertise and is engaged in by a whole raft of highly skilled pro- and anti-establishment forces—both Islamist and extremist—to achieve a bewildering array of ends, from cyber graffiti and web defacement attacks on vulnerable websites, to the full-blown theft of information and identities.

Individual Islamist groups may hold sway in Syria, but the Syrian Electronic Army, a pro-government hacker and activist collective, has emerged as a potent force. The SEA's Facebook site emerged only days after regime protests escalated in Syria in April 2011 and, a mere matter of weeks later, its authorized website was officially registered by the Syrian Computer Society—which acts as the country's domain name registration authority, and was headed by Bashar himself in the 1990s having been established by his brother Bassel. This endorsement of what is in essence a hacker site has led many to believe that it is a state-sponsored group. Though SEA claimed on its webpage to be merely "a group of enthusiastic Syrian youths who could not stay passive toward the massive distortion of facts about the recent uprising in Syria," within three weeks the group's denial of being an official entity had been removed. These were, transparently, organized pro-government cyber-attackers.[15]

The SEA has perpetrated a series of hacks with the support of the Syrian regime. The group went on the

rampage in 2013 and landed a major international blow when it hacked the official Twitter feed of the Associated Press and tweeted a message giving the "breaking news" that there had been two explosions at the White House and that President Obama had been injured. Within minutes it had been retweeted thousands of times, and even caused the Dow Jones Industrial Average to drop sharply. The Syrian Electronic Army had managed to infiltrate one of the largest and most respected news agencies through a phishing scam which sent impressively authentic-looking emails purporting to come from Twitter to AP employees, which, when they logged onto a fake Twitter page, then recorded their keystrokes, gathering their usernames and passwords. Other cyber-attacks perpetrated by the Assad regime and its supporters have been directed against opposition forces, with their social media accounts hacked and made to erroneously pledge support for Bashar.

ISIS claims to study social media profiles to find weaknesses as well as potential recruits; indeed, the FBI and Department of Homeland Security issued a bulletin in November 2014 warning US and Canadian military personnel to limit their social media exposure in light of the October 2014 Ottawa attacks.

For a long time the group calling themselves the "Cyber Caliphate" was thought to be ISIS' own branch of hackers, headed by British extremist Junaid Hussain, an immensely skilled black hat hacker, who was killed in August 2015 by

a drone strike. Security analysts revealed the group to be Russians using the Cyber Caliphate name as a disinformation strategy—though no doubt ISIS has gained hugely from the free publicity, which included hijacking the Twitter accounts of *Newsweek*, the *International Business Times*, and (apparently in retaliation for the killing of Junaid Hussain) over 54,000 individuals, mostly Saudi Arabians. The group also allegedly hacked the US Central Command's Twitter and Facebook accounts, and, audaciously, launched a crippling April 2015 cyber-attack on the government-funded French television network TV5Monde, taking over its channel, websites, transmitters, and social media accounts for some hours, and replacing the TV5Monde logo on the network's Facebook page as well as posting copies of ID cards allegedly belonging to relatives of French soldiers involved in anti-ISIS operations. The message was: "The Cyber Caliphate continues its cyber jihad against the enemies of Islamic State."[16] So, although security establishments around the world now seem confident that ISIS still lacks the ability to carry out a technically sophisticated cyber-attack, the group's recruitment and propaganda remain unmatched—and it seems to have others who will happily do the grunt work.

In Pakistan, militant groups have hacked rival militants' webpages. For instance, Tehrik-e-Taliban Pakistan (TTP) launched an online English-language jihadist magazine,

presumably to attract Western recruits, and, as part of its digital campaign, social networks affiliated with this group carried out cyber-attacks. The pro-TTP Facebook group "Cyber Jihad Media" claimed responsibility for hacking a page supporting the TTP's militant rival, Jamaat-ud-Dawa; indeed the group publicized the hack widely, showing off their cyber-warring prowess. Another pro-TTP page, "Bedari Ummat," urged viewers to do their own hacking and "infiltrate" websites supporting the Pakistani military. These efforts were meant to show that individuals could participate in new ways, in the cause and movement against the "establishment."

Hacking is not only used as a cyber-attack on enemies, or even on established connections. A considerable amount of extremist hacking is proactively geared toward stealing identity information in order to target and make contact with potential recruits, particularly the use of phishing sites to adduce, as well as to steal, personal information.

Cluster Bombs: Malware

Facebook is increasingly being used for high-stakes cyber warfare being waged by Syrian regime supporters against the opposition—specifically as a means to launch malware attacks, and yielding large amounts of intelligence on the strength, movements, and overall strategy of rebel forces. (Of course, this process is two-way: opposition forces in

Syria have used malware to invade the computers and systems of Assad's military forces, yielding much-needed tactical information.) In 2013, links to what purported to be a video about the killing of an opposition commander appeared on the Facebook page of the pro-opposition group Revolution Youth Coalition on the Syrian Coast. In fact, the link downloaded malware that allowed pro-Assad forces, who had planted the posts, to monitor infected computers by logging keystrokes and taking system screen-shots.[17] The internet security firm Kaspersky Labs identi-fied the software used in the cyber-attacks, called njRAT, which is open source and relatively simple. The Facebook page had actually been hacked, too, so that when other members of the Facebook group tried to warn about the dangers of the linked file, their comments were promptly deleted. The same tactic has been used to target specific individuals via email. For instance, one administrator of an NGO was sent an email with a link to a video of the brutal murder of a civilian, again including a malware link that dropped a Remote Access Tool on the system. Even researchers are not immune: links in online articles about the use of malware in the Islamic world have themselves been compromised—and lots of articles now carry editorial disclaimers cautioning about clicking even those links. Information is dangerous.

Non-state actors are more than aware of the real and present danger of surveillance and information leakage,

and so make heavy use of encryption programs to safe-guard their online documents, websites, and emails (more on which below). These are, therefore, a favored target for malware. The Global Islamic Media Front (GIMF), an al-Qaeda-associated extremist propaganda organiza-tion, had to issue a warning in December 2013 that a new encryption program called Asrar al-Ghurabaa, apparently released by ISIS in November 2013, was suspicious "and its source is not trusted."[18] The Front advised its followers only to download encryption tools from its own website or the Al-Fajr Media Center. A large number of suspected malware and fake encryption programs are designed to look as though they have been developed by the GIMF, when in fact they are the work of al-Qaeda. Extremist malware programs are devised so as to keep track of rival groups, and to help in determining whether or not a communication is part of a Western intelligence operation.

Extremists can also succumb to precisely the same sorts of cyber-attack they often launch against others. Junaid Hussain may not have been the head of the Cyber Caliphate, but he was seminal to ISIS' social media strategy and, at the time of his death, third on the Pentagon's "kill list" of ISIS militants due to his huge overseas influence and role in inspiring "lone wolf" terrorism (including shootings in Texas). His death by drone reportedly came about when he himself fell victim to a cyber-attack. *The*

Times claimed that Hussain had clicked on a compromised weblink sent to him on the Surespot messaging app by an undercover agent after GCHQ and its US allies cracked encrypted Islamic State communications.[19]

Computer viruses can also infiltrate and keep many at bay. Islamists and extremists are keen to use viruses— including, as we saw earlier, the Shamoon virus—as a weapon against impenetrable networks and state-run organizations. Malware can also be used by states against states. The US has proven that it is not afraid to pull the trigger in the cyber domain when it comes to offensive operations, the most famous example being the launch of the Stuxnet virus in 2009 and 2010, and possibly also 2008, against Iran's nuclear infrastructure. A joint US–Israel initiative, the virus was designed to set back Iran's ability to produce a nuclear weapon and ended up damaging about one-fifth of the country's centrifuges. This cyber-sabotage was a NATO-defined "act of force" against Ahmadinejad, raising yet more questions about the limits of online warfare, and to what extent it is replacing traditional operations.

The Patriot Missile: Encryption

Because many extremist groups are getting blocked by social media providers, and are exceptionally sensitive to getting caught by governments and Islamist groups, they are relying more and more on encrypted technology.

In order to successfully communicate through the "underground space" of the internet, extremist organizations have made wide use of encryption programs to secure their communication networks. The first appeared in 2007 with the launch of Asrar al-Mujahideen by the GIMF.[20] The program allows users to send encrypted emails from Windows and Mac for a number of purposes: general communications to their members, late-stage recruitment (that is, travel information and other instructions), or to contact other extremist sects. The encryption suite was first announced in the al-Qaeda magazine *Inspire*. Individual encryption keys are offered by various extremist organizations, often via YouTube, Twitter, or Instagram, which offer access to the particular organization's account.[21] Advertisements can be found in various extremist publications, which provide encryption keys for readers to be able to send questions to extremist leaders.

Following the Snowden leaks, extremist organizations harnessed information about the alleged NSA/GCHQ PRISM data surveillance program in order to better secure their communication networks. From just a single extremist encryption service existing in 2007, by 2013 there was a new one being released almost every month. Most function by generating a unique encryption key for each user, often taken from pre-existing or open source encryption programs, which allows for a focus on key users and makes timely information accessible to members. For example,

Asrar al-Dardashah, released by GIMF in February 2013, allows users to encrypt messages sent through the Pidgin instant messaging client, such as Yahoo, Google, AOL, and others. The GIMF's Tashfeer al-Jawwal, released in September 2013 (after the Snowden leaks), focuses on providing encryption for SMS messages on Android OS (Google) and Symbian OS (Nokia) mobile phones, with an updated version, CryptoSMS, released more recently. Amn al-Mujahid, released by al-Qaeda's Al-Fajr Technical Committee in December 2013, is an encryption app for Windows that supports emails, SMS messages, and instant messages; a mobile version was also released for Android OS (Google) in June 2014.

The deepest level of online secrecy can only be reached via the dark web, in which entire websites as well as users can hide their identity and location. It employs the Tor encryption tool (or similar), and users find sites by using the same encryption tool and, crucially, somehow knowing beforehand of the sites' existence and precisely where to look, as URLs need to be typed in directly. There are legitimate uses for the dark web (for instance, for people living in closed, totalitarian societies which block sites and online access), but it has certainly become more and more popular with terrorist groups and other Islamist units which today, because of advances in monitoring technology, can no longer simply confine their hardline activity to specific internet discussion forums, as they did

in the early 2000s. Based on content analysis, it is clear that extremist recruiters are utilizing new platforms (like Diaspora) which provide anonymous IP handles and geolocation scrambling to disguise their users' identity and protect against detection. That is not to say that the more moderate sites are now free of extremists; these are the sites that attract most people, and therefore provide happy hunting grounds for posting links to more radical content on the dark web. An example of such a site is the French-based Ansar al-Haqq, which attracts a good deal of support from women, young people, and Muslim converts, yet is a gateway site to the dark web and channels users thence. There are many trails of crumbs leading to the dark side.

Big Brother Is Viewing You

One reason why encryption is so important is precisely the widespread recognition that governments are increasingly undertaking "cyber policing," such as patrolling websites for dissent, and general online surveillance to counter Islamist and extremist forces that they see as opposing their rule. This surveillance can sometimes be linked to kinetic attacks if the identity and location of the "perpetrator" (in the state's eyes) can be ascertained. Hence, unsurprisingly, in 2012, as the events of the Arab Spring continued to shake the Muslim-majority world, one of the hottest mobile downloads in Turkey, Egypt, and elsewhere was an app that uses a

virtual private network in order to allow anonymous surfing, access restricted websites, and hide IP addresses. Over the course of a single weekend in Turkey in June 2013, downloads of the application Hotspot Shield jumped 1,000 per cent. The app was used widely throughout the Arab Spring revolts, opening up blocked sites like Twitter and Facebook, evading censorship, and cloaking users' identity and location.

Social media is becoming the preferred tool for state actors and government sympathizers, including country intelligence agencies, to not only monitor civil society groups and religious political parties for signs of dissent, but to attack and even ensnare them.

Nowhere was this more evident than in Malaysia in 2013. The national police make no secret of the fact that they monitor opposition blogs, on the lookout for seditious statements.[22] Just a few weeks after the election, four young women were arrested for insulting Malaysia's constitutional monarch, the Yang di-Pertuan Agong. The women apparently crossed the line in a Facebook conversation, posted on one of their walls, which had cast aspersions on the king's honesty and talked of feeling nauseous when they listened to his speech urging Malaysians to accept the disputed election results.[23] So far so (unfortunately) familiar to repressive regimes everywhere. But the Malaysian government seems to have gone much further in its cyber campaign against those it deems to be enemies. In the run-up to the 2013 general election, opposition

groups and media organizations known to be critical of the government were the targets of repeated cyber-attacks. For the two weeks immediately prior to election day, it was almost impossible for Malaysian computers to access Malaysiakini.com, the oldest and most popular opposition news site.[24] In March 2013, CitizenLab, an internet freedom task force, discovered evidence of spyware attached to a downloadable Malay-language Word document which listed all the candidates for parliament in the election. The document contained FinFisher, surveillance software that mimics Firefox and sends information about web usage back to its command server. Since FinFisher is sold only to governments, the group concluded that the Malaysian regime must be operating the program, and thereby censoring the internet, blocking certain sites, and even spying on its citizens—specifically, given the content and language of the document, politically minded Malay speakers (who numbered significantly in the opposition). This put pressure on the opposition.[25]

Even more sinisterly, the "Red Bean Army"—supposedly a group of web-savvy Malaysians who, according to Barisan Nasional, were paid by the opposition to spread lies about the government, incite ethnic hatred, and generally create disruption online—was blamed by the ruling regime for spreading rumors on social media of power cuts at hundreds of polling stations on election day. This was the opposition's pretext for declaring the elections invalid.[26]

The opposition parties, however, vigorously denied that they pay supporters or orchestrate the spread of lies online, and they questioned the Red Bean Army's very existence, of which the government had never produced convincing proof.[27] The regime's accusation that the DAP had financially supported the Red Bean Army to the tune of $30 million over five years was strenuously denied by the party, which argued that it did not have the funds to support such an operation, even if it did exist.[28] The Red Bean Army is a real group, composed of paid employees and unpaid volunteers. It also represents the Barisan Nasional's attempt to understand, and criminalize, Malaysians' growing online activism and the new knowledge economy of the internet, in which rumors and untruths not sponsored by the government can easily circulate across a national audience.

In Bahrain, the government has turned to targeting specific individuals with arrests for their supposedly seditious social media posts.[29] Predictive analysis is a main driving factor behind this monitoring, as government officials strive to counter protests and demonstrations before their onset.[30] The regime in Iran was especially fearful of social media after bystander Neda Agha-Soltan was shot dead during the 2009 election protests, an event that became a rallying point for those angrily disputing Ahmadinejad's election victory. Video footage capturing the murder went viral, and #neda was one of the trending topics on Twitter that day (despite state-controlled media silence). *Time* magazine said

it was "probably the most widely witnessed death in human history."[31] The cause of Neda's death was fiercely disputed, with eyewitnesses reporting that she was shot by a member of the pro-government Basij militia, while officials insisted it was another protestor (even pressurizing Neda's parents to agree this was the case, and accusing the BBC and CNN of doctoring the video footage). Ironically, the regime's insistence on exposing a conspiracy of misinformation revealed their own use of similar online tactics, using fake social media posts to capture and beat unsuspecting protesters.

Perhaps due to the heavy social media presence of Saudi Islamists, Saudi Arabia, one of the most rigorously policed countries in the world, is a leader in cyber patrolling and the repression of speech online. ETIDAL, the Global Center for Combating Extremist Ideology, launched in May 2017, is an attempt to build counter-narratives against extremists. But to date the focus has mostly been on censorship, and the reprisals are harsh. After Saudi novelist Turki al-Hamad tweeted that the government does not practice the correct version of Islam he was arrested and jailed in late 2012, and held without trial for six months.[32] If for other countries social media can be used as a means of highlighting abuses of power, hashtag campaigns in Saudi Arabia which call attention to unpopular government decisions only enable the government and its supporters to monitor dissidents.[33] Even greater powers were passed into law in 2014 with new antiterrorism legislation, ostensibly

brought in to protect the kingdom from any extremist backlash emanating from Syria, as well as to distance the Saudis from recent media allegations of their funding terrorism there. Human rights groups and independent media sources have recognized this as, instead, a state-sponsored campaign against free speech; an editorial published in February 2014 on the independent pan-Arab news website Ra'y al-Yawm argued that the motive was "to silence 'Twitter preachers,'" and, as a web statement by the Saudi Civil and Political Rights Association suggested, "not because they are hardliners, but because they direct their hardline tone toward the authorities, and not just toward society as the government wants them to do."

What is less often seen is a more progressive approach taken by regimes in the region to reform their censorship policies. Tunisia, however, transformed itself from the "internet's enemy" under Ben Ali,[34] a country with "some of the most pervasive internet filtering in the world,"[35] to lifting the majority of its restrictions on the internet, diminishing social media surveillance, and rapidly expanding online freedoms following Ben Ali's ousting (though pornographic sites are still blocked).[36]

Force Multipliers

It is clear that cyber warfare or cyber terrorism is becoming an entrenched aspect of control and resistance in both

offensive and supportive roles. It drives the subjugation of populations, the destruction of enemy forces, and the spread of terror-inducing violence: in other words, most extremist or military activities in cyberspace act as force multipliers for conventional military or non-state violent activity. Cyber warfare allows an Islamist or extremist guerrilla force to maintain a "command and control network"[37] far exceeding its actual military force. Fingers on buttons are rapidly becoming as or more important than boots on the ground.

Cyber warfare is built on alliances: between individual activists, particular groups, hacking communities, or even hackers and political actors. Given their backgrounds— often educated to university level in computer technology or related fields—many Islamists were already members of hacking communities as they were familiar with coding and programming, making the establishment of relationships even easier and more organic. The hacking fraternity brings with it an air of legitimacy that many extremist groups have yet to achieve but, based on content the hacktivists are posting on different social media outlets, it is clear that they are steeped in their allied extremist organization's vision.

Social media has enormous potential as a force multiplier, not only as an offensive cyber-weapon focused on out-and-out attack and intelligence-gathering. Islamist groups are consistently using social media to undermine their opponents, including other armed groups, through the

1 Video clips of the protests following Mohamed Bouazizi's self-immolation in the impoverished town of Sidi Bouzid, Tunisia, in December 2010, triggered the country's uprising and the Arab Spring after being shared widely across social media. This is a still from the first video filmed on the spot outside the government building where Bouazizi set himself on fire. The crowd are themselves filming the police presence—an unconscionable act up to this point.

2 The role of social media in initiating and sustaining the 2011 Egyptian revolution is
acknowledged by this placard in Tahrir Square. The hashtag #Jan25—referring to the
beginning of the uprising on January 2   was tweeted 1.2 million times during the protects.

Egypt... Power to you

3 Emblazoning its slogan across an image of Tahrir Square, in this and other advertisements released in the West after Mubarak had been defeated Vodafone claimed to have been influential in inspiring the Egyptian revolution: "We did not send people to the streets... We did not start the revolution... We only reminded Egyptians how powerful they are." In fact, the company shut off cell service to the Egyptian public at the height of the uprising, allowed the government to access its networks, and even disseminated pro-Mubarak SMS messages.

قادمون يا بغداد
الدولة الإسلامية في العراق والشام

4 A much-viewed 2014 tweet from an extremist's Twitter feed warning "Baghdad we are coming!" The ISIS flag has been Photoshopped on to the top of the Palestine Hotel in Baghdad—the hotel used by many Western journalists covering ISIS' rise. The group's skillful handling of tweet blitzes ensured tweets like this were themselves much covered in the Western press.

Ehsanullah Ehsan @ehsanullah_ttp   3h

@samishah @omar_quraishi How could do disrespect vital organs that protect you from internal poisoning? Sorry, comedians are full of it :>

Expand

Sami Shah @samishah   3h

@ehsanullah_ttp @omar_quraishi Okay, I have to admit, that was a good one. shit.

Expand

Zarrar Khuhro @ZarrarKhuhro   2h

@samishah @ehsanullah_ttp @omar_quraishi You guys should do a standup comedy show together.

Expand

Ehsanullah Ehsan @ehsanullah_ttp   2h

@ZarrarKhuhro We could do a lovely show with @samishah but U would have to come here. Your "liberal fascists" would censor our show in Khi

Expand

Zarrar Khuhro @ZarrarKhuhro   2h

@ehsanullah_ttp @samishah So open-air theatre or cave acoustics?

Expand

Ehsanullah Ehsan @ehsanullah_ttp   2h

@ZarrarKhuhro @samishah We would like you to be as comfortable as possible. We will make you feel at home, without the alcohol and women.

💬 Hide conversation   ↩ Reply ♻ Retweet ★ Favorite ••• More

1   **1**
RETWEET   FAVORITE

6:50 AM - 12 Oct 13 · Details

5 and 6 Extremist groups are sophisticated sculptors of their social media profiles. In 2013, Pakistani comedian Sami Shah found himself playing an unwitting part in humanizing the Taliban when he entered into a humorous Twitter exchange with its then spokesman (left). ISIS is an adept meme-maker, particularly with those geared toward enticing Western youths to the jihadi lifestyle with promises of big cars, glamor, and riches. Though it first appears as a thrilling game (above), the message—and outcome, for many who are recruited—rapidly becomes much more serious.

7 The political wing of the Muslim Brotherhood in Jordan live-blogging over social media to broadcast its boycott of the country's 2013 parliamentary elections. The Jordanian Brotherhood ran a number of public services, embedding itself in impoverished communities, and ensuring that its good work was well documented online in order to capitalize come election time.

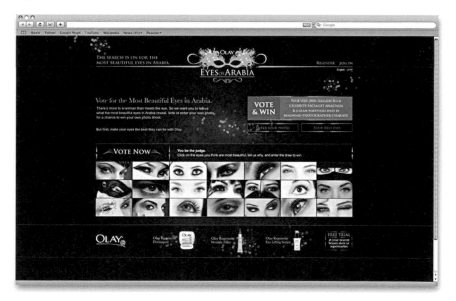

8 Cosmetics company Olay brilliantly utilized social media's personal, direct access to private individuals in their "Eyes of Arabia" online campaign, which encouraged Saudi women to engage with its website in order to enter and vote in a beauty pageant. It was a triumph of marketing, showing how social media can be cleverly and sensitively used to respect cultural norms and transform restrictions on Muslim women into a strength—to sell products.

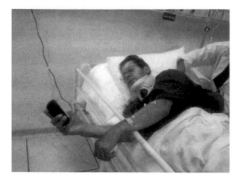

9 Imran Khan tweeting from hospital in May 2013 after tumbling from an elevated platform at an election rally. Khan shared many images like this with his legions of Facebook followers, ensuring that, even from his sickbed, he stayed in the public eye.

@jud_official Jamat 'ud' Da'wah ● 9K followers
#Banmusliminnocence People Start gathering for protests after Jummah Prayers throughout the country - Updates soon #MyProphetMohammed
Sep 14 2012 9:19am GMT (a year ago) 📍 💬 ↩ Reply ⇄ Retweet ★ Favorite

@jud_official Jamat 'ud' Da'wah ● 9K followers
#HurmateRasool Protest at #Chuburji Chowk, #LHR - Massive crowd #Tehreek Hurmat e Rasool leading against Blasphemous Movie #US
Sep 14 2012 10:12am GMT (a year ago) 📍 💬 ↩ Reply ⇄ Retweet ★ Favorite

@jud_official Jamat 'ud' Da'wah ● 9K followers
#HurmateRasool per Jaan Bhe Qurbaan ! #HYD protest at Press Club - #KHI Press Club people coming from all parts of city
Sep 14 2012 10:13am GMT (a year ago) 📍 💬 ↩ Reply ⇄ Retweet ★ Favorite

10 and 11 In September 2012 the film *Innocence of Muslims* sparked protests across the Muslim world, with the flames fanned by social media. Jamaat-ud-Dawa's Twitter feed (above) quickly picked up the story emanating from Egypt and urged followers to action, while in Indonesia the government called for YouTube to remove the video from the viewing eyes of its population, and social media-savvy student-led protests sprang up outside the US embassy in Jakarta (below).

Breaking: Two Explosions in the White House and Barack Obama is injured

↩ Reply ⟲ Retweet ★ Favorite ••• More

1,900
RETWEETS

83
FAVORITES

1:07 PM - 23 Apr 13

12 Associated Press became a high-profile victim of the pro-Assad Syrian Electronic Army's sophisticated phishing scam in April 2013. Having infiltrated AP's official Twitter account, the hacktivist collective tweeted alarming news of explosions at the White House, which even caused a dip in the US stock market.

platforms' fundamental power to connect. For instance, in September 2013, fifty Islamist brigades fighting the Syrian regime merged as one coalition under the banner of Jaysh al-Islam with the mutual goal of toppling Syrian President Bashar al-Assad's forces. Independent of both the Free Syrian Army (FSA) and al-Qaeda-affiliated bands— though funded to the tune of tens of millions of dollars by Saudi Arabia and other countries—Jaysh al-Islam appears to be positioning itself as an alternative to those avowedly secular and virulently sectarian groups, while maintaining strong ties to other anti-Assad Islamist and extremist brigades. The merger was triumphantly announced on Jaysh al-Islam's official Facebook page, and the YouTube channel of Liwa al-Islam (a faction with which many of the brigades had previously been associated) posted a video of the announcement ceremony. Social media provides an outlet to build moral support and generate a community-like feeling during a war-torn period, and in that way contributes a supportive role to the war effort.

Affiliations built and publicized by social media can also propel independent and little-known extremist groups into the broader extremist narrative. Tehrik-e-Khilafat, another Pakistani militant group with a limited history of attacks in the Karachi area, was relatively unknown until it pledged allegiance to ISIS leader Abu Bakr al-Baghdadi via social media in July 2014. The two groups' pan-Islamic rhetoric blends well together, with Tehrik-e-Khilafat announcing

its desire to unite the subcontinent with ISIS territory via "Khurasan" (an outdated term that refers to part of Central Asia and Afghanistan—echoing ISIS' own use of histori-cally loaded terms such as "Levant" and "al-Sham"). Another extremist group, the Ansar Beit al-Maqdis or "Supporters of Jerusalem," operating out of Egypt, also pledged allegiance to ISIS via an audio recording on Twitter in November 2014.[38] It renamed itself "The Sinai Province," insisting that it slotted into the larger caliphate promised by al-Baghdadi, and indeed has now become an official wing of ISIS.

Because in cyber warfare the identity of the perpetrator is so often disguised, "false flag" cyber threats—in which the real assailants deliberately manufacture their assaults to look like the work of others—are quite common, and used with intent: both to hide and to "get away with it," but also to falsely magnify prowess and power. During their 2012 DoS attacks on the US banking sector, the Qassam Cyber Fighters claimed to be part of the al-Qassam Brigades. Forensic investigation of the code that was used revealed that, as Senator Joseph Lieberman explained, it was too complex to likely be the work of the al-Qassam Brigades, but too rudimentary to be that of Iran. It is thought that the Qassam Cyber Fighters enlisted the help of an organ-ized cybercrime group. A more credible theory was that Iran purposefully wrote rudimentary code as a "red herring." A large part of the Qassam Cyber Fighters' first-mover

strategy was to win the "perception war" and send a clear message.

Net Delusions

Islamist and extremist groups use digital strategies in many different ways to wage war against their opponents. It is clear that states—authoritarian more often than not in this region—also employ the same kinds of strategy in counterattacks. Cyber warfare is waged against other Islamist and extremist groups, as seen in Pakistan and Syria; to help Islamist governments, as demonstrated with the Muslim Brotherhood in Egypt; to cripple Islamist governments, as in Turkey; and against key influencers and civil society, as in Syria, Saudi Arabia, and other countries. This varied influence demonstrates the extent of these digital networks' power. But can they be said to really make a difference—and, that is, the right kind of difference?

The major dissenting voice questioning the power of social media—particularly in the sense of it advancing civil society movements and faith-based causes—is Evgeny Morozov, with his "net delusion" theory.[39] Morozov's goal is to burst the bubble of optimism that surrounds many debates about social media. Painting himself as the ultimate social media realist, aiming to bring a dose of candid truth to discussions about the effect of digital technologies on advancing opposition movements, he argues that they

make little, if any, difference. In fact, so his argument goes, they may reinforce dictatorial tendencies and keep the status quo in place; the internet makes it easier for authoritarian governments to repress citizens and abuse power, and individuals waste their time and, worse, aid and abet tyrants by limiting their engagement to a form of "slacktivism," which has little hope of advancing real regime change. The portrait Morozov paints of technology and social revolutions is a dismal one, in which cyber-utopian ideals of information as liberator are not just rejected but inverted. He regards such cyber dreams as counterproductive, even dangerous, to changing countries' realities. (For Morozov's arguments about social media and charitable donations, see Chapter 6.)

While Morozov's critique does raise important points, he fatally overlooks key phenomena, especially in the Muslim world (where he has spent little to no time on the ground), and ignores key incidents and tectonic movements (especially among Islamists) that reverse key assumptions about his argument.

The Islamic world has for decades been the scene of underground movements, because of Muslims' inability to congregate freely. Rather than social media activism being peripheral or self-congratulatory—some sort of glorified pat on the back—digital technologies advanced entrenched political or oppositional programs. From Tunisia to Iran to Pakistan, there are many legitimate social organizations

and faith-based protests that have been facilitated by social media and digital technologies. Neither the Jamaat-e-Islami, nor the Muslim Brotherhood, nor the AKP (Turkey) have become lethargic, asocial, apolitical organizations by using social media to mobilize and compete; rather, social media has complemented their grassroots activities. Social media is a tool, one of many weapons that can harness political mobilization which bypasses state surveillance and structures and presents a credible threat. But it is a viable tool, and one with real consequences.

As one Egyptian Islamist blogger told me, "No matter how powerful a government is, they'll never be more powerful than the World Wide Web. They can't turn that off." The war continues.

FOUR

TRACKING TRANSFORMATION

"THE SO-CALLED 'Arab Spring' of 2011, which changed the political landscape of the Middle East, would not have been possible without the quantum leap driven by social networking." So stated Rahman, a commander in the Badr Organization, a Shiite militia group based in Iraq, in March 2015.[1] Growing up poor and miserable near Karbala, Rahman had been told for too long that a two-room shack, electrical outages, and meager meals scraped together on the few rupees his father earned from working twelve-hour days were the lot of his "kind." His was the age-old rage of the have-nots—a secret fury he seldom spoke of, but which, with the new tech, outlets, and online tools offered by the social media explosion, Rahman could now put to more effective and deadly use than ever.

The new technology had propelled the Badr Organization into a powerful position. In the past, taped

videos from religious figureheads would have had to be smuggled and distributed in order for a group or cause to make an impact. Disseminating the message could take nine months to a year. Activist groups would spend months signing up enough volunteers to field a small company of fighters and it was a costly, time-intensive process. Now, with the acceleration offered by social media, organizations like Rahman's could release their videos and propaganda campaigns across a broad geographical reach instantaneously, to be viewed and talked about within minutes, with the ability to recruit new volunteers in a matter of hours.

"No, we will not relocate our camp," a defiant Rahman firmly told his men after being targeted by enemy aircraft. They would not shrink from any conflict. Their communications team would continue monitoring and messaging 24/7 via their newly acquired SAT phones.

* * *

Much is made of the revolutions inspired—in some sense created—by social media technology in the Islamic world. It is undeniable that social media platforms have drastically changed the time and effort required to foment unrest and outright revolution in Muslim-majority nations. But to what extent? And who has it benefited?

Social media provides us with the ability to measure its own utility—it both empowers and calculates. This chapter explores revolutions and outrages pre- and post-dating

the advent of social media to reveal its game-changing role, and to disaggregate the ways in which Islamists and extremists have used digital technology (or not) to achieve their aims.

A New Spring?

The series of revolutions that became known as the Arab Spring—which kicked off across the Middle East following the self-immolation of Mohamed Bouazizi on December 18, 2010 and which saw protests and demonstrations across the region and regimes toppled in Tunisia, Egypt, Libya, and Yemen—seemed to many to be an entirely new phenomenon. Indeed, the attention it received was, in part, precisely due to the innovative adaptation and effective employment of brand new connective technologies, both in coordinating the movement within particular countries as well as informing the wider region and the world. Yet in many ways it could be said that the Arab Spring began three decades earlier in Iran. In fact, for the Arab Spring (as well as for the many budding resistance movements leading up to it), the 1979 Iranian Revolution proved to be an important historical precedent, organizational under-pinning, and reference point for many groups. Technology, enabling information-rich actors and effective organiza-tion, played a central role in both revolutions. Yet the different technologies that had developed over the

intervening thirty-plus years made for telling shifts in the control and speed of the later uprisings.

The Right Tools for the Right Job

The 1979 Iranian Revolution, spearheaded by Ayatollah Khomeini, was the conservative reaction to the seculariza-tion of Iran under the US- and UK-supported Shah, Mohammed Reza Pahlavi. It was of critical importance because it was the first televised religious revolution in history. The TV images seen by the world would be associ-ated with Islam and/or extremist groups for some time, and technology, however rudimentary, played a crucial part in the formation.[2] It all began with cassette tapes. In 1963, after he was forced to go to Najaf in Iraq because of his opposition to the Shah, Khomeini began using cassettes to help spread the revolutionary spirit. This first involved recordings on tape cassettes, which became the "electronic minbar," or new type of pulpit. On these, Khomeini recorded his diatribes against the pro-Western Pahlavis, gave stimulating sermons, and instructed his followers. His visitors would literally carry the cassettes back to Iran. The intention was to bypass the very specific targeting of Khomeini and his message, as well as to outmaneuver the very limited news and information environment in Iran. Although by 1977, radio covered almost the entire country and 75 per cent of Iranians had television access

due to the Iranian government's ownership of, and operation under the guise of, the National Iran Radio and TV conglomerate, there were only a few outlets supplying information across the country; and most were state-owned and subject to heavy monitoring and censorship.[3] It was only after 1977—when relations between Iran and Iraq had improved, and thousands of travelers, including Shiite pilgrims, were able to visit Khomeini—that the information environment began to change. The Ayatollah's tapes began to garner a following in Iran. Khomeini moved to Paris in 1978, where multiple tape recorders constantly recorded his sermons and pronouncements, which were then transmitted to Iran via international telephone lines. By these means thousands recorded his speeches so that, by 1979, in excess of 110,000 tapes were being passed around in circulation. With 60 per cent illiteracy in Iran in 1977, this was a creative and highly innovative use of technology to reach the greatest number of people, and it was difficult for authorities to monitor. Khomeini's pronouncements and theocratic statements were accessible to the masses, and the emotional and politicized religious beliefs began to build a grassroots movement: "silence and apathy mean suicide, or even aid to the tyrannical regime."[4]

Khomeini's tapes were duplicated and circulated alongside Xeroxed leaflets. These information missives openly opposed the regime for its modernization, encouraged the idea of martyrdom, highlighted the country's tremendous

wealth gap, and eventually gave actionable itineraries for strikes and protests (including the general strike on May 15, 1978). More importantly, they further separated the revolutionaries from the pro-Pahlavi, pro-West faction (and other enemies), and enhanced the polarization of the movement, creating "the binary division between the mostakbarin, the oppressors, and the mostazafin, the dispossessed, the latter term neatly encompassing" the opposition.[5] These leaflets were read or posted in public places (often to be torn down by the regime's police apparatus), dropped into classrooms, and circulated at street demonstrations.

As alternative media countering state censorship and Iran's main media apparatus, these methods clearly represented a skillful circumvention tactic to spread ideas and awareness of the revolution to key influencers and organizers. Once Khomeini recorded a tape or printed a leaflet, it could be duplicated and circulated by his followers. Understanding the limited information environment, Khomeini's cassettes and pamphlets injected fresh ideas from an untraceable and irrepressible platform, which proved highly successful in informing, organizing, and coordinating the masses who were yearning for an outlet for expression. There was, for instance, an unusually high turnout of over 2.2 million Iranians on the streets of Tehran for the now-famous demonstration on December 2, 1978. The tapes and leaflets played a critical role in bringing out all the demonstrators and providing them with a common roadmap.

The enriched information environment which drove the Arab Spring has some important differences. In Chapter 1 we examined the participatory technology on offer in 2011. This was coupled with significant access to internet-enabled computers and smartphones across the affected countries, with a good proportion of social media take-up within those populations: 5.1 million (10 per cent) of the Tunisian population had internet access, with half of them on Facebook, and the country had 87 per cent cell phone accessibility. In Egypt, of the 18 million who had social media access, 6.1 million (19 per cent of the population) were on Facebook.[6] There were also 165,000 bloggers, 25 per cent of whose blogs were political. Moreover, 65 per cent of Egyptians had video-enabled cell phones. With a large contingent of the population digitally connected, access to an enriched information environment in some form was at a majority of the population's fingertips. The feasibility of virtually spreading a revolution increases when a sizable portion of the population is digitally engaged.

Of citizens polled in both Egypt and Tunisia, 88 per cent of Egyptians and 94 per cent of Tunisians reported getting their information from social media sites during many of the events and activities of the fateful Arab Spring. This depth of penetration led to media convergence—the ability of information to travel across platforms as well as borders—which further accelerates and disseminates revolution. As an Egyptian activist said, "We used Facebook to put together

and schedule timing for demonstrations, Twitter to make sure of logistics and that everyone knew the location and YouTube to spread the message out to key audiences." Images, memes, and tweets mixed with videos of atrocities and talking-head soundbites as well as circulating news and blogger articles. Like-minded groups easily mobilized, such as the Facebook group "We are all Khaled Said," created when a young Egyptian activist was murdered by police in Alexandria, which attracted 95,000 followers and translated into 2.2 million protestors in Cairo's main public squares.

Wael Abbas, an Egyptian blogger-activist, was a one-man specimen of media convergence, with his writing featuring embedded pictures, interactive sections, and video clips alongside written updates. Wael's blog attracted over 36,000 views a month and as many as 550,000 during the key events of the Spring. The top twenty YouTube videos received approximately 6 million views each within a month of their posting. The hashtag #Egypt was mentioned 1.5 million times in the first few months of 2011, while #Jan25, in reference to the beginning of the Egyptian Spring, garnered 1.2 million mentions, with #protest amassing 650,000 mentions. In the week preceding Mubarak's resignation, the rate of tweets regarding political change ballooned tenfold with 252,000 tweets a day within Egypt alone, and an average of 2,500 tweets a day sent from adjacent countries drawn into multiple conversations. When the government attempted to turn off the technology—quite literally

blacking out the region by shutting down the internet—workarounds were found: Bluetooth, even when SMS and mobile networks were shut down, allowed activists to stay in touch with each other and was the main way in which the first videos of the murders of Neda Agha-Soltan and other activists were viewed by others.[7] The officials' attempt to control the information environment backfired, with 56 per cent of Egyptians and 59 per cent of Tunisians confirming that that violation of their rights alone motivated their support of the movement.[8] It created a cascade effect.

The Pace of Change

According to Egyptian and Tunisian protestors, during the lead-up to the revolutions Facebook and Twitter were mainly used to spread information as quickly as possible to fellow community-members and the rest of the world—a near-impossible goal prior to the introduction of social media. The Tunisian Revolution lasted just under four weeks and concluded with the ousting of President Zine El Abidine Ben Ali who fled to Saudi Arabia after more than twenty years in power—a stunning change of events. The Egyptian Revolution began on January 25, 2011 and lasted all of two weeks. The then president Hosni Mubarak was overthrown after a thirty-year rule, ending the corresponding three-decade state of emergency. His military administration faced constant pressure. Compare that to the 1979

Iranian Revolution, which took almost nineteen months from the first demonstrations against the Shah to Khomeini assuming the role of Supreme Leader—but around sixteen years from Khomeini's exile, when he really began building the movement, until his accession.[9] Historically, and by political revolutionary standards, this was hardly a quick upheaval—from start to finish it was about the length of most entire movements prior to the advent of social media and the new means of 'rebel' communication.

As has been discussed, social media has accelerated the pace and growth of political activism immensely. This is especially evident in Tunisian and Egyptian uses of Facebook, Twitter, and YouTube during the 2011 revolutions. The technology and its corresponding distribution has allowed greater speed of information-sharing, interactive and dynamic communication, and connection to a much wider audience. As powerful as Khomeini's black audio cassettes and leaflets were, the outside world was limited in its ability to engage with and witness the socio-political events that were unfolding. The capacity to encourage the empowerment of the opposition was technologically bound. Instead of taking months or even years to organize isolated citizens into a coherent movement, the revolution in Tunisia started just one day after Bouazizi's suicide, with the biggest protest occurring on January 11. Ben Ali was deposed just three days later. Egypt's revolution started on January 25, 2011 with the

largest protest on February 8 and Mubarak's ousting on February 11. Virtually anyone could participate in posting or receiving information and could simultaneously read messages and express their solidarity within and outside of their geographical locations. The Arab Spring was documented and tracked in dynamic real time, and the feedback loop—formed by the tens of millions of connections via social media and the web—amplified the efficiency of information exchange and lowered the costs of information. Whereas the Iranian Revolution saw little global media attention until the end of the politico-religious movement neared (it has been said that the revolution came as a surprise to much of the world, which was largely uninformed until the BBC and other world news wires began covering the demonstrations in 1978), social media immediately informed a global audience about the Arab Spring, and, more than that, fashioned a space for regional and global collective identities to emerge. As Oscar Morales, leader of One Million Voices Against FARC, another social media-enhanced revolution, said, these movements no longer snowball, they avalanche.[10]

Net Works

With regard to growth and acceleration, the telling difference between the 1979 Iranian Revolution's use of information technology and the Arab Spring's utilization of

social media for political purposes lies in the prevalence of networks. In the Iranian case there was a single, central point of information production and a focus on the organizing, recruiting, motivating, and agitating of followers rather than on the expansion of the movement. This was driven by the accessibility of media. Today's capacity for much larger populations to participate in demonstrations and revolutions is a result of the new, digitally enabled distributed networks.

Khomeini presided over a decentralized hierarchical network that helped overcome the geographic hurdles. Iran's thousands of mosques (at that time, the only main civic organization independent of the regime) and their linked bazaars were "the organizing nodes of the opposition movement"[11] with access to millions of potential supporters. Mosques, bazaars, and the key figures within the entrenched religious establishment were positioned at the inner radial nodes of the communication system, helping to disseminate information out toward the masses on the periphery. Thus, despite the established networks and inventive use of modern technology, the Iranian Revolution could rely only on a hierarchical organization under Khomeini's guidance, a pyramidal production of information loops, and the top-down unidirectional trickle of information. The general population was far removed from the information's source, and could not spread the message across borders because dissemination

required time-consuming, physical transmission and distribution (such as posting by hand in city centers or handing out in main financial bazaars). The movement was therefore limited solely to Iran and diaspora pockets. Hence, Khomeini's ability to shape the revolutionary narrative was curtailed—a distinct difference compared to the Arab Spring, which overtook the entire Middle East and North African region and allowed for democratic participation in producing and consuming information.

The Arab Spring's peer-to-peer "network of autonomous social actors"[12] flattened the hierarchies of preceding movements and revolutions into demonstrations that resembled the form of the internet, with dispersed nodes in a honeycombed distribution that allow information to bubble up through a democratic distribution of power, and flattened centers that control information.[13] Unlike the 1979 Iranian upheaval, information could travel across the network to the periphery without having to pass through official checkpoints or hubs of authority—what I term "veto players." Whereas a leader used to be able to shape and control information costs, and therefore also the movement—this is the outsized influence of the veto player—distributed networks make movements citizen-centric. Ordinary people become both consumers and producers of information, a new type of information supply and demand. Civic, political, and cyber activists now have the unique opportunity to assume leadership and to leverage their

(local) cause, garnering international support irrespective of any hierarchical containment of information.

Even if "digital political revolution" is not an apt euphemism for the Arab Spring, the participatory culture of these new technologies and the ability to harness and curate media on different platforms undoubtedly is responsible for the mobilization of the maximum number of people in an unbelievably short timeframe, as well as the quick power transitions. The Arab Spring may not have been the high quality, perfectly (centrally) organized political movement that the 1979 Iranian Revolution was, but in amassing and informing the greatest number of people using participatory technology it has greatly altered the acceleration of movements due to the enriched information ecosystem. However, acceleration has not necessarily led to stability.

Eyes of the Storm

The [technologically] empowered citizen knows the technique of getting people to the square, but they don't know what to do with them when they are in the square. They know even less of what to do with them when they have won.

Henry Kissinger[14]

The advent of social media and its introduction into political movement-making allows for a speed that means

revolutions are easier to start but, ultimately, harder to finish. The "loose ends" of the Arab Spring and the destabilized parts of the current Middle East are due to the technologically accelerated momentum having deprived the revolution of any proper gradual leadership development.[15] Who wields the power of a demagogue? Who is at the fulcrum of this faceless movement? This power vacuum grants any organized group the opportunity to hijack leadership. And this happens regardless of their alignment with or support of the revolutionary cause, or their historical links to it.

The slow pace of the Iranian Revolution, in comparison, allowed for a much more stable transference of political power and decision-making. Khomeini's trajectory was long in the making, from when he was sent to the seminary at Qom in 1923 and gradually started to build a movement with his student disciples (many of whom became notable later, including Hojatolislam Mohammad Javad Bahonar and Ali Akbar Hashemi-Rafsanjani). Khomeini would begin to teach Islamic jurisprudence in 1955, be deemed a scholar of the highest accord in 1961, and inspire violent demonstrations by his disciples, inextricably leading to the commencement of the revolution only three years later. Khomeini had a considerable amount of time to build an organization and become a spiritual, if not a political, leader of not only a movement but also of Iran (which still bases its political system on the original 1979 constitution). In

the years following the revolution, when the economy collapsed and the government apparatus had been dismantled, Khomeini drew on the pre-existing religious establishment to shore up his base and consolidate power among his circle. The revolution's gradual development gave him time to cultivate leadership and operational capacity, with which he became the organizer and the face of the revolution, and eventually the highest authority in the state.

As the prolific technologist Jared Cohen notes regarding Kissinger, "Unique leadership is a human thing, and it is not going to be produced by a mass social community."[16] When there is no single leader to focus a political movement—Khomeini, Mandela, Lenin—there may be more and faster revolutions than previously, but there are fewer revolutionary outcomes and scenarios. So when a dictatorship—by definition and decree the sole and strongest institution in a country—is deposed by insurrections like the Arab Spring, what comes into the place of the power vacuum is not dictated by those who have created it. There is no veto-player surrogate for the overthrown power. Information and communication technologies do not, after all, invent new regimes or networks; they amplify existing narratives and make existing networks more accessible, so that—idealistically, perhaps—those networks can further a particular cause.[17]

"As the fates of previous *journées révolutionnaires* warns us, spring is the shortest of seasons, especially when the

communards fight in the name of a 'different world' for which they have no real blueprint or even idealized image."[18] Both Tunisia and Egypt witnessed precisely this lack of a specific revolutionary goal. The power vacuums left in the wake of the deposed governments were hijacked, in both cases, by the Islamists, who were the best-structured, most focused, and most agile groups in the countries. They became the ultimate veto players.

Optimists who had hoped that the Spring would instill liberal values and pillars of democracy within the MENA region were sorely disappointed when the moderate Islamist party Ennahda won Tunisia's first democratic election on October 24, 2011. One report described the victory as a signal to the region that once-banned Islamists were now challenging for power.[19]

For this inaugural Arab Spring country, the citizens of which had not seen a separation of Islam and public life since before Ben Ali's 1987 impeachment of President Habib Bourguiba, this was a shocking win. Ben Ali's repressive regime had banned or demolished competing powers, and, in the absence of strong civil society organizations, the religious institutions and movements had readied themselves for a potential opportunity. The once expelled and reviled Ennahda was legalized in the wake of the protests. Its achievement in making it to the big stage was quite simply due to it being one of the largest and most organized parties.

Ennahda's organization capitalized on social media usage among its key targeted audiences. Recognizing that many university-educated, middle-class, and urban-based youths were struggling with envisaging a future for themselves and their country, Ennahda came up with catchy hashtags, ran social media competitions (asking young people to submit short videos and memes that described its vision of a future Tunisia), and made sure it was a first-responder with constant digital updates on current events, driving news cycles online and leading to take-up by more traditional media. The creative campaigning of Ennahda's social media team made the party more popular with a wide variety of younger audiences (despite them not necessarily agreeing with the party's Islamist heritage), and gave it a ready supply of young volunteers, especially in urban areas. Noah Feldman recognized that Ennahda is, "like the Muslim Brotherhood in Egypt and elsewhere, a social movement as much as it is a political party, which gave it a substantial leg up when it came to organizing dedicated volunteers to motivate voters. The relatively short period of time between the opening of the democratic process and the elections only increased that structural advantage."[20]

So, when the Tunisian electorate was faced with more than eighty parties and hundreds of independent candidates to choose between, the decision had already become much easier. Although some were well-established movements, and others freshly emerged in the wake of the

revolution, Ennahda was well positioned. Years of community work had made it a household name among ordinary and vulnerable populations, and it had people in many of the key districts within cities and rural areas. Ennahda was the only party that covered the entire country and had distinctive strategies and plans for each district. This gave it a distinct advantage. Thus, despite polling poorly in the days leading up the election, Ennahda was able to secure almost double the expected number of voters. It was not a matter of Islam being some defining feature of Tunisian identity—despite the Islamists' claims. Rather, the victory was the natural outcome of the inevitable schism between the nature of the revolution and the readiness of the Islamists for power.

A similar story could be told about the Muslim Brotherhood in Egypt, which gained power when Mohamed Morsi and its Freedom and Justice Party won the country's first democratic presidential election. Despite governmental crackdowns on extremism in the movement, the Brotherhood increased in strength and influence under Mubarak. The Brotherhood worked to become an integral player in student associations and university groups, and shrewdly established welfare projects and social services in disenfranchised villages—all organized, publicized, and augmented through social media. Remarkably, the Brotherhood endorsed Mubarak's candidacy in the 1988 presidential election—which could explain its lack of

evident participation in or support for the revolution. Nevertheless, the group was carefully positioning itself throughout the Arab Spring, "manning checkpoints, providing hot tea to protesters, and chanting 'Welcome to Free Egypt!'" in Tahrir Square.[21] As the revolution entered its final days, the Brotherhood also named it "not a Muslim revolution [but] a revolution against Mubarak"—a revolution that belonged to the people. The strategy was to avoid appearing overly ambitious or threatening. It worked: the Brotherhood emerged as the most organized grassroots political organization in the country with the vital support of key rural and urban populations.

Mahmoud Salem, an Egyptian blogger-activist, noted the problem facing post-revolutionary Egypt: "there is an inability to move past the short-term goal of unseating Mubarak and opening the political system to competition."[22] Unlike in Tunisia, in Egypt there was a clear preference (70 per cent) for an Islamic state. This meant that the onus was on the newly created parties, especially centrist and leftist ones, to clearly outline their plans for a liberal Egypt—very much a foreign idea. Yet none of them was able to present a unifying vision for their country. The Brotherhood, propounding a clear narrative for change, presented a formidable answer to the ills of current Egyptian governance. And, as a religiously inspired community project before it was a political party, it had the organizational discipline and ability to mobilize great electoral

support that other parties could not match. With over 2.5 million followers in Egypt, and having reportedly rallied a 90 per cent turnout, the Muslim Brotherhood mobilized 4 per cent of the country not only to vote for it on election day itself but to support the party and leverage its cause beforehand. Hence, just 15 per cent approval prior to the elections transformed into the Brotherhood taking 40 per cent of the seats in the People's Assembly. Moreover, the party gained the presidency and populated the top leadership positions in order to fulfill its mandate.

* * *

The purpose here is to look at which revolutions are more successful—traditional, centrally organized movements, or those digitally enhanced and propelled through networks. Part of the answer lies in revealing the essential changes that connective technologies (including social media) have introduced into the revolutionary genesis. This is why veto players are so important.

Social media has also sparked different sorts of protest in the Muslim world, ones that have strict religious edicts rather than democracy at their heart, though with the same tendency to transcend borders—and which have been seized on with more vehemence by both Islamists and extremists. Again, it is salutary to track specific instances in order to assess the difference social media has made to the dissemination of, and reaction to, loaded material, and

how different players have used and benefited from it. Again we see the use of media technologies by religious leaders and religiously based political parties who worked— in different or complementary ways—to whip citizens into a frenzy and then to channel their energies into particular modes of protest. Again, the event in and of itself would not have had the same impact had social media not played a role—something we can view starkly and assess in comparison.

Not So Innocent

On September 11, 2012, Americans were shocked to hear of two attacks on US diplomatic outposts abroad: a protest at the American embassy in Cairo which ended with the protestors scaling the embassy walls and removing the American flag; and an attack on the consulate in Benghazi in Libya which ended with the death of the American ambassador, Christopher Stevens. Both attacks were reported to be in response to two similar fourteen-minute YouTube videos called *Innocence of Muslims*, purporting to be a trailer for a forthcoming film, and uploaded in July with a version dubbed into Arabic appearing in early September. The video's laughably poor production values could not disguise the deep offensiveness of its content. Claiming to be a biopic of the Prophet Muhammad, it depicted him as an oafish lecher with a taste for underage girls. The original

scenes were overdubbed with Islamophobic content, against the original intent of the actors.

Innocence of Muslims struck a chord across the globe. Protests erupted in more than forty cities in September 2012, with most occurring in Muslim-majority countries or cities with large Muslim populations. Yet other Muslim countries that were very much aware of the video did not erupt in violent protest. Why? Although the Benghazi attack was later understood to be unrelated to either the Egyptian protests or the video, the Cairo incident, and some fatal protests in Pakistan less than two weeks later, do tell us much about the Muslim world. Understanding what happened in Egypt and Pakistan requires us to understand, among myriad other factors, the competition between religious figures and political parties for power and influence over their respective polities, and the integral part social media plays in that dynamic.

The original *Innocence of Muslims* video was, unsurprisingly given its subject matter and its makers' lack of platform, languishing in obscurity until it was picked up by two ideologues on opposite ends of the spectrum. Florida pastor Terry Jones, infamous in both the US and the Muslim world for his repeated attacks on Islam, endorsed the video (and at roughly the same time that it appeared on the Arabic-language blog of Morris Sadek, an émigré Egyptian Copt and noted Islamophobe). Shortly after, on September 8, Sheikh Khalid Abdallah, one of a new breed

of vociferous hardline Salafi religious TV personalities competing for viewers' attention, featured it on his daily program on the Salafi satellite channel Al Nas.[23] A man quick to interpret any event as an attack on Islam itself—and encouraged by his profit-seeking TV channel to attract large viewing figures[24]—Abdallah nevertheless seemed not to grasp the incendiary material he had in his hands: the video was not the lead story but buried in the final third of his program, and he played just two and half minutes of it. It was more likely his inflammatory rhetoric, rather than the clip itself, that launched *Innocence of Muslims* onto the Egyptian scene.[25] And launch it did. The video became a rallying cry.

The story's rapid course through Egyptian society can be traced most easily on Twitter (which offers far more robust archival tools than other social media platforms such as Facebook). Al Nas did not tweet about the video until Abdallah featured it again on the following days, after 3 p.m. (GMT) on September 8 when the protests were already underway. Other actors led the charge in the interim.

Al Youm, one of Egypt's major dailies, published a story on the morning of September 9 describing the video and pinning blame for it directly on expatriate Copts—having teased the news on its website as early as 9 p.m. the previous night. The story slowly gathered steam on Twitter throughout the day, with tweets linking to the paper rather than

Al Nas' social media (its YouTube channel was not yet featuring Abdallah's program). Some of the earliest interventions were from very significant figures: the Grand Mufti of Egypt, Dr. Ali Gomaa, a major figure in Egyptian politics with more than 350,000 Twitter followers (and now 1.08 million), weighed in via his own account at 5 p.m. local time, which would have brought the film to a new level of attention among Egyptian Twitter users.

One of the most seismic interventions came around the same time, and from a direct competitor of Al Nas: Al Hekma ("Wisdom"), a religious TV channel apparently founded in response to the Danish cartoon controversy (see below),[26] with links to Egypt's main Salafist party, al-Nour. The channel's founder, chairman, and most prominent onscreen presenter, Dr. Wessam El Haddad (also known as Wessam Abdel Wareth),[27] had been perhaps the first Egyptian to tweet about the film, at 5.38 p.m. local time (10.38 p.m. GMT) on September 8, referencing it in a plug for an upcoming TV appearance. El Haddad has long used his position as the head of Al Hekma to promote himself and his political views in support of the increased Islamization of Egypt and of more power for Salafi political parties. His views are conservative rather than extremist (the same day he first tweeted about the video, he declined an invitation to participate in a protest in support of Dr. Omar Abdel Rahman, the so-called "Blind Sheikh" who was convicted of planning the 1993

World Trade Center bombing: President Morsi had pledged to work to free Rahman when he assumed office a few months previously).[28] Before *Innocence of Muslims* came along, he had campaigned on TV and social media on behalf of the Egyptian army and police officers who were being prevented from growing their beards (as many Salafis believe Islam requires men to do), urging his followers to change their Facebook profile picture in solidarity.[29] He clearly jumped on the controversial *Innocence of Muslims* to continue this work.

On the evening of September 9, El Haddad tweeted that a new group, the Dar al-Hekma ("House of Wisdom") coalition, had been founded to defend Islam against those who would "ride roughshod" over it. The name of the new coalition was clearly intended to elevate El Haddad's television station; the link between the man, his channel, and the video would continue throughout the controversy's life. No other religious satellite stations' Twitter feeds mentioned the issue directly, at most responding to the growing ferment with fairly anodyne salutations of the Prophet: after all, why use your own feed to direct viewers toward a competitor? El Haddad exploited the monopoly, tweeting about the coalition constantly over the course of the afternoon of September 10, updating his followers on prominent figures who had announced their support, providing links to newspaper articles (all of which prominently featured his picture), and even crowdsourcing

slogans, asking his followers for ideas about what to chant at a protest the coalition was organizing at the American embassy the following day.

At 2.11 p.m., he announced a major coup: the Salafist Call, Egypt's main Salafi group, and its political arm, al-Nour, were joining the coalition. This significantly altered the stakes for the social media campaign and the protest. Nader Bakkar, a leader of al-Nour, had around 720,000 Twitter followers—twice as many as the Grand Mufti and nearly ten times that of El Haddad—and his announcements about the coalition and the protest (at 2.54 and 3.04 p.m. GMT) were retweeted hundreds of times. If El Haddad was something of a political gadfly, Bakkar was a true power broker, leading a party in the political ascendancy (following their surprise success in the 2012 parliamentary elections) and with huge organizational capacity. His involvement turned the House of Wisdom Coalition from a fringe group into a national movement.

At the embassy protest itself, the movement's leaders were remarkably silent, with Bakkar's only words a quick tweet (at around 7.30 p.m. local time) informing his followers that the Salafist Call had ended its participation in the event shortly before. Dozens of ordinary Egyptians who attended the protests provided real-time reporting on the action, though, tweeting the address of the embassy, updating on the protests' location, and, most spectacularly,

apprising Twitter of the removal of the Stars and Stripes from the embassy's roof. However, social media was never the main tool of those organizing the Cairo embassy protests. Given the relatively shallow penetration of Twitter in Egypt, and the involvement of the established party, it is safe to assume that the real organizational effort took place offline. It was the difference epitomized by El Haddad and Bakker: the first a man whose power lives and dies by his ability to create controversy and draw notice, the second a politician presiding over a more solid base and more entrenched power structure. Yet both were necessary to bring the Egyptian protests to life: El Haddad created a controversy with a valuable pay-off for both himself and Bakker, and Bakker mustered the multitude necessary to turn an internet scandal into a geopolitical crisis.

Twitter did, however, help to push the phenomenon beyond Egypt's borders and, especially, to Pakistan. Jamaat-ud-Dawa (JuD), the Pakistani extremist organization re-formed from the roots of banned terrorist group Lashkar-e-Taiba, was one of the many Pakistani Twitter feeds quick to pick up on the story and to urge action. On the afternoon of September 13, JuD's official account announced that it was holding an emergency meeting to discuss the issue, with a press conference to follow. It provocatively linked to a website recounting how Ka'b bin al-Ashraf, a seventh-century Jewish Arab in Medina who wrote poetry defaming the Prophet, was assassinated by

two members of the Muslim community. Using the hashtags #BanInnocenceofMuslims and #HurmateRasool ("The Sanctity of the Prophet"), JuD used its account to issue ringing condemnations of the video, to call for it to be removed from the internet and its makers brought to justice, to link to videos of worldwide protests, and to instigate similar protests in Pakistan. The JuD Twitter feed closely followed the course of protests around the country the following day, Friday, September 14, giving would-be protesters information about where they could take part and issuing a stream of passionate tweets calling upon Muslims to defend the honor of the Prophet. Some of the tweets could easily be interpreted as encouraging violence.

While the protests on September 14 ended peacefully, they were something of a preview to larger events across Khyber–Pakhtunkhwa on 18 September and Islamabad and Karachi three days later. As it had the previous week, JuD used its Twitter account to raise awareness of the protests. Besides organizing the action, the JuD account offered followers material to deepen their understanding of the issues at stake, such as a religious scholar's video blog about the importance of protecting the sanctity of the Prophet. Naveed Qamar, the amir (chief) of JuD's Karachi branch, tweeted calls to the Pakistani government to cut off trade and diplomatic relations with the countries responsible for the video, and to his listeners to boycott those countries' products. As it had the previous week, the

official JuD account tracked the protests' progress through Pakistan's cities. When they turned violent, JuD turned to Twitter to disavow any association with them, and to emphasize that its own protests were both peaceful and nonsectarian, being held in conjunction with a protest led by a Shiite student organization. At the same time, the JuD tweeted excerpts (in Urdu) from the speeches that party leaders gave at JuD rallies which, while not mentioning violence, used somewhat more inflammatory language than in its English-language tweets, indicating that the JuD modified the messages it intended for different audiences.

The JuD account was only one of many Pakistani Twitter accounts tweeting about *Innocence of Muslims* at this time. Given the fairly small number of Pakistani Twitter users, it was probably impossible for them not to hear about the video and the surrounding furor. A search for tweets geotagged within Pakistan and using the hashtags #MuhammadTheRoleModel, #IshqeRasoolDay, #BanInnocenceofMuslims, #Muhammad, #HurmateRasool, #Blasphemy, and #TerryJones, or containing the phrase "Innocence of Muslims," returns over 11,000 hits for the period September 12–23. Nearly 8,000 of these appeared on September 21, Ishq-e-Rasool ("Love of Prophet Muhammad") Day itself. In total, these tweets appeared in Twitter users' feeds 21 million times, with #MuhammadTheRoleModel the most common hashtag

by a wide margin. On September 21, the day of the protest, during which many were killed or injured in clashes with police, there were 7,954 of these tweets, compared to 330 on the previous day. It seems clear that Twitter activity was more robust in response to the protests—the newsworthy, the traumatic—than it was in motivating and driving them in the first place. But that reporting itself stoked the fire.

The protests continued in Indonesia, a country with a huge moderate Muslim population and a large cohort of web-connected urbanites, though internet penetration remains low at around 28 per cent of the population. Jakarta, however, is widely considered to be the most active city on Twitter.[30] There is evidence that the *Innocence of Muslims* video was widely viewed within Indonesia, particularly as the Indonesian government demanded that YouTube remove or ban the video for Indonesian users. The search "Innocence of Muslims" trended on Google in provinces with majority Muslim populations, although, comparing the Google Trends index with media-reported protests for September 2012, it is clear, rather, that protests were more likely in urban areas than Muslim-majority rural areas. The main organizers of the September 17 protests in Jakarta were the Islamic Society Forum or Forum Umat Islam (FUI) and the Islam Defenders Front (FPI), both members of the country's national clerical body, the Indonesian Ulema Council. While the FUI and FPI both have little presence on social media (fewer than

500 Twitter followers each), information about the protests was quickly spread via tweets disseminating their location. This gave rise to a decentralized, student-led, and truly viral protest at the US embassy, with similar demonstrations held outside well-known American firms.

The September 14 protests in Tunis are thought to have been instigated and organized by Saif-Allah Benhassine, a cleric at the al-Fatah mosque in the city and the leader of the Tunisian chapter of the Salafist organization Ansar al-Sharia—a group thought to be tied to the Benghazi attacks.[31] Benhassine is thought to have delivered an inflammatory sermon at the al-Fatah mosque that called for the resignations of Ennahda officials who had abandoned devout Muslims.[32] Compared with the 2010–11 social media-led protests against then-president Zine El Abidine Ben Ali, which saw French-speaking moderates and more extreme Islamists working together, the 2012 protestors were almost exclusively Salafi, and there was scarce media and social media coverage of the protests. This was likely a reflection of the conservative nature of the Salafi movement and the lack of support from Francophone moderates. Since social media did not play as large a role, the protests were consequently smaller.

The protests in India varied wildly due to the subcontinent's complicated ethno-religious makeup. The most intense protests were in Chennai, capital of the southern, Muslim-minority state Tamil Nadu, in which "Innocence

of Muslims" was the most popular search term for September 2012, even though Muslims account for less than 6 per cent of the population. The September 15 protests there were organized by a coalition of Islamic political organizations including the Tamil Nadu Muslim Munnetra Kazhagam, the Popular Front of India, the Indian Touheed Jamaat, Manithaneya Makkal Katchi, and the Indian National League.[33] Comparing online data with protest reports across India, once again the relationship between viral searches, Islamist participation, and protests has no direct correlation. As internet penetration in India stands at around 10 per cent, Indian political organizations, especially in rural areas, still rely on conventional political networks—though this has changed somewhat since the successful social media campaign of Modi.

In Sudan, however, where social media and internet penetration are low, public outcry over the video was substantial.[34] With the independence of South Sudan and the resultant economic crisis in 2012, the country was well versed in the instigation of protests via social media campaigns targeting relatively wealthy young people with photos of police brutality and economic strife. However, the 5,000 or so protestors who gathered around several embassies in Khartoum (particularly those of the UK and Germany, countries with large diaspora populations) in the days following the release of *Innocence of Muslims* were older and highly sectarian, and the protests were reported

to be larger and more fervent than anti-government protests earlier in the year.[35] There was little use of social media: the crowds had been called to gather after midday prayer by several clerics, who had forbidden their congregations from committing the blasphemous act of actually watching the video. Thus, in this case it seems that it was not the protests that made the video go viral, but the video's viral status that aggravated the protests. (In fact, it is now thought that the protests were planned in response not to *Innocence of Muslims*, but to the Danish cartoons controversy, and were merely launched in early September by opportunists.)[36]

Much as in Sudan, the September 13 protests in Sana'a, Yemen, were intense and violent but have little record in Yemeni social media data—likely a result of low internet penetration in the country.[37] However, they were far more violent than those in Khartoum and Pakistan, breaching the grounds of the American embassy (something even al-Qaeda had failed to do in 2008) by dint of sheer numbers. Extensive dismissals of political actors and military personnel from the national government followed, suggesting—albeit anecdotally—that the Sana'a protests were further aggravated in order to alleviate pressure on the troubled Saleh administration in the wake of several recent power struggles between the president and the country's nepotistic and corrupt elite.[38] As in Egypt, the protests in Yemen and Sudan were a testament to the power of religious authorities in translating online controversy into on-the-ground

action—acting as a kind of internet connection for the masses, and protecting their status with Luddite rhetoric. Or, alternatively, and maybe more accurately, they used a viral sensation as a *casus belli* for a premeditated attack.

Plotting the Google Course

To what extent was this a global trend? And did Islamists and/or extremists drive it? Google searches for the phrase "Innocence of Muslims" in 2012 show that, unsurprisingly, the peak was reached in the week of September 9–15, with a statistically insignificant number of searches in the previous week, and a more gradual tail-off in the subsequent weeks (down 7 per cent the next week, to less than a quarter of the peak volume by September 23–29, and to 5 per cent by September 30–October 6). The pattern is familiar to all those who analyze how knowledge spreads in the internet age, and how quickly one phenomenon can be replaced by other trends or scandals. In Pakistan, while searches ballooned during the week of September 9–15 (to more than a quarter of the peak number), it was only in September 16–22 that searches climaxed—tripling at a time when searches in the rest of the world were declining. Indonesia and Bangladesh followed a similar pattern. Residents of those countries were clearly not responding to what was happening in Egypt with a knee-jerk reaction, and were taking their cues from events other than the Cairo embassy protest.

The phrase "Innocence of Muslims" never came close to "Gangnam Style," the second most popular search in the world in 2012, peaking at just 27 per cent of the song's total searches worldwide.[39] But, disaggregated by country, "Innocence of Muslims" was a far bigger deal in the Muslim world than that might suggest. In the top ten countries by search volume—with Bangladesh first, followed by Pakistan, Sri Lanka, Indonesia, Lebanon, Malaysia, United Arab Emirates, Singapore, Nigeria, and the Philippines— six are majority Muslim, and one is roughly half Muslim.

It is interesting that, with the exception of Pakistan and, to a certain extent, Bangladesh, the countries that experienced the most unrest over the video were not the ones where the search was most popular. There are several possible explanations. It could be that people who actually searched for the video were more likely to be interested in it and less likely to get upset—ready more to laugh or to simply be informed than to be angry. Alternatively, it could be that people living in countries where the video caused uproar did not search for it because it was so prevalent—a link to it was emailed or messaged to them, or they viewed it as a group with friends, teachers, or religious leaders. A third reason may lie in the problem of comparing countries with huge variances in internet connectivity and population sizes. Or, the crucial factor explaining the difference between, say, Pakistan and Indonesia could be the presence of interest groups in the former, which saw a possible

advantage in fanning the flames of the controversy in order to use popular anger to further their own political ends. This does not mean that every religious or political leader who called for a protest against the video was motivated to do so purely by cold-hearted calculation; but, when their interests and their passions aligned, the result was explosive.

Twitter was slow to pick up on the *Innocence of Muslims* phenomenon, but once the topic had broken, it rapidly gained prominence across the world. Looking at the frequency of tweets[40] using some of the common hashtags and phrases associated with the scandal—#Muhammad, #BanInnocenceofMuslims, #MuhammadTheRoleModel, #Blasphemy—there is only a low hum of activity, primarily involving the hashtags #Blasphemy and #Muhammad, before the period in question. After September 11, however, the number of tweets using these and other terms rose rapidly, peaking at more than 26,000 on September 13 and then again at 33,000 on September 21, the day of world-wide protests against the video. Over the course of the two weeks between September 9 and September 23, tweets containing these phrases and hashtags appeared in Twitter users' feeds over 900 million times. On September 21, the phrase "Innocence of Muslims" alone appeared in feeds over 130 million times. As with Google searches, those who tweeted about the issue were disproportionately located in the Muslim world. Remarkably, the far smaller

total number of Twitter users in Pakistan and Saudi Arabia used the phrase "Innocence of Muslims" roughly as often as those in the United States or Indonesia (and barely register on the number of "Gangnam Style" tweets). While tweets clearly associated with *Innocence of Muslims* made up only 0.005 per cent of worldwide Twitter traffic during this period, in Pakistan they made up over 4 per cent. (The next highest percentage was in the United Arab Emirates, with 0.5 per cent of all tweets using one of the associated hashtags.) Pakistani users tweeted about the topic more than 31,000 times, compared with 39,000 in the United States, despite the population of the former being just over half that of the latter, with only 10 per cent internet penetration in Pakistan compared with 84 per cent in the US in 2012.

To put things in perspective, however, searches for both "Innocence of Muslims" and "Gangnam Style" in Pakistan were nowhere near the number of searches for "unblock YouTube"—an increasingly popular search after the Pakistani government cut off access to the site on September 17, 2012. It is clear that both "Gangnam Style" and *Innocence of Muslims* were niche interests. Compared to searches for "Facebook," neither of them figures at all.

Previous Offenders

Innocence of Muslims was not the most sophisticated, nor the first, and nor will it be the last example of how Western

media can inflame Muslims and spur extremists into action. Gleaning the role of social media in spreading awareness and perpetuating this anger, however, is essential if we are to understand the differences in how extremism is cultivated and utilized.

Many examples of Western denigrations of Islam, whether it be of the Koran or the Prophet Muhammad, have failed to inspire the same degree of widespread fury as did *Innocence of Muslims*. In 2008, for example, the right-wing Dutch politician Geert Wilders produced a similarly low-quality film, *Fitna*, which criticized the Koran, and which had the stated aim "to provoke."[41] Media buzz surrounding the release predicted it would cause uproar. Harvard strategic studies expert J. Scott Carpenter anticipated that "When Wilders' film is released, many Muslims (not all) in many countries (not all) will riot; cries will go up far and wide for the West to come to terms with Islam, and the radicals will again try to shift the ground toward them."[42] The Danish government raised the terror threat level from "limited" to "substantial."[43] Yet, despite the predictions (and Wilders' best attempts), the general response to the film was very muted—the reaction in Iran amounting to a minor protest of forty mild-mannered students.[44] Like *Fitna* and *Innocence of Muslims*, Theo van Gogh's 2004 twelve-minute straight-to-television film *Submission* was never in line for an Oscar. With the screenplay written by influential feminist and vocal critic of Islam, Ayaan Hirsi Ali, the drama

took a critical stance against Islam's mistreatment of women. Hirsi Ali and van Gogh both received death threats, and in November 2004 van Gogh was fatally shot by a Dutch-Moroccan Islamist on the street in Amsterdam.[45] This tragic incident aside, however, the film created no international stir on the same level as *Innocence of Muslims*.

The underlying reasons for the dominant domino-effect of *Innocence of Muslims* become clearer if we compare it with the Danish cartoons controversy and the violence that has repeatedly been targeted at the magazine *Charlie Hebdo*—reprisals that have occurred both before the advent of social media and in the full glare of its searchlight.

On September 30, 2005, the newspaper *Jyllands-Posten* published twelve cartoons depicting the Prophet Muhammad in an unflattering manner. Many Muslims argued that this went against the principle of aniconism, which forbids the depiction of the Prophet. This, coupled with the belief that *Jyllands-Posten* was fomenting Islamophobia, provoked a global uproar and at least 139 people died as a result.[46] The Muslim Brotherhood in Egypt posted videos on YouTube and Arabic online forums denouncing the cartoonists and pleading with young believers to join them to fight such "indecency" and the "smearing" of their religion: it is reported that thousands signed up.

In Lahore, where I was when the scandal broke, the long queue of people lining up outside the Jamaat party

field office snaked down the block. It was predominantly made up of highly agitated smartphone users who had seen the coverage on social media and Arabic-language news websites and who were chafing to join the fight against the infidels. One young man told me, "I feel like I need to do something. We can't sit back and let the West get away with these insults and attacks. At least the Jamaat leaders take a courageous stand for our religious beliefs." The reaction in most countries, such as Malaysia, still came from printed media—including the ironic scandal created when a Borneo newspaper printed one of the cartoons alongside a story bemoaning the lack of controversy in the country.[47]

In 2008 the cartoons were reprinted in Danish newspapers to coincide with the Wilders film, and in Afghanistan more than 5,000 protesters took to the streets shouting "Death to Denmark" and "Death to the Netherlands" while burning the Danish and Dutch flags.[48] The incident also affected the Danish economy. An official boycott of Danish goods by Muslims around the world sharply decreased the amount of exports the country sent to the Middle East; trade with Saudi Arabia decreased by 40 per cent, and that with Iran by 47 per cent.[49]

The French satirical magazine *Charlie Hebdo* began its own foray into the controversy by reprinting the *Jyllands-Posten* cartoons in 2006.[50] It drew widespread scorn from such figures as the then president, Jacques Chirac, and from organizations such as the Muslim World

League and the Union of French Islamic Organizations. In November 2011, the magazine again published satire featuring the Prophet, this time with a "guest article" supposedly written by Muhammad himself inside the monthly issue retitled *Charia Hebdo* (a name which poked fun at sharia law). The cover leaked a few days before going to press and quickly made its way around the social media circuit. Unlike incidents that had come before, this provocative gesture rode the social media wave, and in reprisal the magazine's main office was firebombed.[51] Many tweets expressed anger and irritation at *Charlie Hebdo*'s constant irreverence for Islam. It was not until 2015, however, that the culmination of radical anger spilled over into a deadly assault. The French government was already all too aware of the magazine's potential impact; after a particularly offensive edition in 2012, it went as far as to temporarily close twenty of its embassies.[52] On January 7, 2015 these fears came to a head when two gunmen attacked the magazine's offices in Paris, leaving twelve dead and eleven wounded, and allegedly shouting "Allahu akbar" as they made their escape.[53] Only hours earlier, *Charlie Hebdo* staff had published a tweet of ISIS leader Abu Bakr al-Baghdadi.[54] It is uncertain whether *Charlie Hebdo* was a larger target than past transgressors because of its expert in-yer-face handling of social media as well as its print publication, but none of its predecessors had done so to the same extent.

Social media allows for anger to spread to the global stage. Unlike local or regional broadcast services, such as television and radio, social media platforms engage users on a grassroots, cross-border level. One angry individual in Karachi can easily communicate with a like-minded person in Istanbul, Cairo, Belgrade, New York, or Paris. Unlike traditional broadcasting, news on social media is *meant* to go viral, not to abide by local news tastes. The number of times a story is "liked," "shared," or "retweeted" defines its popularity and encourages global consumption of the information.

This is a central defining feature of social media—and perhaps the most important way it distinguishes itself from traditional news broadcasting services. *Innocence of Muslims* and *Charlie Hebdo* turned into violent, global issues because of their trending popularity on social media. *Fitna* and *Submission* were not negligible instances by any means (especially the latter, which inspired an assassination), but they did not motivate the masses to take action. Official outlets and clerics decried the films, but their status never went viral.

The ability of social media to spread awareness and mobilize action is not merely the preserve—as much as the scourge—of the religiously minded, however. Such platforms are key players in the Islamic world's public and private sectors as competing interests vie for market share.

FIVE

CIVIC BOOTY, PRIVATE GAIN

A NEW SHIPMENT of hashish had arrived from the north and all of the men in camp were cut liberal portions. In charge of join the shipment was Tariq, tired from the all-day travel but pleased it had gone to plan.[1] After all, his leadership skills were one of the reasons he had been hired by the Haqqani network—a guerrilla insurgent group running itself as a quasi-private sector entity, with subsidiaries all over the Pakistan–Afghanistan border region, in the fields of logistics, pharmaceuticals, and, the most lucrative of all, illegal drugs.

Tariq had attended a top law school in Kabul but switched career paths after spotting one of the many slick advertisements Haqqani put out through its affiliates on social media channels. These would often use imagery from the Afghan resistance of the late 1970s and 1980s, the Charlie Wilson era, a time when the Afghan mujahideen

were lauded around the world for fighting the Soviets. Such calls to join the patriotic struggle were bolstered in the regional campaigns by the liberal use of religious symbolism, intriguing young Afghans and convincing them to sign up with a seemingly sophisticated organization able to deliver on their promises. Marketing themselves as the special ops of indigenous asymmetric warfare fighting on behalf of Afghans, the Haqqani network certainly meant, and did, business.

Running the drug trade in Afghanistan and Pakistan involved a plethora of people, from truck drivers and teens in training camps to the Fortune 500-esque investors overseeing funds in certain banks and financial outlets. Despite the illegality of its principal revenue generator, the corporation that Haqqani had become meant it could launder its profits and present itself as a force in the private sector.

Tariq had begun working for the corporation as a trader and middleman, associating with a loose federation of Taliban and al-Qaeda that made up the terror ecosystem, planning and executing attacks on US and coalition forces operating in and around the capital, and developing something of a specialty in transporting 'goods' from A to B. In recognition of his skills, he had been promoted—formally inducted into the higher ranks of the Pakistani Taliban. When NATO put a bounty on his head, dead or alive, it greatly increased his prestige. He was given command of a cell, and over the next few years came to control a range of

insurgent forces in several camps, reporting directly to the Grand Emir.

* * *

Social media has become a key aspect of doing private and public sector business across the Islamic world. The historic and dramatic demographic transformation of the Middle East and North Africa (MENA) and South and Central Asia (SCA—specifically the five former Soviet Republics, plus Afghanistan and Pakistan) has empowered youthful populations to take ownership of their own political—and other—choices. It has also high-lighted this tech-savvy demographic as being one that ruling regimes, opposition parties, and private investors would all be wise to have on side. The Arab Spring displayed, among other things, the strength and vibrancy of young people in these regions, and investors see the same generation as an attractive market. Investment from the West and beyond has brought religious and economic actors into the same sphere. And Islamist groups are increasingly incorporating economic, rather than solely religious, messages into their platforms. Time and again, social media has proved to be the chosen conduit in this new arena.

This chapter explores the shared interests and unusual alliances between private sector investment, public sector necessity, and Islamist groups in several Muslim countries,

as many new and established actors attempt to attract the all-important "youth bulge" to win political power and market share. As we have seen, youthful populations can pose a substantial threat to established regimes, but as vast emerging markets they also entice investment. The mixture of religion and commerce is a uniquely powerful blend, one with important political and social implications for the region and the world.

Battle of the Bulge

Understanding the nature and desires of the "youth bulge" is as essential to businesses and governments in the region as it is to those wanting to comprehend the full extent of the complex relationship between private investment, ruling parties, and religious groups there. Analyses suggest that around 55–60 per cent of MENA and SCA populations are under the age of twenty-five, compared with 26 per cent in developed G7 countries.[2] This "baby-faced" population is on track to become even younger on average in both short- and long-term forecasts.[3] This demographic offers immense value in terms of their potential economic productivity and skill-sets, a potential that unfortunately all too often goes untapped in countries with extremely high unemployment rates: it stands at 31.5 per cent in MENA, the highest in the world,[4] and 19 per cent in SCA for those between the ages of fifteen and twenty-four,[5]

though the statistics disguise the relatively menial jobs and accompanying low salaries for those who are "lucky" enough to be employed. These numbers also ignore the "brain drain" of workers seeking employment outside their homelands; Tajikistan, for instance, takes the dubious prize of being "the most remittance-dependent country in the world."[6] It is no secret that revolutionaries and extremists often target this disaffected youth.

This demographic is also more connected than ever before, with more affordable and available communications technology increasingly bringing these markets into the global economy. According to the Arab Advisors Group, 40 million internet users were located in the Arab countries in 2009;[7] by the end of 2018, Google estimates that this number will reach 220 million.[8] With the explosion of 3G and 4G mobile phone towers throughout the Middle East, social media connectivity has skyrocketed. While home internet penetration in the MENA region stands at roughly 46 per cent of the population, 3G and 4G access has ballooned to over 41 per cent. Monthly ISP costs are moderate, and in places like Indonesia, for instance, the price of smartphones has come down 45 per cent in the last year. Forget about laptops—tricked-out smartphones are the future. In Pakistan alone, 3G connection speeds combined with the low price of phones will put some 80 million new social media users online in the next three to five years. According to the World Bank,

both regions already have a higher average mobile subscription rate percentage than the United States.[9] It does not seem to be slowing down anytime soon.

Naturally there is significant (and increasing) investment in information communications technology within the Middle East, one of the top three IT markets in the world for growth. Spending in 2010–12 was three times that in 2006–09, with private ventures by far the largest source of investment in the sector.[10] Total spending in 2015–17 topped $258 billion, with investments in IT projects exceeding $82 billion (an increase of around 7.5 per cent). As private corporations continue to pour investment into the technological infrastructure of the MENA and SCA regions, the value of social media and new information communication technologies will only rise.

These numbers do not go unnoticed by overseas investors seeking new relationships and paths into emerging markets. Thus, as odd as it may seem, some of the most volatile regions of the world are attracting buoyant economic predictions and significant flows of investment. Many Western capitalists have already discovered that they can do good business with Islamists.

Private Temptations

With the growing connectedness of MENA and SCA citizens, companies have increasingly realized that the

technological trends that defined social media's rise can be harnessed for commercial value.

The technology giants themselves see this tech-booming region as a promising growth area. Google has held its "G-Day" conference in Egypt and Jordan,[11] an event which caters to the legions of up-and-coming young IT specialists. It is not just about tech juggernauts coming to town; in a pattern that repeats across all media-savvy businesses operating in the region, they are bending to suit the new audiences and specific market. In some sense, they have to. "The big Western bankrollers have no choice but to do as we say," an Islamist politician in Karachi told me, grinning broadly. "If they don't agree to our terms and the kind of spiritual tunes we want, then we shall declare music unlawful!" He was only half-kidding. Private sector companies know they risk being kept out of lucrative markets if they don't work with and appease the Islamists. The latter can help start an enterprise and get it up and running, or shut the whole operation down with a social media blitz.

Thus, large social media companies have begun to coordinate with local companies. Twitter, for instance, partnered with the Jordanian micro-blogging site Watwet in order to attract new users, allowing cross-posting of updates between the two platforms. This delivered an additional 25,000 subscribers to the US company.[12] Similarly, Yahoo acquired the Arab company Maktoob

for over $160 million in order to get a foothold in the region.[13]

Social media companies were in the vanguard, but they are not the only ones to recognize the further need to mold themselves to suit the specific market. In fact, "native" platforms think they can do better, with a number springing up against the deluge of Western and Eastern sites, many of which purport to offer social media services for the devout: MillatFacebook in Pakistan, Cloob in Iran, and Ummaland for Muslims across the world. Still, slow growth among such native social media outlets suggests that there is room for foreign expansion and entrepreneurship within the MENA and SCA markets.

Although the wealthier cities of the Gulf states are hives of social media activity, such countries have long struggled with the coexistence of the internet and conservative Islam. (It explains their strong preference for private networking sites like WhatsApp, Snapchat, Instagram, and others with friends-only profile access, rather than Facebook and Twitter.) Western businesses have realized that a successful presence in the Muslim-majority world entails negotiating with strict religious mores, which might be strictly antithetical to their own aims. Slowly, they are warming to the idea of working within the confines of conservative Islam, and are devising new, creative advertising solutions harnessing the different powers of social media in order to work their magic within the limits. For example, McDonald's—that

seemingly most brashly Americanized of brands—set itself apart from its competitors in the Arabian Peninsula precisely by developing original but conservative Arabic lifestyle content. Most obviously, its online content was translated into Arabic—the preference of over 290 million social media users, yet accounting for only 4 per cent of content online. The company also produced a sophisticated web-series in the *hakawai* storytelling tradition for Ramadan, which retold fifteen Arabic folktales in a modern but conservative style.[14] The social media-led series appealed cross-generationally, directing adults to the McDonald's site while the graphics, music, and animation entertained a younger audience who would not usually be as enthused by such "traditional" content.

The cosmetics company Olay ran one of the cleverest campaigns in Saudi Arabia. The prospect of advertising a new skin cream to women in a country that places grueling restrictions on their participation in public life—and where it is against the law to reveal any skin outdoors, in print, and even on some websites—was daunting. Olay found a remarkable solution to working under this virtual "privacy veil" which transformed this limitation into a strength. Acknowledging that, in public, Arabian women only showed their eyes, Olay made this the central feature of their marketing campaign. "Eyes of Arabia" was an online "beauty pageant" that invited Saudi women to upload photos of their veiled faces, to vote online for "the most

beautiful eyes," and to interact with other elements of the Olay website (including beauty tips). The company enlisted bloggers to talk about the competition, and paid for banners on other women-focused websites, which ensured publicity for the pageant (and brand) in magazines and social media chatter. It was an instant viral success, with over 80,000 women participating, and almost doubly exceeded Olay's aims to increase its market share and traffic to its website.[15] The combination of a glossy social media campaign, allowing women to uncontroversially participate while celebrating beauty and respecting cultural beliefs, was a winning formula.

Clearly, women, as well as the young, are a key demographic benefiting from the social media business boom and pursuing greater social involvement through the explosive growth of internet-based communication. The power of social media here is not in connecting users, but instead in offering them a degree of anonymity unattainable in the real world, and a freedom that comes from behavior no longer under scrutiny or subject to religious edicts and cultural mores.

While half of Saudi students are female, only 20 per cent of working-age women are in work in Saudi Arabia (compared to 45 per cent in UAE and 56 per cent in Qatar).[16] This lack of formal opportunity in the employment sector has encouraged women to realize the business potential of online platforms. For example, thousands of

Saudi women have taken to Instagram and YouTube—which have seen explosive growth in the region over the last few years[17]—to sell homemade products ranging from jewelry to sushi, with one women starting a successful online barbecue delivery service, "BBQ-Time."[18] One reason for internet-based business enthusiasm is, of course, that it doesn't require one to leave one's house—a particular problem for working Saudi women who face not only social stigma but the practical obstacle of getting to work at all as they are prohibited from driving. New online technologies which have decentralized transportation systems are helping with precisely this; around 80 per cent of Uber app users in Saudi Arabia are women,[19] and more than $2 billion venture capital has been invested in other car-booking app companies, including the home-grown Careem. Its founder, Mudassir Sheikha, estimates that his business has 150,000 regular users and (as of 2017) was growing at a rate of 50 per cent a month.[20]

That growth speaks to Saudi Arabia's increasingly connected reality. And it is technology—particularly the smartphone—that makes life easier in the real world, as well as creating opportunities to speak out about the establishment. For instance, when one cleric proposed that driving might harm a woman's ability to reproduce, a popular hashtag ridiculing the conservative's dubious scientific knowledge was born, using the same technology helping women to navigate those very restrictions. The

hashtag campaign #onlyinSaudi (and its Arabic version) began resonating for younger audiences in urban areas frustrated by the opaque rules. A hashtag that translated as "women driving affects ovaries and pelvis" became popular, too, and was soon joined by many men, hashtagging in Arabic, "I'm a male supporter."[21]

The Real Thing

Drawn by the lure of a young and expanding demographic, one of the most confident, smart, and willing investors in the MENA and SCA regions has been the Coca-Cola Company. Its product and business model gives it a lot of reach in key audience communities—from kiosks in thousands of small villages and cities to established relations with platforms such as Facebook, Twitter, and local alternatives serving as a bedrock of its advertising. It too has manifested a successful "think global, act local" strategy—for instance, invoking the image of Tahrir Square in one advertisement aimed at the newly enfranchised Egyptian youth market. More than that, though, it has interceded in the music market as a way to reach across class divides and religious boundaries to meld Western influences with local culture and concerns, at the same time building on its "cool" brand.

Coke Studio is a TV series and radio station featuring live studio-recorded music performances by various artists,

and even live concerts. Starting in the 2000s, it has become an enormously popular franchise, with outlets now in Pakistan, India, and the Middle East (based in Dubai), and with a sophisticated online presence, including dedicated branded websites, multiple online music channels, web forums and chat sites where users can engage with artists and access additional fresh content, YouTube channels, an app (which allows users to stream and download tracks immediately after a program has finished), and presence on Vimeo, SoundCloud, and Last.fm.

Coke Studio is hugely popular in Pakistan, and was a major impetus for the revival of the country's music industry. One of its central concepts is musical fusion: it brings together established Arab and international artists, as well as up-and-coming and less mainstream musicians, to record an original song meshing two (or more) musical genres. As its own marketing copy enthused:

> Coke Studio prides itself on providing a musical platform, which bridges barriers, celebrates diversity, encourages unity and instills a sense of Pakistani pride ... Now in its third year running, the venture itself has continued to evolve in its outlook and execution. Where Coke Studio One centered on the philosophy of peace and harmony and the appreciation of live music recording, Coke Studio Two was about the Pakistani identity and unity and celebrating individuality. In the

third season, we come full circle but widen the same to encompass all identities as well as be circumspect and retrospect about our own journey—how dreams and goals are created and realized.[22]

The vision is a broad one. On the one hand, Coke Studio's ability to reach across lines of class, geography, and age, its values of cultural openness and respect, and its robust promotion of international pop music and culture, make the station extremely attractive to international investors and businesses, drawing the advertising dollars of many private companies and services keen to associate themselves with it.[23] Young people are a dream audience because they tend to exert a greater consumer demand for new (Western) products and technology, and to be much more receptive to new values and ideas, especially those breaking with tradition.[24] But, on the other hand, the catholicity of the franchise also means that political, religious, national, and even regional views are well represented. The concern of some Pakistanis that corporate sponsorship would mean censorship of any music with a political message proved unfounded. Political music is an important element: the Pakistan Muslim League (a party that employs religious symbolism in democratic politics) ended up using many of Coke Studio's artists in their political campaigns. The Islamist Jamaat-e-Islami organization helped push for *nasheed* (religious songs) to be played by new artists and

guaranteed a loyal fan base if Coke Studio chose to do so. Minority groups in general stand to be the real winners from the proliferation of corporate channels, using such platforms to disseminate their views to a far larger audience than they would otherwise reach.[25]

Coca-Cola certainly benefited from the exposure. Although there is little hard evidence that media channels increase demand for products, brand recognition and advertising revenue certainly make a difference. Before establishing Coke Studio in Pakistan in 2008, Coca-Cola had a 25 per cent market share; four years later, that stood at 35 per cent, encouraging the company to announce a $379 million investment in the opening of three new bottling plants in Pakistan (in Karachi, Multan, and Islamabad) in 2013.[26] (Coca-Cola's biggest rival, PepsiCo, saw its market share drop to 65 per cent after the launch of Coke Studio, down from 80 per cent in the 1990s.[27]) The Coca-Cola conglomerate's confidence in a country which all too often faces upheaval—and has an international reputation for doing so—is very important. The mere presence of Coke Studio, not to mention its wide success, promotes Pakistan as a stable environment for foreign investment and entrepreneurship.[28] Indeed, alongside the many Western political, social, and economic actors who have been and will continue to be increasingly interested in investing in (and profiting from) local communities across the region, the countries' ruling classes and the

Islamists realize that foreign investment is vital to their economies—as well as their own political futures.

Open for Business

Ruling regimes and opposition parties have as much to gain from courting international business as companies wanting to tap the considerable Islamic market. Just one example is Turkey's AKP, many high-ranking members of which hold shares in prominent companies and conglomerates that have prospered under the AKP's watch (see Chapter 6). This may well be a long-term financial strategy across the region, explaining many Islamists' smart investment in legitimate companies and ventures. Islamist political parties also pursue those living in the Muslim diaspora across the globe. Muslim expats in the US, Europe, Canada, and Australia are courted for the influence they may wield abroad (a surprisingly large number hold positions in governments, NGOs, and Fortune 500 companies), the funding they might provide, as well as for their vote back home (as many Muslim nations permit voting by absentee ballot). The first prime minister of the rebellious Syrian opposition National Council, fighting a civil war to oust the dictator Assad, was Ghassan Hitto, an Islamist Syrian-American IT executive from Texas. These offshore constituents can swing an election.

There are challenges, too, particularly centered on businesses' online presence. Social media engages the populace, but its users are unpredictable; governments and conservative groups alike want to exert control over online content; companies need to protect their business models and are reluctant to "pollute" their platforms; the cross-border penetration of online communications can expose a company's tailored campaigns to other audiences who might be left cold or, worse, insulted.

And yet, rulers in the MENA and SCA regions have consistently opened their doors to business—and businesses have crossed the threshold. McDonald's has been a market-leader in synthesizing its global image with local values, and even local palates. The burger giant won praise for its attempt to "glocalize" its menu with such additions as Red Bean Pie in Hong Kong and the potato-patty McAloo Tikki Burger in India. Taste, however, is arguably a secondary factor in McDonald's widespread success. The fast food giant has maintained its global dominance by relying on ties to influential individuals in the countries where it operates. For instance, its first foray into Central Asia—specifically into the 70-per-cent-Muslim Kazakhstan—was led by Kairat Boranbayev, whose daughter is married to President Nazarbayev's grandson.[29] While Boranbayev certainly does not lack in business acumen (having previously held top positions with KazRosGaz, one of Kazakhstan's most successful gas

transportation companies), his political ties stand to be of far greater benefit to McDonald's. Even the sophisticated advertiser Coca-Cola resorted to allying with the local political elite in Uzbekistan, the most populous (and most Islamic) of the Central Asian former Soviet republics, which Coca-Cola saw as its gateway to the whole region. It hired Afghan-American Mansur Maqsudi to head its bottling operation there. He had no previous bottling experience, but was married to Gulnara Karimova, daughter of the country's notorious president.[30] Coca-Cola's time as Uzbekistan's favored soft-drink company was not to last, ending when Maqsudi and Karimova's marriage did in 2002. The inevitably toxic brew of the personal and the political is nothing new, of course, but is a reminder of the potential pitfalls for international companies allying with unsavory local regimes.

Online crowdfunding in the MENA region also brings investors and businesses together, and for many different purposes. The Cairo-based crowdfunding and open innovation platform Yomken (Arabic for "It's Possible") deliberately harks back to the Arab world's Golden Age in its marketing copy, positioning itself very clearly as an enabler bringing together isolated clusters including NGOs, big multinationals, and individual innovators, and increasing the region's economic prosperity: "Yomken's vision is transforming the fahlawa ... that combines wit with innovation, intuition, resourcefulness, and experience—into an economic value

added."[31] The company recruits young, tech-savvy volunteers to help low-tech firms address technical problems.[32] One Dubai company, Aflamnah (Arabic for "Our Films"; it later became Yomken), aimed at facilitating crowdfunding specifically for filmmakers based in the Arab world. Another group, Eureeca, launched in the Middle East and provides an online method for investors to view funding proposals for small and medium-sized businesses. Some innovations and businesses have used this funding to develop new technologies which have become internationally popular, such as the Pocket TV from the UAE or Instabeat from Lebanon. In 2016, crowdfunding sites raised over $41.4 billion for over 3 million campaigns worldwide. And they are not free of politics— especially when used to fund civil society groups and businesses with political agendas.

One who had such an agenda, and benefited from some of that wealth, was the Malaysian politician Tony Pua, a DAP MP, who was fined 200,000 ringgit (about US $61,000) for defaming a private water-services utility in a newspaper interview in which he called the company's financial solvency into question.[33] When the judge refused to wait for the outcome of Pua's appeal before levying the fine, Pua had just six days to come up with the cash. Within five days, Mr. Pua and his party had raised nearly 150,000 ringgit from tens of thousands of Malaysians through a series of websites and social media-sprung community fundraisers.

Public Broadcast

Social media has in fact provided a good way of doing the kind of talking about public services for which Tony Pua was fined. In terms of ruling regimes' attitude toward and use of social media vis-à-vis their citizens, it is certainly not merely a story of conservative clampdowns, censorship, revolutions, and the odd shafts of light. MENA rulers have looked to social media for innovative governmental solutions.

For instance, during the Middle East Respiratory Syndrome (MERS) outbreak in 2012, Saudi Arabian public health went online. The Saudi government realized that nearly half of all its internet-connected citizens were on social media (which was most often accessed via mobile devices on 3G or 4G networks), and sent medical updates en masse via Twitter and Facebook. Saudi women have also benefited greatly from social media spreading awareness of breast cancer—the leading cause of death among women aged 20–59 in the kingdom. In a country which has long struggled with the coexistence of the internet and conservative Islam, and where talking publicly about private body parts is taboo, the internet offers a forum for Saudi women to learn more about their bodies, potential symptoms, and logical next steps in diagnosing this disease.[34] Several Arabic websites, such as Kanzah or Susie in Arabia, provided forums for Saudi women to have such conversations.

In Dubai, too, social media became a tool of social cohesion. Faced with a growing divide between migrant laborers and wealthier residents, Crown Prince Sheikh Hamdan produced the #MyDubai campaign on Facebook, Twitter, and Instagram, which aimed to create an "autobiography" of the state showcasing all residents in an equal light. This followed in the footsteps of Sheikh Mohammed bin Rashid Al Maktoum, the ruler of Dubai and VP of the UAE, who often solicits "help" from the public via Twitter when making legislative decisions—the democratic process crowdsourced by a conservative autocrat.

Even the most apparently enthusiastic political opponents of social media seem to recognize what it can do for them. Index on Censorship reported that, in Iran, "Social media accounts were set up for every candidate in Iran's 2013 presidential elections, despite the fact that Twitter, Facebook, and YouTube are all blocked within the country."[35] Similarly, led by the flagship @UAEGOV set of accounts (now comprising several handles managed by the government), featuring exclusive behind-the-scenes photographs and reports from the UAE's normally reclusive legislative and executive branches, several of its federal ministries have launched Facebook, Twitter, and Instagram profiles in an effort to increase transparency. Social media as an engagement platform is, it seems, irresistible. With presidential contenders joining the social media bandwagon in countries such as Iran, the trajectory certainly

seems to suggest an "if you can't beat them, join them" sort of mentality.

Efforts to establish online platforms that provide a service to people in the region are more often led by NGOs and private sector actors. In Lebanon the #Cheyef7alak program (*cheyef halak* refers to "self-evaluation") was launched in 2011 as an app, Facebook, and Twitter campaign by a Lebanese TV station and a pan-Arab advertising company. (Unsurprisingly it also got some television airtime.) It first mobilized around the issue of road traffic chaos and accidents, which are a leading cause of discontent among Beirut's residents, and which the limited police resources often fail to tackle. It invited citizens to take photographs of traffic violations and upload them to the various social media platforms, notifying police by automatically uploading to law enforcement databases. Recent photos show cars with missing license plates, a motorcyclist texting while driving, and, disconcertingly, numerous bullet holes in car windows and doors. Several cases were followed up using the new data and Beirut's citizens felt empowered, especially in minority neighborhoods. It has led to several new online platforms geared to monitoring bribes and corruption.

In a similar vein, Janaagraha, a Bangalore-based NGO, set up, among other not-for-profit online initiatives, the innovative ipaidabribe.com, which allows users in several African and South Asian countries (presently including

India, Pakistan, Syria, and Morocco) to anonymously document corruption by sending reports via the website. Users can inform of instances when they paid a bribe (to whom, for what reason, and how much), and when they did *not* pay ("Tell us your story. We would like to honor and celebrate you for standing up against corruption"); when they encountered an "honest officer" ("the good guys in the system"); and when they have been victims of a scam. All the stories—including dates, locations, and amounts—are logged and can be accessed and searched on the site, which also informs the authorities so that measures can (hopefully) be taken.[36] These are just some of the examples of the entrepreneurial solutions to lackluster public accountability appearing all over the world. Such crowdsourced anti-corruption initiatives can direct structural change in postrevolutionary environments, sowing the seeds for stability and long-term economic growth.

These social media initiatives aim to change attitudes as well as social conditions. Operating under the slogan "Freedom of speech is allowed within boundaries of respect," the Islamist "network of democratization activists"[37] behind @OnlineBahrain looks at retweets, repostings, the number of followers, time of engagement, resonance of hashtags, and keyword identification in real time, allowing them to customize their postings and what messages they tend to scale up and amplify, such as #weareone, which aimed to create harmony between Sunni and Shiites in Bahrain

(a hotly contested issue). The goal of that campaign was to propound the idea that external actors, not political Islamists, were the problem. It also sent a very clear democratic message through the vehicle of social media.

Such initiatives also effect change by engaging disgruntled citizens in the governance process itself. The Tunisian NGO "Youth Decides" aims to empower young people (particularly to vote) and develops programs of advocacy, cultural promotion, civic engagement, and employment. It was working a range of strategies in the run-up to the 2014 elections to try and encourage the country's young demographic to get involved. Its founder, Wala Kasmi, bemoaned the fact that, despite the slightly embarrassing pop-star references and appearances at rallies, Tunisia's top politicians—the majority of whom are over fifty—were still not focused on young people, and therefore were not attracting them: "Many youth don't feel represented by the politicians . . . They need to speak directly to us."[38] With the central idea that "the technology native generation has an added value to humanity. Technology natives changed the way business worked and they can change the way politics work,"[39] alongside a slick website and excellent social media outreach, Youth Decides has organized petitions and debates online, including a quirky campaign inviting young people to post their candidacy for government roles; a thirty-four-year-old blogger and human rights expert called Tarek Cheniti even nominated himself for prime minister.[40]

SIX

FAITH, DOUGH, AND CHARITY

"Every single antiquity [ISIS] sells out of Palmyra is priceless. It is taking billions of dollars. The market is there; it will take everything on offer, and it will pay anything for it. Daesh is gaining in every single step it takes, every destruction."[1]

Like other extremist groups, ISIS had a clear understanding from its beginnings that in order to achieve its grand territorial ambitions to establish the new caliphate, it would have to raise considerable funds. Unlike other groups, from its beginnings it saw itself as, at core, a "corporation"—a slick money-making operation that could and should establish global networks to buy and sell goods. Getting into the oil business was easy—the group overran numerous productive oil fields as they rampaged across Iraq and Syria. But another income stream, lucrative, cleaner, and more befitting their commitment to

destroy all cultures other than Islam, was to deal in Middle Eastern antiquities. ISIS shot-callers quickly realized they could easily appropriate hundreds of priceless ancient Babylonian artifacts from the territories they conquered, such as the city of Palmyra.

The central problem was how to securely sell them off. One ISIS member named Javaid, a dedicated recruit who had joined the extremists early on, told me how he had sourced potential buyers online, using social media like Telegram to build networks, conversing with leads thousands of miles away in Europe and North America, and then turning to the dark web; and how he conducted the transactions in Bitcoin, and ensured they were untraceable with encryption software.[2] In this way, ISIS' investment in social media propaganda paid off big time. Having built a substantial, networked fanbase as part of its operations on the "information battlefield," it could now do big business in private, cloaked transactions. That was the key: black market sales using digital cash, with no footprints left behind.

And the means of harvesting such antiquities brought its own rewards. Videos of the black-clad terrorists' grab-and-smash, ensuring that no evidence would remain of the treasure-looting, made excellent viewing material to share online. This, too, ISIS has honed to further push its radical propaganda. One French archaeologist who has been monitoring ISIS' destruction across the ancient cities of

the Middle East noted: "It has been learning from its mistakes. When it started on its archaeological destruction in Iraq and Syria, it started with hammers, big machines, destroying everything quickly on film . . . It blew Nimrud up in one day. But that only gave it 20 seconds of footage. I don't know how many people's attention it could capture with that short piece of film." Now, the destruction is prefigured, trailed, teased out piece by horrifying piece. "The planet then has the footage that it releases according to its own schedule." And the longer the destruction lasts, the higher the prices soar.

* * *

The key resources recruited and mobilized by social media-savvy Islamist organizations and extremist groups include not only people, but money. Despite the increasing availability and prevalence of digital technology, most political campaigns are still based primarily on physical mobilization, but social media plays an important role in how parties go about attracting and securing funds, and choosing how to spend them. The function of charitable donations in the region is also contentious, with Islamist groups themselves having cultivated strong links with charitable and philanthropic concerns—and their associated established means of money-collecting online—in order to fund political and even extremist activity.

This is another way that the experience of social media in the Islamic world gives the lie to Morozov's theories of "net delusion." Morozov belittles online communities that support charitable or civic causes because, dividing the amount of money raised by the size of the group, it amounts to mere pennies per member. Many have exposed the weakness of this argument—it is hardly clear that *more* money would be raised in the absence of such platforms, even if more *should* be raised with them—and in the Islamic world, it is even more acute. First, Morozov's view doesn't take into consideration that the majority of those supporting Islamist charitable or civic causes would be prevented from sending any money without online functionality due to the particular security situation in the region. Morozov's calculation also fails to account for the people who might heed an online call to donate by actually doing so in person, which is a common occurrence in Islamic countries. The Muslim Brotherhood has relied on this method for years, soliciting funds on social media and via mobile phone messaging while knowing that the money can be collected directly at early morning prayer (*fajr*) as the congregation members file out.

This is not to say that all uses of collected funds are legitimate. Digital platforms provide twenty-first-century conduits for capital and corruption in the Islamic world, as well as the means for combatting exploitative practices.

Asking For It

"For all of those who aren't joining jihad yet, you can perform jihad with your money. We want to buy 100 grad missiles to shell Qardaha." So read a 2014 tweet by ISIS supporter Abdullah Mohisine. It was retweeted over 900 times, with a Turkish telephone number to call.[3] Social media opens up the possibility of funding to anyone with a telephone and a Twitter account—something that extremist groups like ISIS have been taking advantage of, and with more sophisticated calls than Mohisine's blunt request.

Raising funds through recruiting donors is a vital part of ISIS' entire social media strategy in order to finance the high cost of war. Many groups receive a good deal of funding from people who watch footage of the sins committed against them. Thus, pictures and videos that ISIS posts across YouTube, Flickr, and Instagram document in unflinching detail the atrocities of the Assad regime and its allied forces in Syria, in order not only to fuel the anger of potential recruits in the affected populations, but to loosen the purse-strings of a directly affected regional audience and the considerable number of international humanitarian spectators. More impervious mobile applications such as WhatsApp and Kik are used to organize financial donations from sympathetic followers under the guise of humanitarian aid. It would seem,

ironically, that ISIS is taking a leaf out of international charities' books, which have made donating aid money to relieve disasters—not the least of which is currently being caused by ISIS in Syria—as easy as sending a text.

Being the richest terrorist organization ever, with huge swaths of oil- and gas-producing regions under its (now diminishing) control, the matter of individual donations might not have necessarily kept ISIS leaders awake at night. But it does now—especially since the group has lost a huge chunk of its physical territory. Other Islamist groups also worry about where their funds are coming from.

Most people's picture of who underwrites Islamist groups in the Middle East probably involves wealthy donors from the UAE, Qatar, Kuwait, or Saudi Arabia, benefiting from the lax restrictions and regulations on their money, making underhand deals and wiring their riches to whosoever will best further their cause, or who are most in line with their beliefs.[4] Indeed, some of the largest players in private political funding are the Islamic banks of Saudi Arabia, which have followed their government's lead in regularly channeling money to Islamic enterprises and backing political parties in Turkey and Egypt—specifically in an attempt to enfranchise and/or mold regimes more closely linked to Saudi Arabia. Private donations from Gulf supporters have also contributed to ISIS' funding, though Saudi Arabia and other Gulf nations have recently tried to make it harder for their citizens to donate without government approval—and

certainly harder than when, as during the war in Afghanistan, Saudi supporters could donate money directly at their mosque free from government scrutiny.[5] Twitter, on the other hand, refuses to block personal accounts that solicit funds even when they are quite explicit about what the money might be for, allowing a safe platform for funding messages to be circulated, and further legitimizing organizations like ISIS, but also the Taliban, Hezbollah, and al-Shabaab, and their calls for money.

Because of social media, funding no longer has to come through extremely wealthy individuals with connections, nor even through physical presence. Yet traditional, cash-in-hand collecting is still a major funding channel for many Islamic groups. Some hold regular fund drives at private homes and mosques. At upmarket Kuwaiti fund-raisers, attendees would be asked for donations to help orphans, refugees—"and jihad," impossibly conflating humanitarian rescue and terrorism.[6] A 2013 Brookings Institution report named Ajeel al-Nashmi, one of Kuwait's most senior bankers and a board member for large institutions across the Islamic finance sector, as a lynchpin in the nexus of clerics, extremists, and funds. He is known to have participated in a fundraiser alongside the social media-savvy chief cleric Shafi al-Ajmi, among others, which financed an offensive in Latakia that left several hundred civilians dead. Al-Ajmi himself has admitted that he collected funds, ostensibly for "charity," and delivered

them in person to the ISIS-linked al-Nusra Front.[7] The highly sectarian flavor of these individuals' Twitter feeds gives the impression that they hardly would have condemned the violence. There is, too, an established black market connecting extremist groups with Gulf crooks, through which extremists hold auctions of the spoils of war or other "donated" (heavy on the inverted commas) valuables such as jewelry and cars. The proceeds are channeled back to the shady acquirers.

Cash donations can also be laundered—an unfortunate consequence of the increased economic liberalization in the MENA and SCA regions. Post-revolutionary Tunisia, for instance, became a haven for money laundering, particularly for extremist groups such as al-Qaeda. Illegal flows of money coursed through Tunisian society, working its way toward political parties as criminal networks attempted to buy themselves impunity, thus providing the parties with more resources to finance their campaigns and other activities: "Some highly controversial associations, including but not limited to the League for the Protection of the Revolution, have sources of funding that are still unknown."[8] And, while not every group engaging in this practice has connections to extremists, the unregulated flow of foreign money into Tunisia also flows out again, transiting to fund extremist groups throughout the region.

The reason that the old-fashioned on-the-ground funding remains so crucial for political groups in the region

is precisely the issue of transparency. While some have started looking at social media sites, they remain hesitant, seeing the new technology as bringing with it pressure to lay their cards on the table. Traditional cash transfers are almost impossible to trace, an appealing feature for groups that are interested in hiding the source of some of their donations. For instance, the Turkish tradition of awarding management of state-run enterprises to ardent political supporters creates strong incentives for private citizens to make major investments in political campaigns. The AKP has enjoyed an influx of "green money"—donations from pious Islamist businessmen and Middle Eastern states, who perhaps want a say in Turkish politics or who hope to promote Islamic governance—which is normally kept hidden from the public to avoid the perception of corruption and a possible backlash.[9] The number of high-ranking AKP members who have shares in prominent companies and conglomerates which have prospered under the AKP, and the sheer scale of the inflow of funds—estimated in 2005 to be between US $6 and $12 billion—makes the source of the money a political hot potato.[10] It is not a practice limited to Turkey, of course: many parties use private companies to fund their political campaigns and their actions once in power. It is just that none of them want you to know about it.

Perhaps, as online services continue to gain credibility, political parties, like many other political actors around the world, will increasingly use them to help fund their

campaigns.[11] So, while many groups still recognize the power and usefulness of physical donations, technology is certainly making the process easier and more appealing.

Political Capital

Certain political parties realize the political capital—and actual capital—to be gained from accentuating their charitable appearance. The Muslim Brotherhood in Egypt, Hamas in the Palestinian territories, and Hezbollah in Lebanon have all used the umbrella of charity and social work to increase their grassroots support within their own countries, strengthening their political bases. These efforts particularly target more vulnerable members of society, including poor or refugee populations. Often these organizations will use social media to "brand" their work to potential recruits, volunteers, and mass-media audiences. Associating themselves with the ability to provide social services that authoritarian regimes cannot helps them to gradually chip away at the credibility of the government and to spread their own belief systems. Their investment in communities—and in being seen to be investing—pays dividends. Quite literally so in Turkey, where the AKP's commitment to improving social services, especially housing and health care, has been a major factor in its electoral resilience, and the reason that many Turkish voters tolerate government corruption. It seems that, as long as the average Turkish

voter sees a consistent improvement in the provision of social services, the party is immune to the controversies and scandals that have beset it over the last two years, not the least of which was the failed military coup in 2016.

Perhaps taking inspiration from the AKP, the Muslim Brotherhood has also focused its attention on winning social capital, which can then be transformed into political advantage come election time.[12] Having been granted subcontracts to certain social services by the Egyptian government, the Muslim Brotherhood gained popularity for maintaining hospitals, schools, and shelters all over Egypt (as well as in other nations in the MENA region). By the mid-2000s, the Muslim Brotherhood ran 20 per cent of NGOs in Egypt and operated twenty-two hospitals, welfare programs, and schools in every Egyptian governorate. The Brotherhood in Jordan administered the Islamic hospital in Amman and other services, like wedding and matchmaking programs. In other countries the Islamists operate sports clubs, shelters, food donations, investment programs, and other social facilities. The Brotherhood ensures that its social media team documents and promotes all of these charitable efforts across many platforms, including influential public service announcements, photographs, advertisements, and short videos.

One reason the Brotherhood enjoyed such success in the first elections after the Egyptian revolution was this established history of operating public services that the

government had failed to provide. Another was that Egyptians saw the Brotherhood as free from government bureaucracy and the strongest critic of government ineffi- ciencies.[13] The Brotherhood's social media strategy had inculcated this message, appealing directly to the younger demographic disillusioned with the then-current govern- ment, and swaying many sitting on the fence with its evident good work in the community. It continued after Mubarak's fall with a significant investment of resources. Ikhwanweb and the Brotherhood's websites took an active role in the daily goings on around Egypt, recruiting many younger people to actively engage that demographic and international media attention with quick and catchy updates and responses to critics. (Many noticed how noticeably well-educated and fluent in English the Brotherhood's online workers were, a far cry from the usual "Brother" profile.) It is telling that, when the Egyptian military wanted to destroy the Brotherhood's political base, it first went after the Brotherhood's social service network.

In many ways Ennahda showed how not to do it. Though it, too, staunchly opposed the incumbent and corrupt regime (in its case, that of Ben Ali), and engaged in widespread social programs, from the outset it made a concerted effort to separate its social services work from its political activity, with the intention of dispelling rumors that it provided social services only to win political points. Ennahda was aggressive in its branding of its social programs, and inventively

celebrated the "everyday ambassadors"—ordinary people (volunteers) doing heroic work in their communities—by spotlighting their work on social media. Once the group gained control, however, and the operation of government social services came under the auspices of politically appointed directors and managers, it all crumbled.[14] Like other Islamist parties, Ennahda instituted an old-fashioned spoils system for the civil service, but political appointees were not always capable of—or interested in—effective management. Ennahda itself was soon the subject of criticism for corruption,[15] and for failing to improve social services despite utilizing foreign donations and other inflows of resources to fund them. It quickly became clear that protesting about the inefficient distribution of social services is far easier than actually building efficient bureaucracies. But whereas the Muslim Brotherhood's rise to political and financial power enhanced its Islamic agenda alongside the successful promotion of its commitment to continue its social service programs,[16] Ennahda seemed to succumb to the trappings of office: greater resources and correspondingly greater opportunities for corruption and abuse of power.

The Ties That Bind

The relationships between civil society groups and political parties in the Islamic world are incredibly complex, particularly with regard to the collection and use of

charitable donations. Charity is a central feature of Islamic life: the zakat is one of the five pillars of Islam, an annual contribution for the poor, mandatory for all Muslims. Those who collect zakat thus have enormous funds at their disposal. Charities, and their associated groups, are therefore crucial political players.

Indonesia is a salient example of the complexity of charity and politics. Civil society groups and political parties became intertwined at Indonesian independence, and have only become more so as time has passed. The Indonesian zakat amounts to a considerable sum, and hence the country has witnessed a rise in both state- and community-based zakat collectors, as well as the almost inevitable conflict between them. Indeed, Indonesian political parties have devoted considerable attention to managing state-run zakat agencies, and new political groups have even begun founding their own charities to collect zakat and other contributions: the charities owe much of their financial backing and prestige to their political connections, while the parties are buoyed by the social capital they receive from their association with the charities. It is a symbiosis that brings with it a heightened risk of corruption, as many political groups receive state funding. Furthermore, many of the community leaders who advocated a greater role for NGOs in the distribution of zakat have become a part of a new political class, building more and stronger ties between charities and government officials. Groups also receive

private zakat donations in the name of community development and other social programs.[17]

So too in other countries, zakat collection performs important roles for a number of actors. For the governments of Jordan and other Middle Eastern countries, for instance, zakat collection and distribution legitimizes them in the eyes of Islamists and helps them to maintain political control. Centralized zakat collections therefore represent both a source of income for the state and a connection to the core of Islamic belief.[18] Sometimes the issue of legitimization is more contentious—and costly. In Pakistan, the Muttahida Qaumi Movement's Khidmat-e-Khalq Foundation saw its annual zakat donation drop 20 per cent when the Sindh Rangers, a paramilitary force reporting to the Ministry of Interior, prohibited its members from soliciting donations.[19]

In many Muslim-majority states, charity organizations—not always state-run—are important players in the political arena. The majority of these charities are, at root, politically oriented, and very little of their resources go to non-Islamic recipients. The many more Muslim refugees recently fleeing the civil war in Syria have encouraged Gulf states to send more zakat money in their direction; interviews on the ground suggest that community-based charities run by political parties have had a significant impact on the religious views of the refugee population. The money can be highly disaggregated. Al-Nour, Gamey'ah Shar'iah,

and Ansar al-Sharia in Egypt are examples of charitable organizations that use their services to promote their brand of Islam; the same can be said of the Saudi-based Islamic relief organizations which support the spread of the particular variety of Islam practiced in Saudi Arabia. Organizations and their members often appeal directly to the public for funds as well.[20]

Some charities couple aid distribution with politically based education, paying students to attend classes which are aimed at disseminating certain parties' political propaganda. Other charities distribute succor for specifically religious—even extremist—purposes; there is evidence to suggest that assistance has been given to certain families in Syria if their father or a close relative died as a martyr.[21] Charities associated with the extremist Jabhat al-Nusra have made these sorts of claims, and used them to promote their different platforms.

There is, of course, much evidence of charities and NGOs working efficiently and above board in the region, particularly using social media. Imitating Western sites like Kickstarter, and with a significant focus on marketing, this civic "crowdfunding" allows people to donate to projects with a simple text message or by clicking on a link. Such platforms feature projects such as Bilbaal, "A socially engaging online platform dedicated to connecting pro-bono resources to Palestinian philanthropic initiatives and organizations around the world." And, despite the

occasional difficulties of working in the Middle East, several new groups, such as Zoomaal, which has backing from four major Arab venture capital firms, are attempting to attract people to this kind of donation method. But international secular charities that are operating in the region, such as UNICEF, are wary of partnering local Islamic charities precisely because of their political motivations. The presence of both legitimate and extremist charities causes concern to those who want to donate money for humanitarian interests.

Vying for Power

The Nahdlatul Ulama (NU) in Indonesia and the Gülen movement have both used charities and their funds to aid their political activity.

The NU is a traditionalist Sunni Islam movement, the largest political party in Indonesia, indeed the largest independent Islamic organization in the world. It is a charitable body which sees its role as making up for the government's shortfalls in providing public services. Its size poses several problems, particularly regarding information dissemination and dues collection from its more than 30 million members. (Only a small proportion pay, however, the majority of the party's resources instead coming from individual, group, and business donations.) The NU is very clear about its priorities. While visiting Indonesia I met with several young

men on the staff of NU's sharp social media management team. "We must be efficient at raising money for our projects," an NU official explained. "Fundraising is time-consuming and expensive. We'd rather spend that time pressuring the government and carrying out projects on the ground." As part of this efficiency drive the NU has been exploring how to use technology, such as the online crowd-funding platforms, to help facilitate easier payments. It is already an enthusiastic user of social media. Since its founding at the end of 2010, the NU's Twitter account has put out on average a tweet every hour to its 234,000 followers, its feed very focused on promoting the organization's ideals. It is not only about communication. The NU also uses social media networks to profile its supporters (and the opposition), gathering demographic information and calculating fund-giving patterns. Its core use of online platforms, therefore, is still for the sharing of information and on-the-ground facilitation: maintaining a mailing list (electronic and physical) and a register of party forum members.[22]

If the NU exists to spread Islamic teaching, one of the Gülen Institute's aims is to use education to further more moderate social ideals. This has not made it any less contentious; indeed, though it claims to have no political ties, it is seen as a dangerous competitor in Turkish politics. Based on the ideas of Fethullah Gülen, a Turkish former imam, writer, and Islamic opinion leader, the Gülen

movement—usually referred to as Hizmet (the Service) by its followers or as Cemaat (the Community, or Assembly) by the Turkish public—is regarded as preaching a milder form of Islam. One of the keys to its success is its global network of private schools (numbering somewhere between 500 and 1,000)[23] and universities operating in 140 countries (mostly English-speaking, or relatively wealthy—primarily the US, but also Australia, the UK, Germany, Canada, and Ireland).

With this large source of potential supporters, these institutions of learning allow the group to not only spread its religiously motivated ideology, but also to establish itself as one of the premier transnational Muslim outreach groups with a huge amount of financial backing. Sources under its sway included Feza Publications, a massive Turkish media conglomerate, which echoed the movement's teachings and ideals, and which was shut down by the government in 2016; and Turkey's largest bank, Asya, founded by a Gülen follower and with billions of dollars in assets, which has now also closed down. The movement has also benefited from huge private donations. The Walton Family Foundation, a philanthropic organization established by the famous (and incredibly wealthy) Wal-Mart family, donated at least $2 million to six separate Gülen schools. One, the Magnolia Science Academy in California, received the lion's share—over $1 million.[24] That school was at the heart of a 2011 FBI investigation

into Gülen-owned charter schools in America (a total
of 135 schools with well over 45,000 students).[25] The foundation was accused of diverting federal funds meant for
their charter schools to the Islamist Hizmet Organization,
another wing of the Gülen movement. Supposedly,
state funding was spent on bringing teachers from Turkey
who then donated a portion of their paycheck to the
Gülen movement. According to the state audit, Magnolia
Public Schools "used classroom cash to help six non-
employees with immigration costs. The schools had trouble
justifying another $3 million expense."[26] Given the scale of
private donations, and the considerable lauding of the
Gülen movement as forward-thinking and above reproach,
this improper use of funds is perhaps cause for further
concern.

While Gülen schools provide income and new followers
to the Gülen movement, the larger issue at the forefront of
the Gülen controversy is the political role that the foundation
plays in Turkey and abroad. Each year Gülen schools prepare
1.2 million students to take the YÖS exam (akin to America's
SAT or China's Gaokao), giving the movement a valuable
source of latent followers.

For the Gülen movement, access to the global Turkish
diaspora is essential, thereby making internet-based
communication both a political and a financial priority
for the organization. The Gülen Institute supports its
educational network with social media and other online

activities. Its social media team produces short-content videos, daily online postings, recruitment videos for volunteer work, and charity hashtag campaigns, projecting its vision and adding an important dimension in reaching the Turkish diaspora and interested members in over a hundred countries. Its global ties and ambitions to set up forums for interfaith dialogue connect moderate Islamists in the MENA region with other moderate Muslims and non-Muslims around the world.

While the Gülen Institute insists on its nonpolitical nature, the group's moderate views bring it into political tension with the more conservative governments in the Muslim world, especially given the increasing call for an Islamic solution to MENA regional politics. Its ability to connect globally facilitates professional relationships, which encourages political motivations. And while many Gülen members and sympathizers had been appointed to positions within the Turkish bureaucracy and to other high-level roles, that has now changed following the purge led by the government after the failed military coup in 2016. It was believed that Gülenists in government ministries, such as the Turkish Foreign Ministry, constructed parallel structures and connections, which could bypass official formalities.

So, while the Gülen focus on promoting Turkish culture and language might at first seem a boon to the Turkish state and government, the relationship between the Gülen

movement and Turkish authorities has become downright confrontational. The *Daily Sabah*, which is aligned with President Erdoğan's Justice and Development Party, carried various news articles about the Gülen schools' scandals in the United States and noted that Fethullah Gülen was—and continues to be—"at odds with the Turkish government over the influence he wields inside the Turkish police forces and top judiciary."[27]

Although Gülen institutions are often referred to as "Turkish schools" in the Caucasus and Central Asia, they are far from being state sanctioned today, although they had enjoyed tacit support from the Turkish state previously. After eleven years of broad cooperation—much of which was focused on reducing the influence of Turkey's army and its generals—the AKP and the Gülen movement split over the latter's attempt to use its judicial influence to curtail the National Intelligence Organization.[28] The Gülen movement was understood to be responding to Erdoğan's threat to close its prep schools with revelations of widespread corruption within the Turkish government: Zekeriya Oz, an Istanbul prosecutor widely believed to be a member of the Gülen movement, initiated an early morning raid on dozens of individuals, including the sons of three ministers, an AKP mayor, businessmen, and bureaucrats, exposing millions of dollars stacked in shoeboxes to the press. It was, and was emphasized as, the greatest corruption scandal in recent Turkish history.[29] And, with its substantial media

holdings, the Gülen movement sustained the humiliation, with *Zaman*, its mouthpiece, running articles such as "AKP and the Normalization of Corruption." While pro-Erdoğan groups made forays into the social media sphere with their #Erdoganiyedirmeyiz ("We will not let you 'eat' Erdoğan") and #GuvenimizTamLiderimizErdogan ("Our confidence is fine, our leader is Erdoğan") hashtags, the online prowess of the government was quickly overshadowed by pro-Gülen enthusiasts.[30]

Erdoğan and his party have come to view the Gülen movement as a dangerous and poisonous competitor in Turkish politics: not simply a rival at the polls, but rather a distinct fifth column that could potentially undermine Turkey's stability. The root of this distrust stems from the Gülen movement's own secrecy and lack of transparency; while the organization claims to be a cultural force, it has flexed its political muscle via its large network of supporters. This seems to include political sleeper cells. When the Turkish president ordered police to raid several pro-Gülen news agencies, an anonymous Twitter account, Fuat Avni, began to accurately predict future government crackdowns. With over 700,000 followers, the account became a popular source of information and even predicted when its own feed would be blocked by the Turkish authorities.[31] The extent of the users' impressive insider knowledge suggests that the AKP has more than a few Gülen sympathizers in its inner circle. The popularity of the Fuat Avni

handle, and later leaks of damaging conversations by AKP members, led Erdoğan to block access to Twitter and other social media across Turkey in 2014.[32]

The rise of accounts like Fuat Avni is an important development in Turkish society; analysts suspect that about 65 per cent of Turkish media is under government control,[33] with the pro-Gülen *Zaman* being one of the few independent outlets left. (In 2017, Turkey was placed 15th out of 197 countries in the annual press freedom rankings.[34] The AKP media crackdown also contributed to Turkey dropping eight points on Transparency International's annual Corruption Perceptions Index.[35]) After the corruption scandals, Erdoğan took measures to limit the influence of these media sources and to fight the "parallel state" attempting to undermine his regime—including the arrest of *Zaman*'s chief editor, Ekrem Dumanli, on live television.[36] At first, the police were turned back from *Zaman*'s headquarters by a large group of protesters who had been alerted to the situation by the Fuat Avni Twitter account, though the authorities returned that afternoon to take Dumanli into custody.[37] Ironically, *Zaman* had allegedly worked with the Turkish government to arrest reporters from rival newspapers.[38] While traditional media sources largely ignored the move, Gülen supporters and detractors alike flooded social media—a testament to the impossibility of censorship in a connected age. In response, pro-Erdoğan "netizens" started to "troll" Gülenist Twitter accounts,

making purposefully inflammatory remarks. Proof of the AKP's concern came in the form of a recording that purportedly exposed Erdoğan's daughter Sümeyye directing pro-government powers to discredit Gülenist social media accounts.

The AKP has come to see the Gülenist social media presence as a direct threat to its hold on power in Turkey. In March 2014, after YouTube videos posted to Twitter showed Erdoğan handling large amounts of cash, he threatened to "wipe out" Twitter in response to the "fake" videos. Erdoğan claimed that Gülen supporters within the Turkish government made the videos purely to discredit him.[39] In 2016, the AKP produced videos demonizing Gülen and requested that the US State Department extradite the Pennsylvania-based cleric back to Turkey to face conspiracy charges. Turkish authorities also banned Twitter within the country; Twitter users were urged to use the site's SMS-to-Tweet functionality—itself a reaction to Egypt's Twitter embargo in the early days of the Tahrir Square protests. The ban effectively strengthened the Gülenist position and attracted even more attention to the organization's nearly 200 social media accounts throughout the world.

National and international outreach—which social media expedites and intensifies—is often an attempt on the part of Islamists and extremists to attract resources from within

the region or, more broadly, from around the globe. Online expertise only seems to improve offline mobilization on the ground. Social media is as crucial a tool in Islamic organizations' public diplomacy as it is in their private financing. Again, the ways in which the internet has transformed the spread of information—that is, shifting control from pyramidal, top-down hierarchies into honeycombed, distributed networks—seems to have affected, and benefited, the passage of money too. But it is not only funds that flow across borders. Social media networks have themselves propelled information and people across the world.

SEVEN

ISLAMISTS WITHOUT BORDERS

A S THE ARMORED jeeps draped in black flags rolled along the eerily silent, rubble-strewn suburban streets of southern Raqqa, three students hid in an abandoned house, one of many there that had been pounded with shoulder-launched rockets and heavy-caliber gunfire. The then-dominant ISIS was patrolling the streets of its de facto "capital" looking for dissidents. A loudspeaker crackled an invitation to the neighborhood for cowards to come forward so that the local enforcement squad may have mercy on them, which the students did not heed.

The three young men hunched over their laptops were members of Raqqa Is Being Slaughtered Silently (RBSS), a citizen-journalist group that had first formed to oppose the bloodthirsty Assad regime, but which after ISIS' entry into Raqqa in 2014 had begun to highlight ISIS atrocities and share information with the outside world.[1] RBSS'

goal was to become an uncensored news source for concerned parties outside of Syria. In this way, they aimed to establish a transnational community to put international pressure on Assad and ISIS; RBSS had already inspired other resistance groups in Syria and Iraq. In fact, since the start of the occupation, RBSS had been instilling an increasing level of fear among ISIS elite: with orders to spare no one, the extremists had made a public showing of hunting down and slaughtering any of the group they discovered.

The RBSS cell was engaged in generating a live video feed from concealed cameras to document the latest ISIS purge with visuals that could be made into memes and sent to fellow anti-ISIS campaigners around the world. Earlier, one of the members, Hussam, had slipped outside, pretending to be a farmhand heading to market. Inside his basket was a GoPro camera filming ISIS vehicles and their loudspeaker harangues. The video was being automatically uploaded to the group's cloud-based storage account, and within a quarter of an hour or so it would be edited and packaged for distribution via Facebook, Twitter, and sister blogs like Mosul Eye. Hussam had daringly considered livestreaming the latest ISIS roundup over Facebook, but realized it could give away his location to enemies monitoring the web. The latest tech could spell a death warrant.

The important thing was that they continue to expose ISIS' hypocrisy and its abject lack of support on the

ground in Raqqa, and in this the group's social media strategies were meeting with great success. RBSS used an active Telegram channel, and back at the house, Hussam's colleagues were posting their latest short visuals on Snapchat. One of Hussam's recent Facebook posts had generated hundreds of thousands of hits in less than twenty-four hours. It was becoming obvious that RBSS' dozen or so members had inflicted more damage than any guerrilla force ISIS had faced on the battlefield. With their seat-of-the-pants journalism on a coughdrop budget, the young resistance fighters had made themselves a power to deal with.

ISIS had been humiliated by the worldwide coverage generated by this ragtag coterie of undercover citizen journalists. Certain international media outlets were constantly seeking out and broadcasting RBSS videos as well as running stories based on their on-the-ground reports, such as their use of Google Earth to pinpoint the exact location that the shot-down Jordanian pilot Moaz al-Kasasbeh had burned to death in a cage in 2015.[2] A German digital outlet would pick up the latest "wire" from Hussam and his RBSS team, write it up, and have it quickly translated into French and Dutch. Later that same day, the story would make its way into a three-minute segment on the BBC. TRT World had dedicated two of its journalists to liaise with RBSS members and to use their incoming stories as features in primetime. Turkish audiences especially craved the news reports from RBSS.

Within minutes, Hussam and his team could reach 11 million people in eight countries. It was a new day for the freedom of the press, a new era. Now, when ISIS assassinated people indiscriminately, or was proven to be as corrupt—extorting bribes from local leaders, seeking out young girls for sex—as President Assad's government, people were told about it, backed by visceral, immediate video evidence. With reports having gone viral multiple times, RBSS had built up a twenty-first-century grassroots information powerhouse.

* * *

The central message of the social media revolution was that national borders no longer matter, or even exist. The rise of social media and communication technologies has interconnected the Islamic world, and a transnational Islamic community has begun to rise—and will continue to grow. Social media enables new voices to be heard both locally and internationally, and motivates political actors— including Islamist parties—and extremists to act on the global stage. It is not only citizens who communicate and collaborate over social media: Islamist groups, too, have been influenced by fellow travelers and competitors alike. Social media straddles the local and the global, inviting specific action while garnering worldwide attention— none more so than for the extremist groups radicalizing foreign fighters to defend their "nation of Islam." The

defenselessness of conventional national boundaries has never been more worrisome for the West.

Talking Together and Apart

Digital advances in transnational connectivity have increased communication between extremists sometimes hundreds or thousands of miles apart. Al-Qaeda, under Osama bin Laden, was once without compare in its usage of technology to facilitate communication with cells across the region and the globe. As technology advanced, al-Qaeda continued to evolve its strategy to stay ahead of efforts to track communications. There are reports that al-Qaeda communicated with Abu Sayyaf in the Philippines and groups in Somalia, Chechnya, and other central Asian countries.[3]

Social media, of course, was invented to enable and enhance discourse. With enhanced regional connectivity, transnational Islamic communities are now much more able to communicate with each other, and have adopted a flat, decentralized model facilitated by social media and internet platforms. This has led to such phenomena as a noticeable majority of foreign recruits coming to Syria having been radicalized not by traditional al-Qaeda-affiliated or -supporting clerics, but by the online English-language sermons of clerics based in the US or Australia.[4] But the egalitarian nature of social media has also meant

that other voices of previously marginalized and disen-franchised citizens can be heard by a global audience; it means that citizens "no longer experience injustice in soli-tude."[5] People can express themselves and sympathize with each other over shared experiences. Often, this allows strangers to build a conversation over mutual concerns regarding the pressures of everyday life.

Most Islamic belief was formulated by states and other large domestic religious groups for their own peoples, but, with social media, groups and individuals are more able to debate their religion and other issues with their counter-parts across the globe. For instance, rising food prices is one area of frequent concern: a Pakistani student may tweet a diatribe about Lahore's food prices, as a farmer in West Malaysia shares his concerns over the governmental red tape that drives food prices upward. Islamists from South and Central Asia have begun to discuss Islamic scripture, women's clothing styles, or extremism, of which, until the past five years or so, they had little knowledge and experience. What was once local has now had an interna-tional light shone upon it. Though there is often, and obvi-ously, a clash of cultures, there is also a genuinely interested imparting of information, and this rich sharing of perspec-tives, particularly in global debates about Islamic identity, is far more important to transnational communication.

The way that many Muslims in Europe and around the world have struggled with their Islamic identity under

different types of governance (Western liberal democracies and the Russian authoritarian regime), and the observable drive to redefine Islam amid different societies, is intriguing to many in the MENA region. The transformation of Islam in Turkey has been facilitated by interactions between Muslims there and Turkish Muslims living in Germany. It is too early to say what effect, if any, such sharing of experience might have had on the revolutions of 2011 and later, but at the very least it opened the eyes of some to different possibilities in the political and social arenas.[6]

Muslim women have certainly made up a large proportion of those awakened to and by social media communication. With some national and sectarian variations, studies have shown that Muslim women tend to be more active online, more willing to engage with non-Muslims, and 62 per cent more likely to maintain strong open dialogs than Muslim men. Women tend to stay on closed social networks and password-protected forums, rather than go on sites such as Facebook. Muxlim.com and Alif are popular as they give opportunities to engage in conversation with people from their faith and other faiths (or no faith). Dialog is shaped by, and revolves around, religious issues but also personal details of the respondents' daily lives, families, work, and so on.[7] There is also an element of identity-searching in a good number of conversations, with topics such as how one can be a good Muslim woman in a more modern society coming to the forefront of conversations.

Internet initiatives have also taken a more proactive stance to counter harm to women and to further the sense of a worldwide community of Muslim women. A volunteer-led independent women's rights organization called Young Women for Change, founded in 2011 by two female Afghanis in their early twenties, opened the first women-only internet café in Kabul, called Sahar Gul after a victim of domestic violence. The café gives women a space to access the internet and socialize without facing male harassment, and the owners actually hold sessions where they train girls in how to use social media, inculcating a sense of why it is important to the gaining of more rights for women in Afghanistan.[8] Countering the oppression of Muslim women in sub-Saharan Africa, Ousseina Alidou has argued for the importance of social media campaigns in Kenya to promote an alternative discourse for the representation and self-representation of Muslim women there, which is too often focused solely on their religion. For Alidou, social media campaigns should connect and build relationships between Muslim communities across the globe, especially with women in these communities.[9]

Copycat Campaigning

Islamist political parties and movements throughout the Muslim world influence each other, too. Though Islamists may disagree on religious and political issues, many

groups are eager to share (often by way of social media) strategies and tactics for effective use of online tools to maximize anti-regime propaganda, put in place effective ground tactics, give authoritative pronouncements on sharia law, lure new recruits, and test a grab-bag of fund-raising gimmicks. The increased ability of connected populations to share not only complaints but ideas on how to fix things has pointed the way for Islamist groups to respond with aggressive rhetoric and sophisticated, targeted campaigns.

Some social media ideas are just too good to pass up, spawning a raft of copycat initiatives rather than descending into tit-for-tat rivalry. This transcends even national borders. Thus, when Turkey's AKP runs a popular contest to draw in voters, the PTI in Pakistan soon launches a similar contest. A Malaysian app which tracked official corruption using cartoon caricatures of the incumbent regime became hugely popular with ordinary Malaysians, if not their government, and the app was downloaded in huge numbers. Soon a version of the app began appearing in nearby countries, using the same template, but with other countries' politicians the target of the mockery. A young woman active in the Parti Islam Se-Malaysia (PAS), an Islamist political party dedicated to the long-term goal of creating an Islamic state in the country, told me in an interview: "We watch whatever is working in Egypt or Pakistan. They are our brothers and sisters in Islam. Why

shouldn't we learn from them?" In fact, the PAS did better than that. In the run-up to the 2013 elections it employed the very same social media slogans and campaigns that had been pioneered by Imran Khan in Pakistan and the Muslim Brotherhood in Egypt. In some cases they used exactly the same wording, simply changing the background graphics. No need to reinvent the wheel.

There are many across the Islamic region—in countries such as Iraq, Sudan, and Nigeria—who have taken inspiration from the use of social media during the revolutions in Egypt and Tunisia, not necessarily because they too are Islamist, but because the strategies were initially very successful. Thus Facebook campaigns have appeared everywhere, such as that started by Fadi Quran who wanted to inspire up-and-coming young Palestinians in reuniting Fatah and Hamas, and Iraqis who are organizing rallies and protests to demand better economic and political conditions in their own country. Sudanese activists use social media to organize protests, although many there distrust Facebook as they fear government tracking. Many bloggers have taken up the role of relaying on-the-ground news to netizens and major media outlets—a common practice in revolutionary Egypt, where it was realized that documenting the government crackdown could gain international support. In many states internet-savvy activists are connecting like-minded people, organizing events, and putting pressure on their political leaders, the only

difference between them and Egypt and Tunisia being that they are not calling for the overthrow of their political leaders—at least, not directly.[10]

Political parties are not the only ones scrutinizing social media campaigns. Extremist and terrorist groups have begun to exploit what is most effective in other groups' social media activity. In something of a volte face, considering it banned internet usage in Afghanistan during its period of rule in the late 1990s and early 2000s, the Taliban now tweets merrily about attacks on NATO forces, similar to Nigeria's Boko Haram using Twitter to provide live updates of its assaults, including graphic videos and photos of attacks.

Ruling regimes have also inspired, and been inspired by, the use of social media campaigning. Many countries' social media revolutions can trace some of their ideological origins to Jordan, and the targeting of young people in Amman to engage them in civil society issues. More overtly political in nature, many Jordanian state officials have adopted the pioneering methods of King Hussein, one of the greatest proponents of online outreach, and those of his son, King Abdullah II, for utilizing social media to promote tourism and aid other political motivations. These in turn have inspired the Assad dynasty, which has adopted the same web practices in Syria.[11]

And the inspiration is not simply one-way. In Egypt, "Sinai Cry" is an online media campaign (including slick

YouTube videos) to expose the apparent "war crimes" perpetrated by the Egyptian military in the Sinai Peninsula—probably the first real social media campaign against the Egyptian military after the fall of President Morsi and his Muslim Brotherhood. It is directly inspired by Palestinian campaigns against US drone strikes. Recently, region-wide protestors against the "repressive" Egyptian regime and in support of the Brotherhood have posted videos, graphics, and forum comments, and employed Israeli-Palestinian experiences, images, and videos, to connect the hatred of Israelis with the Egyptian military.

The social media-led spotlight engenders competition between groups, even between revolutions, for the attention of local, regional, and international audiences. The jostling is not always and not necessarily negative; instead, it can inspire communication and influence.

Information Flows

One of the most important aspects of social media's power is its connection to international media outlets in bringing specific issues and grievances to global attention. If Islamist groups are drawing inspiration from the successful communication tactics used by their contemporaries throughout the Muslim world to attract local audiences and effect specific change on their own doorstep, social media can also grab the eyes and ears of the international community,

which can lead to political pressure or even direct intervention, as in Libya.

The earliest instancing of the sheer force of this social media-led connectivity was the Green Revolution in Iran, which the new digital technologies highlighted to Western media outlets and their audiences. In Iran itself, the protests were actually a modest event, but Western media painted them out to be part of a much bigger movement than in reality they were—probably betraying their own fervent desire for the collapse of the Iranian regime.[12] No such amplification occurred, or was necessary, during the seismic Arab Spring revolts. In fact, traditional media outlets in the affected countries, or even in neighboring countries, tended not to cover most of the protests and events. Saudi Arabian media, for example, hardly featured the protests in North Africa for their own political reasons.

But it is the Arab Spring that provides the clearest example of the power of social media's connection to international news outlets, and the pattern of information dissemination that my research uncovered. The early local social media coverage—primarily focused on organizing protests—also aimed to gain the attention of an international audience: social media users from other states in the MENA region, and especially in the West. The idea was that the democratic West would understand what was being fought for, and that Western attention might transmute into eventual intervention or support for the

revolution, lending the revolutionaries and their efforts a good deal of legitimacy. The very style of the social media posts, which contributed to a self-reinforcing narrative, reflected the revolutionaries' attempt to gain as much Western attention as possible. As the opposition persisted and intensified, international news media did begin to cover the events. Their sources of information included local social media posts as well as those of the diaspora networks, made up of groups (such as the UK's Libyan Youth Movement) that passed on news and event information to social media and created websites that garnered thousands of supporters after a few days.[13] The traditional media coverage informed many people abroad who had been relatively unaware of the scale of the protests. The international mainstream media became even more crucial when regimes ramped up censorship. This made it even more dangerous to be on social media and to disseminate information—an intensity of scrutiny not meted out to international news media as they were a known quantity to the regimes, not a new and unruly platform.

The protests of 2011 saw an explosion in the informal "trade" of information, images, and videos between social and traditional media. It benefited the social media revolutionaries, who wanted and needed exposure for their cause, as well as news outlets which needed scoops and original timely content to make power-plays for audience share. Networks like Al Jazeera and Al Arabiya took

information from individuals and groups on the ground in Tunisia, Libya, Egypt, Syria, and Bahrain, rebranded it and sent it off to millions. Those individuals and groups gained further legitimacy for their struggle and more passionate support for their actions.[14]

The decentralized creation and distribution of information has greatly enhanced the information environment by giving ordinary citizens the opportunity to become eyewitness journalists. The rise of "citizen journalism" is one of the greatest changes wrought by social media technology. The miniaturization of quality imaging technology, and most essentially the camera phone, has changed the dynamics entirely. The Arab Spring depended not just on social media, but specifically on social media on mobile phones—the software and the hardware—which allowed for real-time reporting and updating as people walked the very streets they were calling for protests on. As the internet went down, phones became vital when the texting-to-tweet workarounds came on stream. During the uprising against Mubarak, Al Jazeera received over 1,000 videos recorded on cell phones.[15]

Such protesters now fill a void left by professional journalists and foreign correspondents, who are often prevented from entering countries, or denied access to information, or (if they are known to the authorities, and contrary to them) followed closely by government handlers or otherwise specifically targeted by official forces. Indeed, such traditional

correspondents are becoming thinner on the ground: CNN has cut staff precisely in favor of profiling eyewitness accounts instead.[16] Netizens are now able to curate their own content, amplifying the citizen voice past national borders while giving everyone a greater stake in the revolution.

Traditional news outlets have, of course, themselves established a presence on social media, which makes it easier for them to follow movements on these sites and gather information. That presence also shaped the narrative of the Arab Spring. Occurring at around the same time the "Timeline" function came to Facebook, it was the mainstream channels' reposting and recycling of images and comments from the pages of individuals who were perhaps too close to events to take a "long view" (even if that had been top of their list of concerns at the time) that shaped the revolution into a narrative about the struggle for democracy. The established players knew that this narrative was the best way to portray the revolution to Western media and politicians.[17]

Social media cannot do it all. Even during the revolutions of 2011, television was and still is the primary way for many in the MENA region to receive news. However, then and now, many doubt local and state media outlets and have turned their attention to social media and other international sources for their information. Online newspapers have risen in popularity in most Islamic countries as a more viable alternative to print. Yet even traditional online media sites, such as Al Jazeera, are rebuffed in favor of social media

because the latter has no boundaries on topics for discussion.[18] Countering the deficiencies of mainstream, state-run, and therefore often biased or censored media—which, as at times of revolution, become insufferable—more people are encouraged to turn to online media, and to come into contact with transnational political and social conversations.[19]

Overawed, and Over Here

The impression social media gives of being more authentic, truthful, local, and intimate, in comparison to commercial or mainstream media channels, is exploited by extremists and local coordination committees to disseminate propaganda and recruit followers and fighters from the world over. This new kind of "nation," comprised of foreign combatants, is another—and more worrying—kind of extreme community made possible by social media's disregard for national borders.

The number of foreign fighters joining the struggle against the Assad regime has been one of the most interesting aspects of the Syrian conflict. In February 2017 counterintelligence officials estimated that over 12,000 foreign fighters (down from a peak of 30,000) from more than ninety different countries were still in Syria[20]—many from the broader Middle East region, but close to 3,400 reportedly from Europe or other Western states, and over 150 from the US. That number leveled off as ISIS came under heavy military pressure and called instead for recruits to stay

in their "native lands" to carry out operations there: "No need to travel the world," stated an ISIS post on Telegram following the August 2017 Barcelona attacks. "Just pick the main city. Find a hub spot for tourists. Choose you [sic] weapon."[21] Many nations are worried about what their radicalized citizens might do on home turf—and with good reason. The November 2015 attacks in Paris were apparently in retaliation for France's involvement in the civil wars in Iraq and Syria. Led by Abdelhamid Abaaoud, a Belgian-Moroccan Islamic terrorist who had joined ISIS while fighting Assad in Syria in 2013 and who operated as a link between ISIS in the Middle East and French terror cells, the attacks were, in François Hollande's words, "planned in Syria, organized in Belgium, perpetrated on our soil with French complicity."[22] Links to terrorist cells in France and Belgium are, at time of writing, also being pursued in relation to the attacks in Catalonia.

The role of the internet in radicalization is a complex one. Rather than driving it per se, it accelerates the process. The major attacks committed by extremists on European soil in recent years—the recent Paris massacre, the 2014 Boston Marathon, the 2013 murder of Fusilier Lee Rigby—demonstrate the mixture of online influence, international links, and other more personal factors. The local influence is still strong. For instance, although radical mosques seem to be a declining influence (radicalization through mosques accounts for less than 2 per cent of

documented radicalization cases in the UK), Michael Adebolajo, one of Lee Rigby's killers, converted to Islam in London and attended the banned British terrorist organization al-Muhajiroun's meetings and demonstrations, and Abdelhamid Abaaoud grew up in Molenbeek, a district of Brussels now notorious and scrutinized for its radical Salafist presence. Abaaoud also spent time in prison, as did Adebolajo (in Kenya, when he had been arrested attempting to train with al-Shabaab). This is an increasingly important factor in radicalization: Muslims account for more than 50 per cent of France's prisoners, but only 10 per cent of its population.[23] Other factors that exacerbate online radicalization might be mental ill-health and substance abuse. The Chechen Tsarnaev brothers, who targeted Boston, claimed to be motivated by extremist Islamic beliefs, though they were not affiliated to any known or particular groups; other analysts suggest that their Caucasus sympathies and problems with becoming fully integrated into American society may have played more of a part. Radicalized individuals are predisposed to radical content before they actually encounter it online, and in some cases it seems not to really matter what that content might actually be.

Too Much Information

We have already outlined the refined movie-making and gamification techniques that ISIS brings to its social media

propaganda, in its recognized efforts to appeal to potential Western recruits and to have its content circulate on various social media platforms. Having such visual content readily sharable also makes ISIS' activities more "newsworthy"—more likely to be picked up in international media and, in a sense, unavoidably showcased. A *Vice* magazine article on young Britons waging extremist wars in Syria quoted fighter Abu Qa'qaa's Tumblr account where he said, "Britain posting our pictures in newspapers. They don't realise it inspires more to come jihad and don't worry, we never wish to come back. :)"[24] This documentation of terrorism on the international stage is what these once tiny, insignificant forces want. And it is a problem recognized by Western observers and some news media.

Foreign fighters have a complex, international relationship with social media. They are, of course, some of the most active participants in perpetuating precisely those social media outreach tactics that captured their own interest—knowing very well how effective they are. They also use social media more straightforwardly to communicate with their families back home, and with the families and friends of their fallen comrades, usually accompanying the news of the death with a message inviting the recipients to join the same group their loved one fought for and with. They are among the most active users to send memorial tweets in honor of ISIS fighters who have died in battle, feeling themselves to also be on the path to jihadi Paradise. Although *Vice* noted

that, "one by one, these social media accounts have been going silent, presumably because their owners have been killed,"[25] it is the online connection that provides these users with a psychological sense of purpose that they will live on after their deaths—in more ways than one.[26]

And it is not only the extremists' accounts which forward extremist propaganda. The majority of the photos and videos posted in the twenty-four hours after the Syrian chemical weapon attacks in summer 2013, documenting the horrendous effects on ordinary Syrians, originated from more moderate accounts and not those of extremist groups. ISIS makes use of affiliated media outlets which broadcast its propaganda across the web.[27] Since June 2014, ISIS-affiliated media outlets have produced over 625 Islamist propaganda videos.[28] These are in English (as well as Russian, Arabic, French, and other languages), making them readily sharable across large expanses of the world; and their moral abhorrence—particularly the executions of US journalists James Foley and Steven Sotloff—makes them a must-view for all, quite apart from their specific targeting of violent individuals to encourage them to join ISIS in combat.[29]

There are also a number of actors whom the London-based International Centre for the Study of Radicalisation and Political Violence terms "disseminators"—unaffiliated individuals, primarily living in Western Europe or the US, who rarely show allegiance to any specific group, but

whose social media accounts are sympathetic to their causes. In many cases, and particularly in Syria, they are on the frontline of information access and are becoming the main point of contact and source of news about the conflict and events on the ground for mainstream media, the West, and Islamist fighters in the country themselves. These disseminators gather raw content piecemeal from authorized and anecdotal sources—Islamist fighters' private social media accounts, official and unofficial group accounts, and official reports coming from the Assad regime and NGOs—and then translate, edit and, package this content (be it video, audio, or text) into propaganda shared with the larger world mainly through Facebook pages and, to a lesser extent, Twitter.[30] Furthermore, disseminators are generally more personally responsive and more likely to build a bond with the fighters than are organizations, which usually do not engage at all with their supporters or detractors through their official social media accounts.

Against the Tide

If social media has broken down the traditional land walls, what can halt the online tsunami of extremist action? Especially if the same factors that led to the expansion of social media and the explosion in digital engagement so crucial to vital opposition movements—a young and

digitally engaged demographic; discontented populations seeking outlets for political expression; and the overall splintering of conventional hierarchies into decentralized networks—actually play into the hands of ISIS and other groups like them? ISIS' phenomenal and formidable digital success could even prove to be social media's undoing, providing repressive governments and censors in the region with a prime example of why monitoring online communication and stifling freedom of expression are so necessary.

One counterblast has been issued by the religious establishment, particularly the more conservative and traditional Islamists of the Middle East who have been dismayed by the ISIS rampage. As the struggle in Syria has gone on, too, locals have complained of the sense that these "cowboys" have hijacked their struggle. Tempering the videos of luxuries pilfered from the Assad regime is more "traditional" footage of more "traditional" Islamists: men in balaclavas posing with weapons and pick-up trucks, urging others to join their sacred struggle against an infidel tyrant.[31]

Countermoves have also been made by Islamic authorities themselves. The Grand Mufti had already spoken out against ISIS in 2014, claiming that the extremists are "far from the correct understanding of Islam." The Grand Mufti heads Dar al-Ifta, a long-established government-affiliated Islamist institute (and the body that issues fatwas), which launched an online campaign urging media outlets to refrain from referring to the extremists as being

associated with some "Islamic State" in a bid to change perceptions and stop the ingraining of a stereotype. It preferred the term "al-Qaeda Separatists" and invited Facebook users to follow Dar al-Ifta's page to promote that initiative.[32] "In keeping pace with the huge developments in the field of communications," states its website, "Dar al-Ifta undertakes huge tasks imposed by the qualitative transition brought about by the new era of means of communications." It now "achieve[s] the 'highest degree of effective communication'" with the Islamic world; its English-language Facebook page has over 345,000 likes.[33] It is not the only historic Islamic watchdog to enter the twenty-first-century fray. Egyptian clerics at Al-Azhar, a Sunni Islamic institution founded in 970, have created "a YouTube channel to counter Islamist propaganda."[34]

In January 2015, President Abdel Fatah al-Sisi called upon Islamist leaders to help combat extremism and radicalization through a more modern interpretation of Islam in a speech at the Al Zahar Islamic learning center in Cairo. There are of course many Western governments calling for more forceful, urgent, and altogether more secular action against ISIS. But governments are not the only civil society actors who are uniting against extremism in online campaigns.[35] Many groups and individuals are challenging extremist tactics and ideologies, and using social media itself to do so—staying online and open, rather than the regimes' preference for shutting off and

down. This is a crucial point in the discussion about the benefits and pitfalls of social media. While ISIS certainly stands to gain from digital freedom, denying access to individuals across the region effectively silences their own criticism of radicalism.

Reflecting ISIS' favored strategy of (ab)using popular and already trending hashtags in order to hype its message in front of a fresh, broad international audience, netizens have turned the extremists' own hashtags against them. For example, the hashtag #amessagefromISIStoUS, which began appearing in 2014, accompanies different threats from the group and its supporters alongside menacing photos. The hashtag was quickly hijacked by Westerners, who either accompanied it with jokes or insults, or returned the compliment using hashtag #amessagefromUStoISIS to threaten, or more often mock, the group in turn. ISIS had not accounted for the satirical evolution devised by their huge and varied audience, and mounted little comeback. Poking fun at ISIS' open and obliging outreach strategy on such sites as Ask.fm, British comedian Lee Hurst started the satirical hashtag #AskIslamicState in August 2014, which kicked off an onslaught of hilariously ridiculous questions for ISIS full of "First World problems" and trivialities. It became the second most popular hashtag on Twitter that month, and spoke to the power of laughter in the midst of a deadly serious situation. Not even barbaric murderers are immune to trolling.

Some groups have been more earnest in their fight back. The #NotInMyName campaign, organized by the Active Change Foundation, uses the popular hashtag to give individuals a voice in declaring that—as Dar al-Ifta is at pains to propound—ISIS does not speak for all Muslims. And in the wake of the November 2015 Paris attacks, the hacktivist collective Anonymous declared war on ISIS via its French arm's YouTube page, vowing that "we will hunt you down ... We as a collective will bring an end to your reign of terror. We will no longer turn a blind eye to your cruel and inhumane acts of terrorism ... The War Is On." Its #OpISIS campaign had already scored some successes, with around a hundred ISIS and ISIS-related Twitter accounts seized, social media accounts hacked, more than 100,000 Twitter accounts flagged for takedowns, 5,000 propaganda videos reported, and DoS strikes launched to bring down the ISIS website. One major Anonymous Twitter account, @GroupAnon, announced that "we won't stop opposing #IslamicState. We're also better hackers."[36]

It is clear that a strong, unified coalition of government, private sector, and civil society actors is needed to challenge the extremist narrative and confront the presence of extremist groups on social media. This multilateral approach must include an effort to mitigate the "us versus them" mentality and educate partners about the theological sources and teachings that extremists use to

justify terrorism and hatred of Western societies—reducing the demand for radical content rather than attempting to counter radicalization once it is already in progress.[37] A sound policy agenda would include establishing a multi-lateral forum to deal with online extremism, improving schools' teaching of online digital literacy and critical thinking, operating social media accounts to debunk and clarify official policies and ideologies, and establishing a central body to offer seed funding and training for grass-roots online counter-extremism action.[38] Social media is one part of the larger problem of extremism and instability, but the scale of support, power, and funding granted by social media platforms cannot be allowed to continue flowing to extremist groups unchallenged. Because in a world where one hacked Twitter account can cause billions of dollars of damage—the Syrian Electronic Army's hacked tweet about the White House attack caused the New York Stock Exchange to lose $136 billion in three minutes[39]—the cost of further inaction or ineffective action will only escalate.

CONCLUSION

The Next Battlefield

IT WAS A late autumn day and I was in London for meetings at the Foreign & Commonwealth Office on the pressing matter of "breaking" ISIS' brand and status as a "superpower" of terror. The next round of meetings of the seventy-one-nation Global Coalition to defeat ISIS, which had been set up in September 2014 to coordinate local, regional, and global efforts, was also being organized. Getting countries to pony up cash and combatants to strike at the terrorist group with something a little stronger than rhetoric was tricky and laborious work, outright dicey at times. The focus was on finding ways to strengthen civil society voices, while working with IT companies to optimize counter-ISIS strategies and defeat the group's communications online. After all, tech companies are in the business of reaching the same audiences targeted by ISIS' innovative use of social media—they know to

communicate with and impact those audiences with a different message. We in the West have our tragedies, but we also have our heroes.

During lunch in the House of Lords, a close colleague and friend, Tobias Ellwood MP, spoke about his recent travels in the Middle East. We traded "war stories" and talked about young people in the Middle East who often find themselves on the front lines. After lunch, Tobias escorted me around the back of the picturesque Foreign & Commonwealth building to a beautiful monument facing St James's Park, on which are carved the names of 202 British citizens who lost their lives in the 2002 Bali bombings, known to have been perpetrated by al-Qaeda and affiliated groups. Tobias spent a few moments in silence, then reached out and caressed a particular name: Jonathan Mark Ellwood, Age 37. This was Tobias' older brother, an academic historian who had been researching in Bali, the frontier of lost hope, working to further cross-cultural understanding. His goal, Tobias explained, had always been to teach tolerance and faith in humanity. He had been killed by extremists to whom such understanding and compassion were anathema.

As had happened in Bali—and Brussels, and Stockholm, and Berlin, and Paris—terror struck again on March 22, 2017, this time in the heart of London, just a short walk from where Tobias and I had contemplated terrorism's deeply personal impact. The self-radicalized Khalid

Masood's eighty-second rampage across Westminster Bridge and through the gates into New Palace Yard killed four people and injured fifty. Chaos and panic spread like wildfire as Parliament was put on lockdown and thousands fled the scene. ISIS later claimed Masood, who was shot dead at the scene, as one of its "soldiers."

While many rushed for cover inside the Houses of Parliament and frantically tried to call loved ones, one MP ran in the opposite direction, toward the attack, his earlier army training and instincts taking over. He discovered the bloodied PC Keith Palmer on the floor, having been repeatedly stabbed by Masood, and instantly started CPR as others watched on, although tragically, his efforts were in vain. That MP, later hailed for his quick thinking and courageous efforts, was my friend Tobias Ellwood.

Not even three months later, following a suicide bombing at Manchester Arena on May 22, claimed by ISIS, which killed 22 and injured 116, and a frenzied attack on June 3 by three men who drove into pedestrians on London Bridge before stabbing members of the public as they shouted "This is for Allah!" leaving eight dead and forty-eight injured, Prime Minister Theresa May stood outside of 10 Downing Street and spoke to a nation still reeling and in shock:

We believe we are experiencing a new trend in the threat we face as terrorism breeds terrorism and

perpetrators are inspired to attack, not only on the basis of carefully constructed plots after years of planning and training, and not even as lone attackers radicalised online, but by copying one another and often using the crudest of means of attack. We cannot and must not pretend that things can continue as they are.[1]

May voiced a recognition of precisely what this book has laid out, and the problem it has diagnosed—online radicalization, new battlefields, and the implications of digital guerrilla warfare. As the UK attacks demonstrated, violent extremists like ISIS have not only undermined stability in Iraq, Syria, and other conflict regions, but they also pose a threat to international peace and security more broadly, and in places as far afield as Europe and Southeast Asia.

We continue to see new twists in ISIS' strategy, the latest being the weaponization of fear using tweets, memes, and encrypted protected postings. Around the world, ISIS' communicators spend their days on social media platforms interacting with would-be terrorists, methodically feeding each recruit's deranged desire to develop local networks or carry out attacks in their own countries. As we have seen in incidents from Nice and Berlin to Orlando and San Bernardino, social media is ISIS' best weapon for turning a recruit into a radicalized attacker. With recent figures suggesting that 85 per cent of British jihadists convicted for terrorist offences have never been to Syria or

Iraq,[2] it seems clear that ISIS is no longer wooing people primarily to travel to the so-called "caliphate," but increasingly to the "digital caliphate."

Understanding ISIS 3.0 and the New Virtual Safe Haven

As ISIS loses more ground on the physical battlefield, and its call for followers to join them there becomes increasingly futile, the group knows it must ensure it can maintain influence in the battlefield of ideas. This has forced ISIS to alter and accelerate its messaging tactics. Enter the digital realm, a new virtual safe haven.

Today, the group's messengers tell supporters more and more, "Stay where you are. Wage war in ISIS' name wherever you live." Its brand is shifting from that of an ideological organization seeking territory to an umbrella faction united by grievance, psychopathy, and a warped hatred. Instead of recruiting to gain terrain and a bountiful utopia, ISIS is promoting a clandestine, decentralized, international insurgency for marginalized and impressionable youth.

Meanwhile, foreign terrorist fighters who were once encouraged to trepidatiously make their way to ISIS training camps in the Middle East are now heading in the other direction, seeking to escape the battlefield and return to their home countries, from where they can develop local

networks and launch attacks. The target audience is no longer the group—the more the deadlier—but the individual. Combined with ISIS' presence on encrypted social media platforms and the dark web, these trends are a double-edged sword: ISIS is reaching fewer people in these private venues, but its noxious call is more personalized, and thus more persuasive, easier to heed. Halting its ability to leverage these private spaces has now become crucial to defeating ISIS.

Those who speak for ISIS are using the dark web and encrypted applications to communicate with little fear of detection. The dark web is often the preferred medium for terrorist groups because it is difficult to navigate and thereby police, allows for full encryption, and can make certain accounts nearly impossible to access. It is also completely anonymous and allows users to hide their IP address, even as they are accessing a worldwide network of computers, including those used by financial services.

These challenges increase the difficulty in identifying and tracking the inspired, self-radicalized attacker, as was seen in Nice, Dhaka, Medina, Kabul, Ansbach, and elsewhere. Keeping on top of this digital underworld has become critical to the safety of the US and other nations around the world. How to counter these violent extremists' anonymous use of the internet is a core focus in the fight to defeat ISIS, particularly for law enforcement and those working on counter-messaging strategies in both

political office and the private sector. US government, the Global Coalition, and the technology private sector are making it increasingly difficult for ISIS to spread its poisonous ideology to vulnerable audiences. For example, the ubiquitous Twitter has sped up the process of removing terrorist accounts and their regenerated online handles, suspending over 635,000 ISIS-related or affiliated accounts which abused the platform since mid-2015.[3] Global Coalition members are also beginning to employ a range of new (and still classified) analytic tools while sharing intel with allies to get ahead of the curve, to stymie online recruitment wherever possible. At the same time, the Global Coalition's own Twitter accounts (in Arabic, French, and English) continue to build a strong following with messages aimed at counteracting ISIS' online presence.

Building resistance to extremist propaganda and countering the use of the internet for terrorist purposes have become vital in the fight to defeat ISIS anywhere and everywhere. These efforts have thus far shown progress. Counter-ISIS content is now more prevalent online than ever before—research suggests the group's online opponents outnumber ISIS supporters online upward of six-to-one on some social media platforms—and pro-ISIS content is declining in open forum social media channels.[4] As a terrorist group, ISIS is increasingly struggling in the face of these more organized and sophisticated initiatives, many of them spurred by the Global Coalition.

Caught at the Digital Crossroads

"Among the peoples of the world," wrote Marshall McLuhan in the 1960s, "strange new vortices of power will appear unexpectedly."[5]

Many of the young people interviewed for *Digital World War* represent the new social media revolution, which has pushed the Islamic world into the eye of the storm, shifting the pivots of power, the production and consumption of information, even the structure of society. This is the youth that "took media into their own hands" to create the bottom-up, citizen-driven revolution that supplanted top-down totalitarian regimes during the Arab Spring.[6]

Yet, as compelling an avenue for political change as it often is, social networking cannot ensure that a resultant political regime will reflect the values of the media messaging that helped to bring it into power. Those Islamist regimes that have benefited from digitally driven revolutions and counter-revolutions to achieve and retain power are not transparent, liberal, or secular, despite the hazy notion some hold that social media is essentially democratic in nature and will help force regimes into line. Yes, it may lead toward such a positive outcome, but that's not a given, nor is it a scenario that will have an immediate effect.

Actually, the opposite may be the case. With the appearance of new, more democratically inclined regimes, which

are more concerned than ever about their image, public opinion, and dissent, Muslim governments are pushing back hard, and in the open, via the World Wide Web. Newly installed Islamist regimes want to quickly assert their independence from—and defiance of—Western hegemony, particularly in the wake of disastrous combat interventions in the region. The Islamists' ultimate goal remains what it has always been: all Muslim nations partnered under some connection to religious authority. In some cases, this certainly means less freedom, not more, and will bring on a retrograde de-democratization. Some may call this a fatalistic view; others are sure it's realistic.

As *Digital World War* has demonstrated, social media can be used for a multitude of purposes. Its empowerment of millions, giving a voice to those who before had none, may be one of the most important power shifts of all time. The social media consumer represents a new kind of global citizen, one with a fresh take on global relations, who knows he or she is being heard by an international audience and who plays to that crowd. In recent years, the main establishment opposition—Islamist political parties and movements—have found an effective way to fight entrenched power structures by reaching out to the masses through the increasingly important online public space. They have assumed power, and lost it again (as in Egypt). The use of social media by these newly emerging Islamic political machines has already fundamentally changed the

nature of elections and electoral politics. Core middle-class voters want to see Islamists continuing to kick out the old ways and taking their countries in new directions, while Islamic political power-players exploit the internet's riches to propagate their conservative sociopolitical and religious messages.

Based on my research on the ground and the surveys and interviews I've conducted, it has become very clear that social media platforms are now playing a—indeed *the*—pivotal role in getting millions of young people to participate in political activities for the first time. The Islamists are remaking the Muslim world's political order as for over a century we have known it. They are looking to establish a hybrid form of government—part Islamic, part secular. As *Digital World War* shows, these events have significant implications for the West and our alliances with Muslim-majority nations, as well as for our war on terror.

Looking Forward and Backward

Digital World War underscores the fact that twenty-first-century communications and consumer technology demands awareness of the broader context—the history and motivations underlying the actions of Islamists and extremists. Such awareness will vastly improve the ability of foreign policymakers to successfully navigate the ever-changing and often bewildering political terrain that is so

visible online. Oversimplified and uninformed depictions of Islamist opposition politics (and in particular, misperceptions of the role of social media in Islamist recruitment and mobilization) has affected international policy in negative ways. The result has been clumsy mismanagement or total neglect of potentially vital relationships. Understanding how Islamic organizations are motivated by both pragmatic political and religious considerations will greatly help Western governments deal with Islamic political actors, both allies and antagonists. More specifically, an understanding that extremist politics are not always driven solely by ideological absolutism will open new opportunities for diplomacy.

The lack of official engagement with important groups outside of the executive branch is most pronounced when weighing how international governments deal with Islamists, especially regionally important Islamists. Since 2001, and at various times since, the Islamists have been a potent political force in Egypt, Tunisia, Libya, Lebanon, Syria, and Iraq. However, Western governments' contact with these leaders has been not only limited, but even actively avoided in most cases. The same "hands off" approach has informed relations with other networked and hierarchical Islamist groups in key areas of strategic importance. More than simply refusing to engage these parties, much of the West's policies toward Islamists have been designed to suppress, disable, or circumvent their

solid hold on power. This is reflected in the antagonism found on social media toward these newly emerging groups.

Founded on the conventional but faulty wisdom that political Islamism is driven by economic disenfranchisement and militaristic zeal, many international governments have undertaken to weaken confessional Islamic parties by limiting their engagement, providing few avenues for cooperation and "capacity building." *Digital World War* calls into serious doubt the motivational assumptions underlying these policies, clearly suggesting that such efforts might well be counterproductive for all concerned. It is likely that the Islamists and their social media outreach will remain an integral fixture of the political landscape, regardless of third-party efforts to eradicate or stymie them. Though Islamic parties can—critically—be differentiated from extremist groups, in some instances they do have loose ties. More commonly, they have complex interactions with violent extremists, but are invested in the electoral political process and would not gain from a transition to autocratic religious rule. Despite their rhetoric on social media, and their depiction in the mainstream press, these parties are important potential allies to Western interests. Fortunately, some Western policymakers are starting to realize this.

The historical conduct and core interests of Islamist opposition parties suggest that they could be useful

partners in the effort to limit the spread of violent extremism, if they are properly incentivized. While Islamist parties have recently deemed it an electoral advantage to affiliate, in varying degrees, with militaristic organizations, the likes of Jabhat al-Nusra or the Taliban are uneasy bedfellows, and are actively working to destabilize the political system on which Islamist parties depend for their own survival. Rather than pushing Islamic parties further into the arms of extremists through policies of suppression, Western powers would be wise to exploit tensions between these groups and to look for points of shared interest with Islamic parties, interests that may well serve as the basis of dialogue and cooperation.

Walking the Digital Walk

With the information battlefield wide open, this new outreach approach will require a major realignment of perspectives. Western nations must interact with political parties that are considered moderate within the Arab or Middle Eastern context, not only those seen as moderate by Western norms. To be sure, this shift poses domestic political challenges for the United States and its Western allies. There is a risk of being seen as cooperating with polarizing groups, especially those who employ heavy anti-Western rhetoric and are known to maintain connections with extremists. However, Western policymakers would do

well to look beyond the rhetoric of Islamic parties, to determine their underlying motivations, and to create innovative ways to provide support to those groups that espouse antiviolence measures. Social media provides useful insights into their "mass market" strategies; and the new accountability of social media (as with "crowd-sourcing" journalism) provides several innovative ways to help shape these groups' positive influence.

In the area of public diplomacy, and particularly regarding education, we should be directly challenging the idea that the West is absolutely opposed to Islam (a tough nut to crack these days). Social media is ripe with conspiracy theories, with certain extremists actively seeking a declared war between Islam and the West. That is their goal, and the basis on which they target niche audiences (that is, foreign fighters). We should send the message that expanding quality education is a priority across the Muslim world and that religious schools play an important role (as they do in the West). Western powers should emphasize that the problem is not with madrassas but with murderers. We should stress that for the Muslim world, and for the West, the important issue involves countering the drivers of violent radicalism. Radicals who are out to kill should be pinpointed, pursued, and prosecuted wherever they are based, whether state or non-state actors. The task on social media is not to endorse or agree with all groups, but to keep channels of dialogue open, to challenge the wilder

inaccuracies and misconceptions about Western policy. Websites like SoulPancake and Reddit offer content that allows young people to discover key answers about extremism. These platforms are also able to highlight core messages regarding the West's long-held respect for religious concerns and traditions, pressing the point that it is terrorism that is the problem, not the righteous tenets of Islam.

Building workable relationships with Islamist parties is necessary in order to ensure that new international development aid is effectively directed toward modern healthcare and education initiatives. As their use of social media makes clear, in many cases Islamists are striving to provide a positive alternative narrative to violence. Unfortunately, Islamists have been wary of outside influences and resources that could undermine their own patronage structures and thereby usurp or outshine local authority. With the increasing use of social media platforms, Islamist parties and extremist groups have continued reaching out to new segments of voters and supporters. In some cases, these groups take credit for new schools, roads, water systems, and clinics, which were actually built by Western money and know-how. In other instances, security concerns have halted projects and led to high personnel turnover.

There will remain, of course, some Islamist political actors with whom direct or even indirect cooperation is impossible. Although *Digital World War* has argued that it

is counterproductive for the West to view all Islamists as either ideologically intransigent or wholly opposed to Western interests, some individuals or local offshoots are indeed so closely linked to violent extremists that there is no longer any light between them. In some cases, targeted efforts to disempower these dangerous political actors may be required. Since Islamist politicians derive much of their power from their mutually reinforcing control over local religious institutions, proposals for better internet governance may be one of the most promising strategies for undermining militant extremist groups.

Breaking the "Brand"

Muslim nations have a long history of imperialism, colonialism, regionalism, feudalism, and factionalism, which makes them more likely to foster religio-political power dynamics. The power and resources that have historically been attached to religious leaders have long stood in tension with secular, feudal, political power, now expressed by proxy through democratic electoral politics. Islamic political parties combine both types of power, but with specific limits. Those who strongly favor religious identity are restricted in their access to electoral means, and vice versa.

The Islamists' online drive toward deepening engagement in electoral politics and "branding" is, it would appear,

strategic rather than ideological. There are now more incentives to participate electorally (rather than extra-electorally) in ways other than religiously derived politics. Despite Islamist parties being systematically excluded by the ruling elites, and unable to dominate the national parliaments of Muslim countries, they have significant electoral power at a local level and thus should never be ignored. As a matter of broad policy importance, they are also susceptible to persuasion that is not ideological, regardless of their often bold anti-Western postures.

Voter behavior and aspirations within Muslim-majority countries must also be considered when shaping international policy. We must accept the legitimate autonomy of Islamic groups; the sharp differences in sect, ethnicity, and region; and the uneven distribution of material resources in these countries. The latter sets the stage for practices among Muslim voters. At the national level, they are more likely to vote for Muslim democrats (or even secular parties) who are incorporated into state networks and therefore predisposed to provide material benefits and support. Locally, they may be more inclined to elect Islamists who offer both spiritual and material benefits, the nature of which can vary widely.

* * *

Few areas of study are more relevant to assisting Western foreign policy than today's communications networks. The

advance of web technology, social media platforms, and the rise of Islamist politics dominates the current political terrain. In the wake of the 2016 presidential election in the United States there has been an outpouring of books, articles, and commissioned reports on how we should communicate with the Muslim world. Numerous conferences on strategic communications and messaging have been organized. The new US administration has been met by a flurry of public diplomacy proposals, generally calling for revised budgets, input in policy creation, and for new public diplomacy offices within and outside of government in cooperation with the private sector. Diverse internal efforts and recommendations, such as improving the language skills of US Foreign Service Officers, have also been proposed. Nonetheless, in spite of the deluge and the implementation of some recommendations, we are still wrestling with questions about the effectiveness of public diplomacy in Muslim countries.

Understanding the operating environment is the basis of any good business plan or military strategy, though this is generally precisely what is missing in the case of public diplomacy. Previous studies of the social media phenomenon have downplayed or ignored outright what Muslim populations collectively think or do. These studies have overlooked the explosive nature of social media networks and the symbolism of Islamist politics. Instead, the focus has been on what the West can do unilaterally, not what

the West can do vis-à-vis the attitudes and practices found on the ground. An essential part of understanding the public environment in Muslim countries involves examining the political organizations that represent them and how they communicate on the information battlefield. Too much is at stake to ignore it.

NOTES

Introduction: The Medium is the Message

1. https://www.uturn.me/i/about.php
2. Shirky, 2011.
3. Gladwell, 2011; Penny, 2011; Kravets, 2011.
4. Scott, 1986.
5. See Mecham, 2006.
6. For my purposes, an organization is defined as "extreme" if it meets two of the following three criteria: (1) it adopts exclusionary policies based on rigid classifications of morally valid behavior (Wintrobe, 2006); (2) it uses inflammatory rhetoric about the divide between the morally upright and the morally corrupt as a mobilization tool and incitement to action; (3) it engages in extra-electoral tactics, including militant action and violent enforcement of religious practice.
7. Ahmed, 1985, cited in Waseem & Mufti, 2009.
8. Any use of the term "sharia" must come with some caveats. J.M. Otto, for instance, identifies four different senses of sharia, of which the first and most universal is the abstract law of Allah as revealed in the Koran. But, since the Koranic law must be applied (and, according to some, interpreted), sharia in the modern sense also includes the works of the classical jurisprudes: the historically and geographically contextual bodies of interpretation produced by Muslim courts over the past thousand years; and finally the contemporary "spectrum of principles, rules, cases, and interpretations that are developed and applied at present." In most Muslim societies, therefore, "the variety of meanings of sharia has given rise to a flexible ... discourse about sharia and law which moves smoothly from one definition of sharia to another" (Otto, 2008). The result of sharia's long historical development has been a multiplicity of interpretive schools, or *fiqh*, each with its own understanding of the

particulars of the law. In Pakistan, in particular, this diversity is increased by the different ideological and theological groundings of the Islamist parties.
9. Warrick, 2013 Nov. 4.
10. Laville, 2014.
11. Goodspeed, 2012.

1 The Weaponization of Information

1. Interview with Khalid, Dubai, May 24, 2016.
2. Vachon, 2011.
3. Stalinsky & Sosnow, 2015.
4. Mekhennet & Miller, 2016.
5. Berger, 2014.
6. Alexander, 2013. The full name of the group is Harakat al-Shabaab al-Mujahideen, hence "HSM."
7. Berger, 2014.
8. Ibid.
9. According to Nielsen, a global communications firm, YouTube content reaches more adults in the United States between the ages of 18 and 34 than any television network (Strickland, 2015), and most videos are posted by users in that age bracket (Hussain & Saltman, 2014).
10. Beaumont, 2011.
11. Weimann, 2014; Ackerman, 2012.
12. Strickland, 2015.
13. Weimann, 2014.
14. Alexander & Beach, 2014.
15. Yaqub, 2013.

2 Just Watch Me

1. Interview with Waris, One Central, Dubai, February 23, 2016.
2. Interview with Sami Shah, 2014.
3. Geo News Urdu, 2017.
4. Halkon, 2015.
5. *The Economist*, August 30, 2014.
6. Liljas, 2013.
7. Alexander & Beach, 2014.
8. https://twitter.com/ISILCats
9. Vice News, 2014.
10. Wagner, 2014.
11. Fears, 2014.
12. Saul, 2014.
13. Fears, 2014.
14. Saul, 2014.
15. A number of videos depict fighters chanting in languages other than Arabic, which certainly reflects a concern with appealing to individuals from around the world, emphasizing global continuity for the ISIS cause (CNN, 2014). In fact, it would seem likely that consolidating their worldwide

appeal is a priority for ISIS given recent reports claiming that foreign fighters from over 80 countries have joined the group (Ackerman, 2014).

16. CNN, 2014.
17. Herrera & Lotfy, 2012.
18. See Social Bakers, 2014.
19. Herrera & Lotfy, 2012.
20. Zennie, 2014.
21. Coughlin, 2014.
22. Bleiberg & West, 2014.
23. Paraszczuk, 2014, December 30.
24. Weimann, 2014.
25. Pearlman, 2012.
26. Stone, 2014.
27. According to the Friendica global directory, the social network maintains approximately 9,200 total users (http://dir.friendica.com/). No such official number of users is maintained by Diaspora (https://blog.diaspora-foundation.org/2-how-many-users-are-there-in-the-diaspora-network), but a voluntary poll conducted by one Diaspora user recorded over 1.1 million responses (Robinson, 2014).
28. Nahon & Hemsley, 2013.
29. Gais, 2014.
30. Weimann, 2014.
31. Brachman & Levine, 2011.
32. Sani & Khalili, 2012.
33. Mullany, 2013.
34. Weiss, 2009.
35. Mohamad, 2008. Dr. Mohamad now blogs at chedet.cc.
36. Tan, 2013, May 5.
37. Kong, 2013.
38. Dudley, 2013.
39. Kong, 2013.
40. www.youtube.com/watch?v=BMGfsWgIujk
41. www.youtube.com/user/videoDAP?feature=watch
42. www.youtube.com/user/umnohq/videos
43. Mahavera, 2014.
44. Welsh, 2013.
45. *Asian Image*, 2011.
46. Kully, 2010.
47. *The News*, 2011.
48. *The Dawn*, 2011.
49. Najafizada & Nordland, 2011.
50. Erdbrink, 2012.
51. Deutsche Welle, 2012.

3 Guerrilla Webfare

1. Interview with Salman, Jarir Bookstore, Doha, July 13, 2015.
2. See http://instagram.com/najib_razak, www.najibrazak.com/ and www.facebook.com/najibrazak. Razak's Twitter handle is @NajibRazak.

3. From the blog of a Malaysian Islamist.

4. Nakashima, 2012.

5. Reuters, 2012, December 9.

6. In May 2014, five members of Unit 61398, the cyber division of China's national army, were indicted by the US Justice Department on charges of industrial espionage, having hacked into the computer networks of Westinghouse Electric, US Steel Corp., and other companies—tech firms that hold strategic importance to US national security (5 *United States v. Wang Dong*, Criminal No. 14-118. W.D. Pa. May 1, 2014). This has been the only official response to a cyber threat on America so far—and, even so, only on legal grounds, and largely symbolic. North Korea was accused by the FBI in December 2014 of hacking into Sony Pictures as a reprisal for the film *The Interview*, about a CIA plot to assassinate North Korean leader Kim Jong-un. Messages appeared on Sony employees' computer screens, including "Remember the 11th of September 2001"—clearly riding on the wave of the al-Qaeda atrocity. Most recently, in April 2015 US officials reported that Russian hackers had gained access to White House and State Department emails the previous year, which, though not classified, were sensitive, and included those belonging to officials corresponding with President Obama.

7. In fact, Anonymous petitioned the White House to recognize DDoS as a legitimate form of protest (Kersey, 2013).

8. Somaiya, 2011.

9. Ashokan, 2011.

10. Singh, 2011.

11. Shenker, 2011.

12. Hamill, 2014.

13. Iasiello, 2013.

14. Gonsalves, 2013.

15. Norman, 2011.

16. Constantin, 2015.

17. Galperin et al., 2013.

18. Zelin, 2013.

19. Cartledge, 2015.

20. *Recorded Future*, 2014.

21. Stalinsky & Sosnow, 2014.

22. Mustafa, 2013.

23. *Malaysian Digest*, 2013.

24. Mullany, 2013.

25. Marquis-Boire, 2013.

26. *Business Times*, 2013.

27. Kaur, 2013.

28. Lim, 2013.

29. Shahbaz, 2014.

30. Reuters Canada, 2011.

31. *Time*, 2009.

32. Young, 2012.

33. Black, 2013.

34. Freedom House, 2013.

35. Lamer, 2012.
36. Reporters Without Borders, 2011, February 10 and August 16.
37. Hannigan, 2014.
38. Kirkpatrick, 2014.
39. Morozov, 2011.

4 Tracking Transformation

1. Interview with Rahman, House of Prose, Dubai, August 14, 2015.
2. I am indebted to Retter, 2013, pp. 5–26, for the following account of the use of technology in the Iranian Revolution and the Arab Spring.
3. Galloway, 2004, p. 33.
4. Sreberny-Mohammadi, 1990, p. 358.
5. Ibid., p. 363.
6. Retter, 2013, p. 21.
7. Galloway, 2004, p. 31.
8. Ibid.
9. Retter, 2013, p. 12.
10. Ibid., pp. 16–17.
11. Sreberny-Mohammadi, 1990, p. 345.
12. Galloway, 2004, p. 33,
13. Retter, 2013, p. 22.
14. Schmidt & Cohen, 2013, p. 23.
15. Retter, 2013, p. 25.
16. Schmidt & Cohen, 2013, p. 131.
17. Ibid., p. 23.
18 Davis, 2011.
19. Amara & Lowe, 2011.
20. Feldman, 2011.
21. Sennott, 2011.
22. Quoted in Schmidt & Cohen, 2013, p. 131.
23. Ghosh, 2012. Al Nas was a religious satellite television station which specialized in a hardline Salafi interpretation of Sunni Islam. Founded in 2006 by a Saudi investor, Mansour ben Kedsa, who hoped to attract viewers with a schedule that interspersed religious programming with more secular entertainment, Kedsa ultimately hired a team of clerics to transform it into "the station that takes you to paradise." While it claimed to be open to all interpretations of Islam, Al Nas' clerical batting order was nearly entirely Salafi.
   A number of satellite channels continue to serve religious Egyptians. Field and Hamam (2009) speculate that the Mubarak government had encouraged Salafi television as a counterweight to the Muslim Brotherhood, yet religious satellite TV has also taken full advantage of the increasingly religious atmosphere of post-Mubarak Egypt, including the lifting of restrictions on veiled female presenters, and fewer government restrictions on what can be discussed (Shull, 2012). Furthermore, in the Egypt of September 2012, when the nature of the state itself seemed up for grabs, satellite television was part of the larger Salafi effort to define Islam and set the terms for an Islamic Egyptian state (Salt, 2012)—an effort, however,

that was far from being unified or even coordinated, with various factions among the Salafi tendency espousing different visions of the ideal state (al-Anani & Malik, 2013). Thus, while these channels may be for-profit or nonprofit, Salafi or broader based, they are all engaged in a stiff competition for viewers and influence, which results in the relentless search for a story that will rise above the clamor: *The Innocence of Muslims* became such a story, although it required careful management.

24. Field & Hamam, 2009.
25. Meo & Freeman, 2012.
26. Rabie, 2007.
27. Ibid.
28. Lynch & Hauslohner, 2013.
29. Al Arabiya, 2012, July 5.
30. Lipman, 2012.
31. Al Arabiya, 2012, September 17.
32. Walt, 2012.
33. IBN Live, 2012.
34. This relationship is indicated in the data, as Google Trends has insufficient data to generate an index, while the GDELT Project database indicates a substantial increase in online and print media reports of protests in early September compared to the same period in other years.
35. Malik, 2012.
36. *The World Post*, 2012.
37. Google Trends has insufficient data to generate an index, though the GDELT database shows a noted increase in online and print media reports of protests in early September compared to the same period in other years.
38. Coombs, 2012.
39. The most-searched term for 2012 was actually "Whitney Houston." "Gangnam Style" is the preferred comparative term here as the Korean pop song was truly a global phenomenon, and because it was trending at roughly the same time as the *Innocence of Muslims* video.
40. Tweet volumes are calculated using absolute numbers, without taking into account the number of Twitter users in each country. Thus a country with a large number of users is likely to show a high number of tweets for almost any subject, while a country with only a few users will not, even if every Twitter user tweeted about the topic.
41. Mostaghim, 2008.
42. Carpenter, 2008.
43. Thomasson, 2008.
44. Mostaghim, 2008.
45. Leung, 2005.
46. Harding, 2006.
47. Fouché, 2006.
48. Masood, 2008.
49. BBC News, 2006.
50. *The Economist*, 2015.
51. Jolly, 2011.

52. Weisenthal, 2012.
53. Bilefsky & Baume, 2015.
54. *Washington Times*, 2015.

5 Civic Booty, Private Gain

1. Interview with Tariq, Doha, July 18, 2015.
2. Some sources claim as high as 60 per cent (Torchia & al-Khalida, 2012), though data from the CIA World Factbook suggests a more conservative 46 per cent.
3. Fisher, 2013, October 31.
4. Murphy, 2014.
5. World Bank, 2017.
6. Trilling, 2014.
7. Center for International Media Assistance, 2011.
8. Statista, 2017.
9. World Bank, 2015.
10. Thompson, 2014.
11. Trzcinski-Clément, 2010.
12. Ghannam, 2011.
13. Kincaid, 2009.
14. *Saudi Gazette*, 2015
15. www.creamglobal.com/search/17798/29313/eyes-of-arabia-/
16. Arab News, 2017.
17. Paudyal, 2015.
18. Amos, 2015.
19. Jones & Al Omran, 2014.
20. Farber, 2016.
21. Global Voices, 2013.
22. www.last.fm/music/Coke+Studio/+wiki
23. Qatar Culture Club, 2012.
24. Ibid.
25. Tanweer, 2014.
26. Baloch, 2013.
27. Lowe, 2011.
28. Kehar, 2012.
29. Lillis, 2014, November 17.
30. Lillis, 2014, February 27.
31. http://yomken.com/beta/about
32. Chen, 2013.
33. Pua, 2012, July 6.
34. Kiefer, 2015.
35. Shahbaz, 2014.
36. http://www.ipaidbribe.pk
37. Diamond & Plattner, 2012, p. 24.
38. Petré, 2014.
39. www.linkedin.com/in/walakasmi
40. Mahjoub, 2015.

6 Faith, Dough, and Charity

1. Fisk, 2015.
2. Interview with Javaid, Amman, Jordan, March 13, 2015.
3. Abi-Habib, 2014
4. Lavizzari, 2013
5. Alexander & Beach, 2014.
6. Di Giovanni et al., 2014.
7. Ibid.
8. Tagine, 2013.
9. Rubin, 2005.
10. Rubin, 2005.
11. Snoj, 2014.
12. Bohn, 2011.
13. Rohac, 2012.
14. Kirkpatrick, 2011.
15. Albawaba, 2013.
16. Brooke, 2014; Berman, 2003.
17. Latief, 2013.
18. Wiktorowicz, 2001, pp. 64–70.
19. Ali, 2015.
20. Lavizzari, 2013.
21. Hasselbarth, 2014.
22. Assyaukanie, 2009, p. 180.
23. Pandya, 2012, p. 1.
24. See http://gulencharterschools.weebly.com/magnolia-science-academy-ctd. html
25. Strauss, 2012.
26. Gilbertson, 2014.
27. Soylu, 2014.
28. Uras, 2013.
29. Akyol, 2014.
30. Tremblay, 2013.
31. The Turkafile, 2014.
32. Avasthy, 2014.
33. Larson, 2014.
34. Freedom House, 2017.
35. Orocoglu, 2015.
36. *Hurriyet Daily News*, 2017.
37. BBC News, 2014.
38. Gutman, 2014.
39. Avasthy, 2014.

7 Islamists Without Borders

1. Interview with Hussam, DIFC Tower, Dubai, March 10, 2016.
2. Spencer, 2015.
3. Zanini & Edwards, 2001.

4. The ISCR reported the clerics in question to be, namely, Ahmad Musa Jibril and Musa Cerantonio (Carter et al., 2014).
5. Schmidt & Cohen, 2013, p. 23.
6. Bertilotti, 2003.
7. MediaBadger, 2011.
8. *The Dawn*, 2012.
9. Crane, 2012.
10. DeLong-Bas, 2015.
11. Ghannam, 2011.
12. Khilafah, 2011.
13. Harb, 2011.
14. Mason, 2013; Aday et al., 2012.
15. Batty, 2011.
16. Weprin, 2012.
17. Lengel & Newsome, 2012.
18. Dennis et al., 2013.
19. Nguyen, 2013.
20. Reuters, 2015.
21. Warrick, 2017.
21. www.bbc.co.uk/news/world-europe-34835046
22. Hussain & Saltman, 2014.
23. Roussinos, 2013.
24. Ibid.
25. Laville, 2014.
26. Bleiberg & West, 2014.
27. Banco, 2014.
28. Winter & Clarke, 2017.
29. Carter et al., 2014.
30. Laville, 2014.
31. Meky, 2014.
32. Fayed, 2015.
33. Mourad & Bayoumi, 2015.
34. Mahmood, 2013.
35. Hern, 2015.
36. Weimann, 2014.
37. Hussain & Saltman, 2014.
38. Fisher, 2013, April 23.

Conclusion: The Next Battlefield

1. *Time*, 2017.
2. BBC News, 2017.
3. Global Coalition, 2017.
4. Bodine-Baron, Helmus, Magnuson & Winkelman, 2016.
5. Quoted in Baglow, 2011.
6. Schmidt & Cohen, 2013, p. 23.

REFERENCES

Abi-Habib, M. (2014, June 26). Call to Jihad. ISIS Recruiting is Way Up. Peace and Freedom. https://johnib.wordpress.com/tag/britains/

Ackerman, S. (2012, July 17). Syrian Rebels Use YouTube, Facebook for Weapons Training. *Wired.* www.wired.com/2012/07/syria-youtube-facebook/

Ackerman, S. (2014, October 30). Foreign Jihadists Flocking to Iraq and Syria on "Unprecedented Scale"—UN. *Guardian.* www.theguardian.com/world/2014/oct/30/foreign-jihadist-iraq-syria-unprecedented-un-isis

Active Change Foundation (2014, September 10). #NotInMyName: ISIS Do Not Represent British Muslims. YouTube video. www.youtube.com/watch?v=wfYanI-zJes

Aday, S., Farrell, H., Lynch. M., Sides, J. & Freelon, D. (2012). New Media and Conflict After the Arab Spring. United States Institute of Peace. www.usip.org/sites/default/files/PW80.pdf

Ahmed, I. (1985). *The Concept of an Islamic State: An Analysis of the Ideological Controversy.* Stockholm: Edsbruck.

Akyol, M. (2014, January 3). What You Should Know About Turkey's AKP-Gulen Conflict. Al-Monitor. www.al-monitor.com/pulse/originals/2014/01/akp-gulen-conflict-guide.html#

al-Anani, K. & Malik, M. (2013). Pious Way to Politics: The Rise of Political Salafism in Post-Mubarak Egypt. *Digest of Middle East Studies* 22(1): 57–73.

Al Arabiya (2012, July 5). Egyptian Policemen Not Allowed to Grow Beards, Rules Court. *Al Arabiya News.* www.alarabiya.net/articles/2012/07/05/224577.html

Al Arabiya (2012, September 17). Tunisian Salafi Leader Escapes, Mosque Siege Ends. *Al Arabiya News.* http://english.alarabiya.net/articles/2012/09/17/238582.html

Albawaba (2013, December 14). Tunisian Political Parties in Talks to Announce New PM. *Albawaba News.* www.albawaba.com/news/tunisia-prime-minister-540406

254

Alexander, H. (2013, September 22). Tweeting Terrorism: How Al Shabaab Live Blogged the Nairobi Attacks. *Telegraph*. www.telegraph.co.uk/news/worldnews/africaandindianocean/kenya/10326863/Tweeting-terrorism-How-al-Shabaab-live-blogged-the-Nairobi-attacks.html

Alexander, H. & Beach, A. (2014, August 23). How Isil is Funded, Trained and Operating in Iraq and Syria. *Telegraph*. www.telegraph.co.uk/news/worldnews/middleeast/iraq/11052919/How-Isil-is-funded-trained-and-operating-in-Iraq-and-Syria.html

Ali, R. (2015, July 7). "Extorted Donations": Karcahi's Multi-Million Dollar Charity Business. *Express Tribune*. http://tribune.com.pk/story/916674/extorted-donations-karachis-multi-million-dollar-charity-business/

Al Jazeera (2014, June 13). Iraq "Blocks Facebook, Twitter, YouTube." Al Jazeera. http://stream.aljazeera.com/story/201406131947-0023834

Amara, T. & Hammond, A. (2011, October 24). Moderate Islamists Claim Win in Tunisia's Arab Spring Vote. Reuters. http://in.reuters.com/article/2011/10/24/idINIndia-60100220111024

Amara, T. & Lowe, C. (2011, October 26) Islamists head for win in Tunisia's Arab Spring Vote. Reuters. http://uk.reuters.com/article/2011/10/26/uk-tunisia-election-idUKTRE79L27P20111026

Amos, D. (2015, May 11). Saudi Women Can't Drive To Work; So They're Flocking to the Internet. Parallels. www.npr.org/sections/parallels/2015/05/11/405885958/saudi-women-cant-drive-to-work-so-theyre-flocking-to-the-internet

Andrejevic, M. (2002). The Work of Being Watched: Interactive Media and the Exploitation of Self Disclosure. *Critical Studies in Media Communication* 19(2), 230–48.

Arab News (2017, March 14). Women to Constitute 28% of Saudi Arabia's Work Force by 2020. Arab News. http://www.arabnews.com/node/1068131/saudi-arabia

Ashokan, S. (2011, December 6). The "Hacktivists" of Telecomix Lend a Hand to the Arab Spring. *Washington Post*. www.washingtonpost.com/lifestyle/style/the-hacktivists-of-telecomix-lend-a-hand-to-the-arab-spring/2011/12/05/gIQAAosraO_story.html

Asian Image (2011, March 22). Preacher Burns Quran in Church. www.asianimage.co.uk/news/8923045.Preacher_burns_Quran_in_church/

Assyaukanie, L. (2009). *Islam and the Secular State in Indonesia*. Singapore: Institute of Southeast Asian Studies Publishing.

Avasthy, D. (2014, March 21). Turkey's Erdogan Blocks Access to Twitter Accusing Gülen of Social Media Attacks. *International Business Times*. www.ibtimes.co.uk/turkeys-erdogan-blocks-access-twitter-accusing-gulen-social-media-attacks-1441196

Baglow, J. (2011). For the Arab Spring, the Media is the Message. The Mark. https://uk.news.yahoo.com/arab-spring-medium-message-120301319.html#A0JxO0D

Bakejal, N. (2015, January 8). French Twitter Users Say #JeSuisCharlie Isn't For Everyone. *Time*. http://time.com/3659534/charlie-hebdo-social-media-hashtag-je-suis-charlie/

Baloch, F. (2013, May 21). Coke and Pepsi Bank on Showbiz to Fight Cola Wars. *Tribune*. http://tribune.com.pk/story/552055/coke-and-pepsi-bank-on-showbiz-to-fight-cola-wars/

Banco, E. (2014, December 13). Inside the Video Battle for Followers Between ISIS and Al-Qaeda. *International Business Times*. www.ibtimes.com/inside-video-battle-followers-between-isis-al-qaeda-1752033

Barber, E. (2014, December 28). ISIS Executed Nearly 2,000 People in Syria Over the Past Six Months. *Time Magazine*. http://time.com/3648160/islamic-state-isis-isil-executions-syria/

Batty, D. (2011, December 29). Arab Spring Leads Surge in Events Captured on Cameraphones. *Guardian*. www.theguardian.com/world/2011/dec/29/arab-spring-captured-on-cameraphones

BBC News (2006, September 9). Cartoons Row Hits Danish Exports. http://news.bbc.co.uk/2/hi/europe/5329642.stm

BBC News (2014, December 2014). Turkey arrests: Raids Target Gulen-Linked Critics of Erdogan. www.bbc.com/news/world-europe-30468199

BBC News (2017, July 6). UK Terror Convictions Rising, BBC Jihadist Database Shows. www.bbc.co.uk/news/uk-40483171

Beaumont, P. (2011, February 25). The Truth About Twitter, Facebook and the Uprisings in the Arab World. *Guardian*. www.theguardian.com/world/2011/feb/25/twitter-facebook-uprisings-arab-libya

Berger, J.M. (2014, June 16). How ISIS Games Twitter. *The Atlantic*. www.theatlantic.com/international/archive/2014/06/isis-iraq-twitter-social-media-strategy/372856/

Berman, (2003). Islamism, Revolution, and Civil Society. Apsanet.org. http://carnegieendowment.org/pdf/files/berman.pdf

Bernard, D. (2014, June 18). ISIL Wages Skilled Social Media War. Voice of America. www.voanews.com/content/isil-wages-skilled-social-media-war/1939505.html

Bertilotti, T. (2003, November). "Transnational" Islam Independent of Migration Chains or Shared Ethnic Identity. Review of Allievi and Nielsen, *Muslim Networks and Transnational Communities in and Across Europe*. Hnet. www.h-net.org/reviews/showrev.php?id=8434

Bilefsky, D. & Baume, M. (2015, January 7). Terrorists Strike Charlie Hebdo Newspaper in Paris, Leaving 12 Dead. *New York Times*. www.nytimes.com/2015/01/08/world/europe/charlie-hebdo-paris-shooting.html

Black, I. (2013, November 7). Syria Crisis: Saudi Arabia to Spend Millions to Train New Rebel Force. *Guardian*. www.theguardian.com/world/2013/nov/07/syria-crisis-saudi-arabia-spend-millions-new-rebel-force

Black, I. (2013, December 17). Saudi Digital Generation Takes on Twitter, YouTube, ... and Authorities. *Guardian*. www.theguardian.com/world/2013/dec/17/saudi-arabia-digital-twitter-social-media-islam

Bleiberg, J. & West, D.M. (2014, October 20). The United States Must Respond to the Islamic State Threat (on Twitter). Brookings Institute. www.brookings.edu/blogs/techtank/posts/2014/10/20-islamic-state-social-media

Bodine-Baron, E., Helmus, T.C., Magnuson, M. & Winkelman, Z. (2016). Examining ISIS Support and Opposition Networks on Twitter. RAND.

www.rand.org/content/dam/rand/pubs/research_reports/RR1300/RR1328/RAND_RR1328.pdf

Bohn, L.E. (2011, November 18). The Muslim Brotherhood Takes Twitter. *Foreign Policy*. http://foreignpolicy.com/2011/11/18/the-muslim-brotherhood-takes-twitter/

Brachman, J. & Levine, A. (2011, April 13). The World of Holy Warcraft: How Al Qaeda is using Online Game Theory to Recruit the Masses. *Foreign Policy*. http://foreignpolicy.com/2011/04/13/the-world-of-holy-warcraft/

Breuer, A. (2012). The Role of Social Media in Mobilizing Political Protest: Evidence from the Tunisian Revolution. German Development Institute discussion paper. http://poseidon01.ssrn.com/delivery.php?

Brooke, S. (2014, January 31). Why Do Islamists Provide Social Services? Middle East Political Science. http://pomeps.org/2014/01/31/why-do-islamists-provide-social-services/

Brooking, E.T. & Singer, P.W. (2016, November). War Goes Viral: How Social Media Is Being Weaponized Across the World. *Atlantic*. https://www.theatlantic.com/magazine/archive/2016/11/war-goes-viral/501125/

Brooks-Pollock, T. (2014, August 21). "Soft" Images of Cats, Kebab-Shops and Children "Could Lure British Muslims to Middle East." *Telegraph*. www.telegraph.co.uk/news/uknews/terrorism-in-the-uk/11048199/Soft-images-of-cats-kebab-shops-and-children-could-lure-British-Muslims-to-Middle-East.html

Business Times (2013, May 26). "Anwar Using Red Bean Army to Incite Hatred." *Business Times*. www2.nst.com.my/business/anwar-using-red-bean-army-to-incite-hatred-1.286656

Carpenter, J.S. (2008, March 2). Overcoming "Fitna." Middle East Strategy at Harvard. http://blogs.law.harvard.edu/mesh/2008/03/overcoming_fitna/

Carr, S. (2011, December 26). A Year in Review: Egypt's 5 Most Controversial Figures of 2011. *Egypt Independent*. www.egyptindependent.com/news/year-review-egypt%E2%80%99s-5-most-controversial-figures-2011

Carter, J., Maher, S. & Neumann, P. (2014). #Greenbirds: Measuring Importance and Influence in Syrian Foreign Fighter Networks. ICSR. http://icsr.info/wp-content/uploads/2014/04/ICSR-Report-Greenbirds-Measuring-Importance-and-Infleunce-in-Syrian-Foreign-Fighter-Networks.pdf

Cartledge, J. (2015, September 16). Isis Terrorist Junaid Hussain Killed in Drone Attack After Boffins 'Crack Group's Code'. *Birmingham Mail*. www.birminghammail.co.uk/news/midlands-news/isis-terrorist-junaid-hussain-killed-10069425

Center for International Media Assistance (2011). Social Media in the Arab World: Leading up to the Uprisings of 2011. Center for International Media Assistance. www.cima.ned.org/wp-content/uploads/2015/02/CIMA-Social_Media_in_the_Arab_World-Highlights.pdf

Chen, R. (2013, August 20). Could Civic Crowdfunding Improve Governance in the Middle East? Cipe Development Blog. www.cipe.org/blog/2013/08/20/could-civic-crowdfunding-improve-governance-in-the-middle-east/#.U3uFN15U1g0

Christensen, C. (2011). Twitter Revolutions? Addressing Social Media and Dissent. *Communications Review* 14(3): 155–57. www.tandfonline.com/doi/full/10.1080/10714421.2011.597235

CNN (2014, June 21). ISIS Recruiting Western Youth With English-Language Video. YouTube video. www.youtube.com/watch?v=jdgzCbrPqzQ

Cohen, R. (2011, 5 June). The White House and Pentagon Deem Cyber-Attacks "An Act of War." *Forbes.* www.forbes.com/sites/reuvencohen/2012/06/05/the-white-house-and-pentagon-deem-cyber-attacks-an-act-of-war/

Constantin, L. (2015, April 9). Islamist Hackers Take French Broadcaster TV5Monde Off Air. *Computerworld.* www.computerworld.com/article/2908355/islamist-hackers-take-french-broadcaster-tv5monde-off-air.html

Cooke, S. (2014, February 27). Does Social Media Enhance Political Participation and Representation? Politics@Surrey. https://blogs.surrey.ac.uk/politics/2014/02/27/does-social-media-enhance-political-participation-and-representation-3/

Coombs, C. (2012, September 16). The Innocence Protests Expose Deeper Tensions in Yemen. *Time.* http://world.time.com/2012/09/16/the-innocence-protests-expose-deeper-tensions-in-yemen/

Coughlin, C. (2014, November 5). How Social Media is Helping Islamic State to Spread its Poison. *Telegraph.* www.telegraph.co.uk/news/uknews/defence/11208796/How-social-media-is-helping-Islamic-State-to-spread-its-poison.html

Crane, C. (2012, December 11). Muslim Women, Activism, and New Media in Kenya. BCRW Blog. http://bcrw.barnard.edu/blog/muslim-women-activism-and-new-media-in-kenya/

Crilly, R. (2014, July 9). Pakistani Terror Group Swears Allegiance to Islamic State. *Telegraph.* www.telegraph.co.uk/news/worldnews/asia/pakistan/10955563/Pakistani-terror-group-swears-allegiance-to-Islamic-State.html

Davis, M. (2011) Spring Confronts Winter. *New Left Review* 72. http://newleftreview.org/II/72/mike-davis-spring-confronts-winter

The Dawn (2011, March 25). Province-Wide Demos Held Against US Pastor. www.dawn.com/news/615794/province-wide-demos-held-against-us-priest.

The Dawn (2012, July 24). Afghans Embrace Social Media as Nato Pullout Nears. www.dawn.com/news/736845/afghans-embrace-social-media-as-nato-pullout-nears

DeLong-Bas, N. (2015). The New Social Media and the Arab Spring. Oxford Islamic Studies Online. www.oxfordislamicstudies.com/Public/focus/essay0611_social_media.html

Dennis, E., Martin, J. & Wood, R. (2013, April 24). How People in the Middle East Actually Use Social Media. *The Atlantic.* www.theatlantic.com/international/archive/2013/04/how-people-in-the-middle-east-actually-use-social-media/275246/

Deutsche Welle (2012, February 24). Extremist Propaganda and Illiteracy Fuel Afghan Protests. www.dw.com/en/extremist-propaganda-and-illiteracy-fuel-afghan-protests/a-15767031

Diamond, L. & Plattner, M.F. (2012). *Liberation Technology: Social Media and the Struggle for Democracy.* Baltimore: Johns Hopkins University Press.

Di Giovanni, J., Goodman, L., & Sharkov, D. (2014, November 6). How Does ISIS Fund Its Reign of Terror? *Newsweek.* www.newsweek.com/2014/11/14/how-does-isis-fund-its-reign-terror-282607.html

Djerejian, E. (2003). *Changing Minds, Winning Peace: A New Strategic Direction for U.S. Public Diplomacy in the Arab and Muslim World.* Washington, DC: Advisory Group on Public Diplomacy for the Arab and Muslim World.

Douglas, W. (2013, November). Engaging the Muslim World. http://csis.org/files/publication/131011_Douglas_EngagingMuslimWorld_Web.pdf

Dovlatov, D. (2011, January 4). Pepsi Takes Lead in Russia's Dairy and Juice Market. *Telegraph.* www.telegraph.co.uk/sponsored/rbth/business/8239184/Pepsi-takes-lead-in-Russias-dairy-and-juice-market.html

Dudley, R. (2013, March 6). Web Campaign Will be Game-Changer. *New Straits Times* (Malaysia). www2.nst.com.my/nation/social-media-web-campaign-will-be-game-changer-1.229379

The Economist (2014, August 30). It Ain't Half Hot Here, Mum. www.economist.com/news/middle-east-and-africa/21614226-why-and-how-westerners-go-fight-syria-and-iraq-it-aint-half-hot-here-mum

The Economist (2014, September 13). A Virtual Revolution: Why Social Media Have a Greater Impact in the Kingdom Than Elsewhere. www.economist.com/news/middle-east-and-africa/21617064-why-social-media-have-greater-impact-kingdom-elsewhere-virtual

The Economist (2015, January 10). Terror in Paris. www.economist.com/news/leaders/21638118-islamists-are-assailing-freedom-speech-vilifying-all-islam-wrong-way-counter

Erdbrink, T. (2012). Iran Denounces Florida Pastor Over Koran Burning. *New York Times.* www.nytimes.com/2012/05/01/world/middleeast/iran-denounces-florida-pastor-over-koran-burning.html?_r=0

Farber, M. (2016, December 19). Uber's Middle East Rival Just Got a $1 Billion Valuation. http://fortune.com/2016/12/19/careem-uber-rival-1-billion/

Fayed, H. (2015, January 2). Al-Azhar Responds to Sisi's Call for "Religious Revolution." *Cairo Post.* www.thecairopost.com/news/132144/news/al-azhar-responds-to-sisis-call-for-religious-revolution

Fears, D. (2014, November 1). ISIS Gives Tips on How to be a Good Jihadi Wife. *New York Post.* http://nypost.com/2014/11/01/isis-media-wings-tips-on-how-to-be-a-good-jihadi-wife/

Feldman, N. (2011, October 30). Islamists' Victory in Tunisia a Win for Democracy. Bloomberg View. www.bloombergview.com/articles/2011-10-30/islamists-victory-in-tunisia-a-win-for-democracy-noah-feldman

Field, N. & Hamam, A. (2009). Salafi Satellite TV in Egypt. *Arab Media and Society*, 8. www.arabmediasociety.com/?article=712

Fisher, M. (2013, April 23). Syrian Hackers Claim AP Hack That Tipped Stock Market by $136 Billion. Is it Terrorism? *Washington Post.* www.washingtonpost.com/blogs/worldviews/wp/2013/04/23/syrian-hackers-claim-ap-hack-that-tipped-stock-market-by-136-billion-is-it-terrorism/

Fisher, M. (2013, October 31). How the World's Populations are Changing, in One Map. *Washington Post*. www.washingtonpost.com/blogs/worldviews/wp/2013/10/31/how-the-worlds-populations-are-changing-in-one-map/

Fisk, R. (2015, September 2). Isis Profits from Destruction of Antiquities by Selling Relics to Dealers – and Then Blowing Up the Buildings They Come from to Conceal the Evidence of Looting, Independent. http://www.independent.co.uk/voices/isis-profits-from-destruction-of-antiquities-by-selling-relics-to-dealers-and-then-blowing-up-the-10483421.html

Fouché, G. (2006, February 10). Malaysia Gans Muhammad Cartoons. *Guardian*. www.theguardian.com/media/2006/feb/10/pressandpublishing.race

France24 (2008, March 28). Fitna is Just a Really Bad Film. http://observers.france24.com/content/20080328-fitna-geert-wilders-anti-islam

Franceschi-Bicchierai, L. (2014, September 12). Russia's "Facebook" Cracking Down on ISIS Accounts. Mashable. http://mashable.com/2014/09/12/isis-islamic-state-vkontakte-russia/

Freedom House (2013). Tunisia: Freedom on the Net. www.freedomhouse.org/report/freedom-net/2013/tunisia#.VISl29KueCo

Freedom House (2014). Press Freedom Rankings. https://freedomhouse.org/report/freedom-press-2014/press-freedom-rankings#.VI9wRc5dWXg

Freedom House (2017). Press Freedom Rankings. https://freedomhouse.org/report/freedom-press/freedom-press-2017

Gabriel, A. (2013, July 21). Malaysia's Media Firms Click to Next Page. *Straits Times* (Singapore). http://news.asiaone.com/print/News/AsiaOne%2BNews/Malaysia/Story/A1Story20130722-439037.html

Gais, H. (2014, October 3). Fighting Extremists One Tweet at a Time. US News and World Report. www.usnews.com/opinion/blogs/world-report/2014/10/03/fight-against-islamic-state-group-hits-twitter-and-social-media

Galloway, A.R. (2004). *Protocol: How Control Exists After Decentralization*. Cambridge, MA: MIT Press.

Galperin, E., Marquis-Boire, M. & Scott-Railton, J. (2013, December 22). Quantum of Surveillance: Familiar Actors and Possible False Flags in Syrian Malware Campaigns. Electronic Frontier Foundation. www.eff.org/files/2013/12/28/quantum_of_surveillance4d.pdf

Geo News Urdu (2017, April 26). Former TTP Spokesman Ehsanullah Ehsan Admits RAW, NDS Using Terrorists to Destabilise Pakistan. https://www.geo.tv/latest/139525-Confessional-video-of-former-TTP-spokesman-Ehsanullah-Ehsan-released-pakistan-army

Ghannam, J. (2011, February 3). Social Media in the Arab World: Leading up to the Uprisings of 2011. Center for International Media Assistance. www.cima.ned.org/wp-content/uploads/2015/02/CIMA-Arab_Social_Media-Report-10-25-11.pdf

Ghosh, B. (2012, September 13). The Agents of Outrage. *Time Magazine*. http://world.time.com/2012/09/13/the-agents-of-outrage/

Gilbertson, A. (2014, July 21). Charter Schools: Audit Finds Missing, Misused Funds at LA Network. KPCC. www.scpr.org/blogs/education/2014/07/21/17031/audit-finds-missing-misused-funds-at-la-charter-ne/

Gladwell, M. (2011, February 2). Does Egypt Need Twitter? *New Yorker.* www.newyorker.com/online/blogs/newsdesk/2011/02/does-egypt-need-twitter.html

Global Coalition (2017, March 22). Working to Defeat Daesh. http://theglobalcoalition.org/en/the-global-coalition-working-to-defeat-daesh/

Global Voices (2013, September 29). Saudi Clergyman Delivers Ground-Breaking Science on Why Women Shouldn't Drive. Global Voices. http://globalvoicesonline.org/2013/09/29/saudi-clergyman-delivers-ground-breaking-science-on-why-women-shouldnt-drive/

Gonsalves, A. (2013, April 2015). Islamic Group Expands Targets In Bank DDoS Attacks. www.networkworld.com/article/ 2165676/byod/islamic-group-expands-targets-in-bank-ddos-attacks.html

Goodspeed, P. (2012, April 21). Goodspeed Analysis: The Arab Spring May Have Helped Usher In A New Era Of Government Surveillance. National Post. http://news.nationalpost.com/full-comment/goodspeed-analysis-governments-could-soon-record-and-store-everything-their-citizens-do-from-birth-to-death

Gorman, S. & Barnes, J.E. (2011, 31 May). Cyber Combat: Act of War. *Wall Street Journal.* www.wsj.com/articles/SB10001424052702304563104576355623135782718

Gutman, R. (2014, December 15). Amid Silent Press, Turkish Journalists Use Social Media to Condemn Editors' Arrests. McClatchy DC. www.mcclatchydc.com/news/nation-world/world/middle-east/article24777460.html

Halkon, R. (2015, July 27). ISIS Opens "Souvenir Gift Shop" Selling Branded Baseball Caps and Replica Execution Swords. *Mirror.* http://www.mirror.co.uk/news/world-news/isis-opens-souvenir-gift-shop-6148419

Hamill, J. (2014, June 27). Anonymous Hacktivists Prepare for Strike Against ISIS "Supporters." *Forbes.* www.forbes.com/sites/jasperhamill/2014/06/27/anonymous-hacktivists-prepare-for-strike-against-isis-supporters/

Hannigan, R. (2014, November 3). The Web is a Terrorist's Command-and-Control Network of Choice. *Financial Times.* www.ft.com/cms/s/2/c89b6c58-6342-11e4-8a63-00144feabdc0.html#axzz3dDVKxIzA

Harb, Z. (2011). Arab Revolutions and the Social Media Effect. *M/C Journal* 14(2). http://journal.media-culture.org.au/index.php/mcjournal/article/viewArticle/364

Harding, L. (2006, September 30). How One of the Biggest Rows of Modern Times Helped Danish Exports to Prosper. *Guardian.* www.theguardian.com/world/2006/sep/30/muhammadcartoons.lukeharding

Hasselbarth, S. (2014). Islamic Charities in the Syrian Context in Jordan and Lebanon. Friedrich-Ebert-Stiftung. http://library.fes.de/pdf-files/bueros/beirut/10620.pdf

Herbert, D. (2013). *Creating Community Cohesion: Religion, Media and Multiculturalism.* New York: Palgrave Macmillan.

Hern, Al. (2015, November 2015). Anonymous "At War" With Isis, Hacktivist Group Confirms. *Guardian.* www.theguardian.com/technology/2015/nov/17/anonymous-war-isis-hacktivist-group-confirms

Herrera, L. & Lotfy, M. (2012). E-Militias of the Muslim Brotherhood: How to Upload Ideology on Facebook. *Jadaliyya*. www.jadaliyya.com/pages/index/7212/e-militias-of-the-muslim-brotherhood_how-to-upload

Hurriyet Daily News (2017, January 26). Turkey Ranks 75th in Corruption Perceptions Index Amid Continued Downfall. http://www.hurriyetdaily news.com/turkey-ranks-75th-in-corruption-perceptions-index-amid-continued-downfall.aspx?pageID=238&nID=108999&NewsCatID=339

Hussain, A.J. (2007). The Media's Role in a Clash of Misconceptions: The Case of the Danish Muhammad Cartoons. *The International Journal of Press/Politics* 12(4): 112–30.

Hussain, G. & Saltman, E. (2014). Jihad Trending: A Comprehensive Analysis of Online Extremism and How to Counter It. Quilliam Foundation. www.quilliamfoundation.org/wp/wp-content/uploads/publications/free/jihad-trending-quilliam-report.pdf

Iasiello, E. (2013) Cyber Attack: A Dull Tool to Shape Foreign Policy. 5th International Conference on Cyber Conflict. https://ccdcoe.org/publications/2013proceedings/d3r1s3_Iasiello.pdf

IBN Live (2012, September 19). Chennai: 20,000 Take to Streets in Anti-Islam Film Fury. http://ibnlive.in.com/news/chennai-20000-take-to-streets-in-antiislam-film-fury/293152-62-130.html.

International Monetary Fund (2014, January). World Economic Outlook (WEO) Update. www.imf.org/external/pubs/ft/weo/2014/update/01/

Jolly, D. (2011, November 2). Satirical Magazine is Firebombed in Paris. *New York Times*. www.nytimes.com/2011/11/03/world/europe/charlie-hebdo-magazine-in-paris-is-firebombed.html

Jones, R. and Al Omran, A. (2014, October 17). Ban on Women Drivers in Saudi Arabia Gives Taxi Apps a Boost. *Wall Street Journal*. www.wsj.com/articles/ban-on-women-drivers-in-saudi-arabia-gives-taxi-apps-a-boost-1413456923

Jorquera, R. (2013, May 8). Protest at the Speed of Light: Social Networking the Revolution. Links. http://links.org.au/node/3334

Kaur, J. (2013, July 14). The Red Bean Army Witch-Hunt. *The Malaysian Insider*. www.freemalaysiatoday.com/category/opinion/2013/07/14/the-red-bean-army-witch-hunt/

Kehar, T. (2012, July). Blessing in Disguise. SA Global Affairs. www.saglobalaffairs.com/back-issues/1249-blessing-in-disguise.html

Kendzior, S. (2013, February 10). Twitter's Dangerous Lack of Transparency on Terrorism. Al Jazeera. http://www.aljazeera.com/indepth/opinion/2013/02/201321015712442895.html

Kersey, B. (2013, January 9). Anonymous Petitions the White House to Make DDoS Attacks a Legal Form of Protesting. The Verge. www.theverge.com/2013/1/9/3856202/anonymous-wants-ddos-attacks-to-be-protected-under-free-speech

Khilafah (2011, June 21). Social Media and Islamic Revival. www.khilafah.com/social-media-and-islamic-revival/

Kiefer, B. (2015, June 2). In Saudi Arabia, Social Media Prompts Culture Change. Campaign. www.campaignlive.com/article/saudi-arabia-social-media-prompts-culture-change/1349552

Kincaid, J. (2009, August 25). Confirmed: Yahoo Acquires Arab Internet Portal Maktoob. TechCrunch. http://techcrunch.com/2009/08/25/confirmed-yahoo-acquires-arab-internet-portal-maktoob/

Kirkpatrick, D. (2011, October 22). Financing Questions Shadow Tunisian Vote, First of Arab Spring. *New York Times*. www.nytimes.com/2011/10/23/world/africa/tunisia-election-faces-financing-questions.html?pagewanted=all&_r=1

Kirkpatrick, D. (2012, January 21). Islamists Win 70% of Seats in the Egyptian Parliament. *New York Times*. www.nytimes.com/2012/01/22/world/middleeast/muslim-brotherhood-wins-47-of-egypt-assembly-seats.html.

Kirkpatrick, D. (2014, November 10). Militant Group in Egypt Vows Loyalty to ISIS. *New York Times*. www.nytimes.com/2014/11/11/world/middleeast/egyptian-militant-group-pledges-loyalty-to-isis.html

Kong, L. (2013, April 7). Malaysian Politicians Go All A-Twitter; Upcoming General Election Promises Action on the Ground and in Cyberspace. *Straits Times* (Singapore).

Kravets, D. (2011, January 11). What's Fueling Mideast Protests? It's More Than Twitter. Wired. www.wired.co.uk/news/archive/2011-01/28/middle-east-protests-twitter

Kully, S. (2010, September 19). In True New York Spirit—Who Cares? blog. dawn.com. http://blog.dawn.com/2010/09/19/in-true-new-york-spirit-%E2%80%93-who-cares/

Lamer, W. (2012). Twitter and Tyrants: New Media and its Effects on Sovereignty in the Middle East. *Arab Media & Society*, 16. www.arabmediasociety.com/articles/downloads/20120826084958_Lamer_Wiebke.pdf

Larson, V. (2014, December 16). This Mysterious Twitter User Predicts Turkish Government Crackdowns. *Foreign Policy*. http://foreignpolicy.com/2014/12/16/this_mysterious_twitter_user_predicts_turkish_government_crackdowns/

Latief, H. (2013). The Politics of Benevolence: Political Patronage of Party-based Islamic Charitable Organizations in Contemporary Indonesia. Muhammadiyah University of Yogyakarta. www.academia.edu/6255381/The_Politics_of_Benevolence_Political_Patronage_of_Party-based_Islamic_Charitable_Organizations_in_Contemporary_Indonesia

Laville, S. (2014, April 15). Social Media Used to Recruit New Wave of British Jihadis in Syria. *Guardian*. www.theguardian.com/world/2014/apr/15/social-media-recruit-british-jihadis-syria-twitter-facebook

Lavizzari, A. (2013, May 22). The Arab Spring and the Funding of Salafism in the MENA Region. International Security Observer. http://securityobserver.org/the-arab-spring-and-the-funding-of-salafism-in-the-mena-region/

Lee, J. (2014, September 22). #Notinmyname: Muslims Speak Out Against Islamic State. *USA Today*. www.usatoday.com/story/news/nation-now/2014/09/22/notinmyname-islamic-state-muslims-speak-out/16039911/

Lengel, L. & Newsome, V. (2012). Framing Messages of Democracy Through Social Media: Public Diplomacy 2.0, Gender, and the Middle East and North Africa. *Global Media Journal*. http://scholarworks.bgsu.edu/cgi/viewcontent.cgi?article=1001&context=smc_pub

Leung, R. (2005, March 11). Slaughter and "Submission." www.cbsnews.com/news/slaughter-and-submission-11-03-2005/

Lidsky, L.B. (2012). Incendiary Speech and Social Media. UF Law Scholarship Repository. http://scholarship.law.ufl.edu/cgi/viewcontent.cgi?article=1216&context=facultypub

Liljas, P. (2013, November 27). "My Afro Is Melting": Syrian Rebels Want Hair Products and iPads. *Time.* http://world.time.com/2013/11/27/my-afro-is-melting-syrian-rebels-want-hair-products-and-ipads/

Lillis, J. (2014, February 27). Uzbekistan's Coca-Cola Problem: Is It the Real Thing? Eurasianet. http://www.eurasianet.org/node/66608

Lillis, J. (2014, November 17). McDonald's Partners with Gas Tycoon to Open First Store in Kazakhstan. *Guardian.* www.theguardian.com/world/2014/nov/17/mcdonalds-partner-gas-tycoon-open-first-restaurant-kazakhstan

Lim, I. (2013, June 3). Malaysia's Pendrive Man Denies Links to "Red Bean Army" Fabrication. *Malaysian Insider.* www.themalaysianinsider.com/malaysia/article/malaysias-pendrive-man-denies-links-to-red-bean-army-fabrication/

Lipman, V. (2012, January 30). The World's Most Active Twitter City? You Won't Guess It. *Forbes.* www.forbes.com/sites/victorlipman/2012/12/30/the-worlds-most-active-twitter-city-you-wont-guess-it/

Lowe, A. (2011, December 3). Turmoil in Arab World Tests PepsiCo's Growth Strategy. Gulf News Retail. http://gulfnews.com/business/sectors/retail/turmoil-in-arab-world-tests-pepsico-s-growth-strategy-1.942304

Lunden, I. (2014, September 16). Mail.ru Takes Over "Russia's Facebook" Vkontake in $1.47B Deal, Settles Durov Suit. Tech Crunch. http://techcrunch.com/2014/09/16/mail-ru-pays-1-47b-to-take-over-vkontake-russias-facebook-settles-durov-suit/

Lynch, C. & Hauslohner, A. (2013, January 28). Release "Blind Sheik" Omar Abdel Rahman from Prison, Islamists Urge U.S. *Washington Post.* http://articles.washingtonpost.com/2013-01-28/world/36585616_1_egyptian-cleric-islamists-blind-cleric

Lynch, S. (2013, September 26). Muslim Brotherhood Down, Not Out, in Egypt. *USA Today.* www.usatoday.com/story/news/world/2013/09/25/egypt-muslim-brotherhood/2868647/

Mahavera, S. (2014, February 8). PAS Counters Race-Baiting With "Turun" Campaign. *Malaysian Insider.* www.themalaysianinsider.com/malaysia/article/pas-goes-to-the-ground-to-remind-malaysians-on-the-real-issues

Mahjoub, S. (2015). Coding, Designing, Branding, and Business Modeling for an Economic Inclusion of Tunisian Youth. IndieGoGo. www.indiegogo.com/projects/wecode-inno-tech-for-tunisian-youth#/story

Mahmood, F. (2013, March 6). Social Media in the Muslim World: A Discussion. Fletcher Forum. www.fletcherforum.org/2013/03/06/pandit/

Malaysian Digest (2013, June 3). UPDATED: Insulting The Agong, Will Melissa Gooi Please Stand Up? *Malaysian Digest.* www.malaysiandigest.com/news/63911-insulting-the-agong-will-melissa-gooi-please-stand-up.html

Malik, N. (2012, September 18). Sudan's Hashtag-free Protests Over Innocence of Muslims. *Guardian.* www.theguardian.com/commentisfree/2012/sep/18/sudan-protests-innocence-of-muslims.

Malik, S. (2014, 28 November). Support for Isis Stronger in Arabic Social Media in Europe than in Syria. *Guardian*. www.theguardian.com/world/2014/nov/28/support-isis-stronger-arabic-social-media-europe-us-than-syria

Marquis-Boire, M. (2013, May 1). For Their Eyes Only: The Commercialization of Digital Spying. Citizen Lab and Canada Centre for Global Security Studies, University of Toronto. https://citizenlab.org/storage/finfisher/final/fortheireyesonly.pdf

Mason, P. (2013, February 5). From Arab Spring to Global Revolution. *Guardian*. www.theguardian.com/world/2013/feb/05/arab-spring-global-revolution

Masood, A. (2008, March 22). Afghans Chant Death in Cartoon Protest. Reuters. www.reuters.com/article/2008/03/22/us-afghan-cartoons-idUSISL1279420080322?pageNumber=1&virtualBrandChannel=0

Maubert, C. (2013, September 4). Jihad 2.0: How Social Media Supports Islamist Agendas in Syria. INPEC. http://inpecmagazine.com/2013/09/04/jihad-2-0-how-social-media-supports-islamist-agendas-in-syria/

Mecham, Q. (2006) From Sacred to State. Unpublished doctoral dissertation, Stanford University.

MediaBadger (2011, April 4). Muslim Women and Social Media: An Overview. MediaBadger. www.wunrn.com/news/2011/06_11/06_20/062011_muslim.htm

Mekhennet, S. & Miller, G. (2016, October 4). This ISIS Defector Said He Was an Innocent Bystander. A New Video Questions His Story. *Washington Post*. www.washingtonpost.com/world/national-security/how-a-former-isis-recruit-and-media-darling-edited-his-own-story/2016/10/04/5740ff50-8582-11e6-a3ef-f35afb41797f_story.html

Meky, S. (2014, August 24). Egypt's Dar al-Ifta: ISIS Extremists Not "Islamic State." Al Arabiya English. http://english.alarabiya.net/en/News/middle-east/2014/08/24/Islamic-authority-Extremists-no-Islamic-State-.html

Meo, N. & Freeman, C. (2012, September 15). Middle East Protests: Meet The Hardline "Tele-Islamist" Who Brought Anti-Islam Film to Muslim World's Attention. *Telegraph*. www.telegraph.co.uk/news/worldnews/africaandindianocean/egypt/9545515/Middle-East-protests-meet-the-hardline-tele-Islamist-who-brought-anti-Islam-film-to-Muslim-worlds-attention.html

Mohamad, M. (2008, June 16) Openness. dr-chedet.blogspot.com. http://dr-chedet.blogspot.com/2008/06/openness.html.

Money Jihad (2011, March 29). Muslim Aid in Foreign Politics. https://moneyjihad.wordpress.com/2011/03/29/muslim-aid-in-foreign-politics/

Morozov, E. (2011). *The Net Delusion: The Dark Side of Internet Freedom*. New York: PublicAffairs.

Mostaghim, R. (2008, April 5). Observations from Iraq, Iran, Israel, the Arab World and Beyond. http://latimesblogs.latimes.com/babylonbeyond/2008/04/iran-dutch-fitn.html

Mourad, M. & Bayoumi, Y. (2015, May 31). Special Report: Egypt Deploys Scholars to Teach Moderate Islam, but Skepticism Abounds. Reuters. www.reuters.com/article/2015/05/31/us-egypt-islam-azhar-special-report-idUSKBN0OG07T20150531

Mullany, G. (2013, May 9). In Malaysia's Election, a Free Press Was Elusive. *New York Times Blogs (IHT Rendezvous)*. http://rendezvous.blogs.nytimes. com/2013/05/09/in-malaysias-election-a-free-press-was-elusive/?_r=0

Mulrine, A. (2014, December 1). Why Did FBI Urge US Troops to Scrub Social Media Accounts? *Christian Science Monitor*. www.csmonitor.com/ USA/Military/2014/1201/Why-did-FBI-urge-US-troops-to-scrub-social-media-accounts-video

Murphy, E. (2014, November 4). Youth Challenges in the MENA Region. Middle East Monitor. https://www.middleeastmonitor.com/articles/ guest-writers/15067-youth-challenges-in-the-mena-region

Mustafa, M. (2013, April 10). 26 Political Blogs Under Police Watch. *New Straits Times* (Malaysia). www2.nst.com.my/sports/soccer/26-political-blogs-under-police-watch-1.252166

Nahon, K. & Hemsley, J. (2013). *Going Viral*. Cambridge, UK: Polity.

Najafizada, E. & R. Nordland (2011, April 1). Afghans Avenge Florida Koran Burning, Killing 12. *New York Times*. www.nytimes.com/2011/04/02/ world/asia/02afghanistan.html?pagewanted=all.

Nakaohima, E. (2012, 26 October), When is a Cyber-Attack an Act of War? *Washington Post*. www.washingtonpost.com/opinions/when-is-a-cyberattack-an-act-of-war/2012/10/26/02226232-1eb8-11e2-9746-908f727990d8_story.html

The News (Pakistan) (2011, March 24). Rallies Staged Against Desecration of Holy Koran. www.thenews.com.pk/Todays-News-13-4846-Rallies-staged-against-desecration-of-Holy-Quran

New Straits Times (2013, March 17). Khairy: Battle for GE13 Will Take Place in Cyberspace. *New Straits Times* (Malaysia). www2.nst.com.my/streets/ northern/khairy-battle-for-ge13-will-take-place-in-cyberspace-1.236291

New Straits Times (2013, June 11). Necessary Regulation. *New Straits Times* (Malaysia). http://www.highbeam.com/doc/1P1-216762831.html

Nguyen, D. (2013, June 8). Transnational Public Spheres on the Internet: On the Versatility of Political Discourse in the Age of Digital Communication. Kosmopolitika.http://kosmopolitica.org/2013/06/08/transnational-public-spheres-on-the-internet-on-the-versatility-of-political-discourse-in-the-age-of-digital-communication/

Norman, H. (2011, May 30). The Emergence of Open and Organized Pro-Government Cyber Attacks in the Middle East: The Case of the Syrian Electronic Army. Infowar Monitor. www.infowar-monitor. net/2011/05/7349/

Orocoglu, B. (2015, January 6). Why Turkey's Mother of All Corruption Scandals Refuses to Go Away. *Foreign Policy*. http://foreignpolicy. com/2015/01/06/why-turkeys-mother-of-all-corruption-scandals-refuses-to-go-away/

Otto, J.M. (2008). *Sharia and National Law in Muslim Countries*. Amsterdam: Leiden University Press. https://openaccess.leidenuniv.nl/bitstream/ handle/1887/20694/Sharia%20and%20national%20Law%20in%20 Muslim%20countries.pdf?sequence=1

Pandya, S. (2012). Introduction: The Hismet Movement Abroad. In S. Pandya & N. Gallagher, *The Gulen Hizmet Movement and its Transnational Activities*. Boca Raton, FL: Brown Walker.

Pannier, B. (2015, June 28). Russian Soft Power in Central Asia. Radio Free Europe. www.rferl.org/content/russian-soft-power-in-central-asia/27098601.html

Paraszczuk, J. (2014, October 31). How To Be a Good Islamic State Wife. Radio Free Europe Radio Liberty. www.rferl.org/content/battle-snacks-video-editing-how-to-be-good-islamic-state-wife-syria-iraq/26668491.html

Paraszczuk, J. (2014, December 30). Islamic State Magazine Lauds Sydney Hostage-Taker, Calls for More "Lone Wolf" Attacks. Radio Free Europe Radio Liberty. www.rferl.org/content/islamic-state-dabiq-sydney-lone-wolf-attacks/26769336.html

Paudyal, N. (2015). Interesting Data Showing the Worldwide Social Media Trends. Lifehack. www.lifehack.org/articles/work/interesting-data-showing-the-worldwide-social-media-trends.html

Pearlman, L. (2012, November). Tweeting to Win: Al-Shabaab's Strategic Use of Microblogging. *Yale Review of International Studies.* http://yris.yira.org/essays/837

Penny, L. (2011, February 15). Revolts Don't Have to be Tweeted: Laurie Penny on a Force Bigger Than Technology. *New Statesman.* www.newstatesman.com/blogs/laurie-penny/2011/02/uprisings-media-internet

Petré, C. (2014, December 19). What Messages Do Tunisian Youth Have For the Next President? World Bank. http://blogs.worldbank.org/arabvoices/what-messages-do-tunisian-youth-have-next-president

Pew Research Center (2013, April 30). The World's Muslims: Religion, Politics and Society. www.pewforum.org/2013/04/30/the-worlds-muslims-religion-politics-society-overview/

Pua, T. (2012, July 6). Tony Pua Ordered to Pay RM200,000 Damages to SYABAS. *Philosophy Politics Economics.* http://tonypua.blogspot.com/2012/06/tony-pua-ordered-to-pay-rm200000.html

Pua, T. (2012, July 10). SYABAS Insists on RM200k Payment by 16 July 2012. *Philosophy Politics Economics.* http://tonypua.blogspot.com/2012/07/syabas-insists-on-rm200k-payment-by-16.html

Pua, T. (2012, July 15). "Tony Pua v. SYABAS" Fundraiser: Mission Accomplished. *Philosophy Politics Economics.* http://tonypua.blogspot.com/2012/07/tony-pua-vs-syabas-fund-raiser-mission.html

Qatar Culture Club (2012, September 19). Coke Studio. Qatar Culture Club. http://qatarcultureclub.blogspot.com/2012/09/coke-studio.html

Rabie, P. (2007, August 22). New Islamic Channel Launches on NileSat. Masress.com. www.masress.com/en/dailynews/115867

Recorded Future (2014, August 1). How Al-Qaeda Uses Encryption Post-Snowden (Part 2)—New Analysis in Collaboration With Reversing Labs. www.recordedfuture.com/al-qaeda-encryption-technology-part-2/

Reddy, M. (2013, August 15). Can Social Media Sustain a Revolution? E-International Relations. www.e-ir.info/2013/08/15/can-social-media-sustain-a-revolution/

Religion of Peace. (2006). Charity and Disaster Relief. www.thereligionofpeace.com/Quran/027-disaster-relief.htm

Reporters Without Borders. (2011, February 10). Reporters Without Borders in Tunisia: A New Freedom That Needs Protecting. Reporters Without Borders. http://en.rsf.org/tunisie-reporters-without-borders-in-10-02-2011,39519.html

Reporters Without Borders (2011, August 16). Tunis Court Upholds Order Requiring Filtering of Porn Sites. http://en.rsf.org/tunisia-court-to-take-crucial-decision-for-01-07-2011,40566.html

Retter, J. (2013, July). Technology and Revolutions. McGill Political Science Journal.

Reuters (2012, December 9). Aramco Says Cyberattack Was Aimed at Production. *New York Times.* www.nytimes.com/2012/12/10/business/global/saudi-aramco-says-hackers-took-aim-at-its-production.html?_r=0

Reuters (2015, February 10). Foreign Fighters Still Flowing to Syria, U.S. Intelligence Says. http://www.reuters.com/article/2015/02/11/us-mideast-crisis-fighters-idUSKBN0LE2YX20150211

Reuters Canada (2011, September 28). Insight: Social Media—a Political Tool for Good or Evil? http://ca.reuters.com/article/technologyNews/idCATRE78R3CM20110928?pageNumber=2&virtual BrandChannel-0

Robinson, J. (2014, December 31). The Federation—a Statistics Hub. http://pods.jasonrobinson.me/

Rohac, D. (2012, October 31). The Secret of Islamist Success. Cato Institute. www.cato.org/publications/commentary/secret-islamist-success

Ross, M. (2012, April 11). Coke Studio Debuts in the Middle East. *Rolling Stone.* http://archive.is/xo61I

Roussinos, A. (2013, December 5). Jihad Selfies: These British Extremists in Syria Love Social Media. Vice. www.vice.com/en_uk/read/syrian-jihadist-selfies-tell-us-a-lot-about-their-war

RT (2012, September 17). Indonesian Police Use Tear Gas to Disperse Anti-US Protest. http://rt.com/news/police-jakarta-us-embassy-303/

Rubin, M. (2005). Green Money, Islamist Politics in Turkey. *Middle East Quarterly.* www.meforum.org/684/green-money-islamist-politics-in-turkey

Safranek, R. (2012, March). The Emerging Role of Social Media in Political and Regime Change. ProQuest Discovery Guides. www.google.co.uk/url?s a=t&rct=j&q=&esrc=s&source=web&cd=2&ved=0CCcQFjAB&url=http %3A%2F%2F188.129.255.234%2Funi%2Felectronic_library%2Fdo wnload%2F298&ei=pxuNVYLJOcLC7Aa6qoHoBQ&usg=AFQjCNHaJ ca7eMqkNb9vot3GJnWHkRqm6w

Salt, J. (2012). Containing the Arab Spring. *Interface* 4(1): 54–66.

Sani, R. & Khalili, S. (2012, July 22). Keeping Online Misconduct in Check. *New Straits Times* (Malaysia). www2.nst.com.my/business/latest/trends-keeping-online-misconduct-in-check-1.323686/facebook-comments-7.467890

Saudi Gazette (2015, July 21). McDonald's launches first independently-produced TV series this Ramadan. www.saudigazette.com.sa/index.cfm?method=home.regcon&contentid=20130725174695

Saul, H. (2014, October 31). Isis Now Targeting Women With Guides on How to be "the Ultimate Wives of Jihad." *Independent.* www.independent.co.uk/news/world/middle-east/isis-now-targeting-women-with-guides-on-how-to-be-the-ultimate-wives-of-jihad-9830562.html

Schmidt, E. & Cohen, J. (2013). *The New Digital Age: Reshaping the Future of People, Nations and Business.* New York: Knopf.

Schroeder, C. (2013, January 28). 3 Opportunities the West Misses in the Middle East. *Fortune.* http://finance.fortune.cnn.com/2013/01/28/middle-east-investing/

Scott, J. (1986). *Weapons of the Weak.* New Haven, CT: Yale University Press.

Sennott, C. M. (2011, February 7). Egypt: Muslim Brotherhood Influence Felt at Tahrir Square. *Global Post.* www.globalpost.com/dispatch/egypt/110207/egypt-muslim-brotherhood-tahrir-square

Shahbaz, A. (2014, January 21). Three Years After Arab Spring Officials Thwart Digital Dissent. Index on Censorship. www.indexoncensorship.org/2014/01/three-years-arab-spring-officials-thwart-digital-dissent/

Shenker, J. (2011, June 3). Fury over advert claiming Egypt revolution as Vodafone's. *Guardian.* www.theguardian.com/world/2011/jun/03/vodafone-egypt-advert-claims-revolution

Shirky, C. (2011). The Political Power of Social Media. *Foreign Affairs.* www.foreignaffairs.com/articles/2010-12-20/political-power-social-media

Shull, H. (2012, October 3). Egypt's Maria TV Pitches Strict Vision of Islam. *Washington Post,* http://articles.washingtonpost.com/2012-10-03/world/35498801_1_abdallah-egyptian-women-coptic-christian.

Singh, U. (2011, January 31). Some Weekend Work That Will (Hopefully) Enable More Egyptians To Be Heard. *Google Public Policy Blog* http://googlepublicpolicy.blogspot.co.uk/2011_01_01_archive.html

Smith, M. (2013, January 28). Twitter Will Run Ads in Middle East to Target "Arab Spring" User Base. Business Insider. www.businessinsider.com/twitter-will-run-ads-in-middle-east-to-take-advantage-of-arab-spring-user-base-2013-1?IR=T

Snoj, T.N. (2014, May 19). Crowdfunding—the New Source of Venture Capital in the Middle East. BQ. http://www.bqdoha.com/2014/05/crowdfunding-new-source-venture-capital

Social Bakers (2014). Egypt Facebook Statistics. www.socialbakers.com/facebook-statistics/egypt

Somaiya, R. (2011, February 2). Hackers Shut Down Government Sites. *New York Times.* www.nytimes.com/2011/02/03/world/middleeast/03hackers.html?_r=0

Soylu, R. (2014, July 16). Scandal Ridden Gülen Schools Spark Disturbance Amongst Parents in US. *Daily Sabah.* www.dailysabah.com/politics/2014/07/16/scandal-ridden-gulen-schools-spark-disturbance-amongst-parents-in-us

Spencer, R. (2015, February 4). Anti-Islamic State Group Says It Believes It Knows Where Jordanian Pilot Was Burned Alive. *Daily Telegraph.* www.telegraph.co.uk/news/worldnews/islamic-state/11390643/Anti-Islamic-State-group-says-it-believes-it-knows-where-Jordianian-pilot-was-burned-alive.html

Sreberny-Mohammadi, A. (1990). Small Media For a Big Revolution: Iran. *International Journal of Politics, Culture, and Society* 3(3), 341–71.

Stalinsky, S. & Sosnow, R. (2014). Al-Qaeda's Embrace of Encryption Technology—Part II: 2011–2014, and the Impact of Edward Snowden. *Inquiry & Analysis Series Report* (No. 1086). http://cjlab.memri.org/lab-projects/tracking-jihadi-terrorist-use-of-social-media/al-qaedas-embrace-of-encryption-technology-part-ii-2011-2014-and-the-impact-of-edward-snowden/

Stalinsky, S., & Sosnow, R. (2015). As Twitter Removes Some ISIS Accounts, Al Qaeda's Branch in Syria Jabhat Al Nusra (JN) Thrives, Tweeting Jihad and Martyrdom to Over 200000 Followers. The Cyber & Jihad Lab. http://cjlab.memri.org/lab-projects/tracking-jihadi-terrorist-use-of-social-media/as-twitter-removes-some-isis-accounts-al-qaedas-branch-in-syria-jabhat-al-nusra-jn-thrives-tweeting-jihad-and-martyrdom-to-over-200000-followers/

Statista (2017). Internet User Penetration in Middle East and Africa from 2015 to 2020. https://www.statista.com/statistics/325703/middle-east-africa-internet-user-penetration/

Stone, J. (2014, August 22). Blocked on Twitter and YouTube, ISIS Turns to Diaspora and VKontakte to Disseminate Message. *International Business Times*. www.ibtimes.com/blocked-twitter-youtube-isis-turns-diaspora-vkontakte-disseminate-message-1666758

Strauss, V. (2012, March 27). Largest Charter Network in U.S.: Schools Tied to Turkey. *Washington Post*. www.washingtonpost.com/blogs/answer-sheet/post/largest-charter-network-in-us-schools-tied-to-turkey/2012/03/23/gIQAoaFzcS_blog.html

Strickland, J. (2015). How YouTube Works. howstuffworks. http://money.howstuffworks.com/youtube3.htm

Strom, S. (2012, March 6). Web Sites Shine Light on Petty Bribery Worldwide. *New York Times*. www.nytimes.com/2012/03/07/business/web-sites-shine-light-on-petty-bribery-worldwide.html?_r=0

Tagine, S. (2013, December 3). Is Tunisia Becoming a Hotbed for Money Laundering? Al-Monitor. www.al-monitor.com/pulse/security/2013/12/tunisia-post-revolution-hotbed-money-laundering.html#

Tan, C.C. (2013, May 5). Our First "Social Media Elections." *New Straits Times*. www.highbeam.com/doc/1P1-215724814.html

Tan, C.C. (2013, June 30). "Transforming MCA is a Do-Or-Die Mission Now." *Business Times*. www2.nst.com.my/business/latest/transforming-mca-is-a-do-or-die-mission-now-1.310245

Tanweer, B. (2014, May 5). Coke Studio, Pakistan. Interactive. http://interactive.net.in/coke-studio-pakistan/

Taspinar, O. (2012, April). Turkey: The New Model? Brookings. www.brookings.edu/research/papers/2012/04/24-turkey-new-model-taspinar

Thomasson, E. (2008, March 6). Dutch Raise Threat Level Ahead of Anti-Koran Film. Reuters. http://in.reuters.com/article/worldNews/idINIndia-32339620080306

Thompson, D. (2014, March 21). What Will Drive Economic Growth in the Middle East? Middle CFA Institute. http://meic.cfainstitute.org/2014/03/21/what-will-drive-economic-growth-in-the-middle-east/

Time (2009, December 8). Top 10 Heroes: Neda Agha-Soltan. *Time*. http://content.time.com/time/specials/packages/article/0,28804,1945379_1944701_1944705,00.html

Time (2017, June 4). Read Prime Minister Theresa May's Full Speech on the London Bridge Attack. http://time.com/4804640/london-attack-theresa-may-speech-transcript-full/

Torchia, A. & al-Khalida, S. (2012, January 17). Insight: In Arab Spring, Economic Gain May Trump Pain. Reuters. www.reuters.com/article/2012/01/17/us-arabspring-economies-idUSTRE80G0CH20120117

Trager, E. (2014, May 19). The Muslim Brotherhood Thinks It's Winning Again. *New Republic*. www.newrepublic.com/article/117820/egypts-muslim-brotherhood-thinks-its-winning-war-future

Tremblay, P. (2013, December 19). Pro-AKP Media Flop as Corruption Charges Swell. Al-Monitor. http://www.al-monitor.com/pulse/originals/2013/12/pro-akp-media-flop-corruption-charges-credibility-failures.html#ixzz3fdorgAZx

Trilling, D. (2014, October 31). World Bank Downbeat on Tajik Economy, Lays Bare Dependence on Russia. Inside the Cocoon. http://www.eurasianet.org/node/70716

Trzcinski-Clément, S. (2010, September 23). Our First Ever G-Days in Egypt and Jordan. Google Code. http://googlecode.blogspot.co.uk/2010/09/our-first-ever-google-days-in-egypt-and.html

Tucker, N. (2014, May 18). The Central Asia Digital Islam Project: How the Internet and Social Media are Reshaping the Islamic Marketplace in Central Asia. Registan. http://registan.net/2014/05/18/the-central-asia-digital-islam-project-how-the-internet-and-social-media-are-reshaping-the-islamic-marketplace-in-central-asia/

The Turkafile (2014, August 5). Twitter Phenomenon Fuat Avni Banned in Turkey. www.turkafile.com/hot-topic/2014/08/05/twitter-phenomenon-fuat-avni-banned-in-turkey/

Ufen, A. (2009). The Transformation of Political Party Opposition in Malaysia and its Implications for the Electoral Authoritarian Regime. *Democratization* 16(3): 604–27. www.academia.edu/4210424/The_Transformation_of_Political_Party_Opposition_in_Malaysia_and_its_Implications_for_the_Electoral_Authoritarian_Regime

Uras, U. (2013, December 24). Turkish Probe Marks AKP-Gulen Power Struggle. Al Jazeera. www.aljazeera.com/indepth/features/2013/12/turkish-probe-marks-akp-gulen-power-struggle-2013122473646994231.html

Vachon, C. (2011, January 25). Tonight in Cairo, the Parliament is Surrounded. The Awl. http://www.theawl.com/2011/01/tonight-in-cairo-the-parliament-is-surrounded

Vice News (2014, July 11). ISIS Releases Recruitment Video of Militants Giving Candy to Children. Youtube video. www.youtube.com/watch?v=i2fAofF39Eg#t=33

Voices from the Blogs (2014, October 27). ISIS: Perception on News On-Line and Social Media Considering Only Posts and Articles Written in Arabic Language. https://voicesfromtheblogs.files.wordpress.com/2014/11/isis_on_newssocialmediavoices.pdf

Wagner, M. (2014, August 23). Apparent ISIS Terrorists Take Photos with Nutella to Seem Softer, Friendlier to West. www.nydailynews.com/news/world/isis-fighters-photos-nutella-friendly-article-1.1914450

Walt, V. (2012, September 21). After Protests, Tunisia's Salafists Plot a More Radical Revolution. *Time*. http://world.time.com/2012/09/21/after-protests-tunisias-salafists-plot-a-more-radical-revolution/

Warrick, J. (2013, September 21). Private Donations Give Edge to Islamists in Syria, Officials Say. *Washington Post*. www.washingtonpost.com/world/national-security/private-donations-give-edge-to-islamists-in-syria-officials-say/2013/09/21/a6c783d2-2207-11e3-a358-1144dee636dd_story.html

Warrick, J. (2013, November 4). Islamist Rebels in Syria Use Faces of the Dead to Lure the Living. *Washington Post*. www.washingtonpost.com/world/national-security/islamist-rebels-in-syria-use-faces-of-the-dead-to-lure-the-living/2013/11/04/10d03480-433d-11e3-8b74-d89d714ca4dd_story.html

Warrick, J. (2017, August 18). ISIS's Propaganda Machine Is Thriving as the Physical Caliphate Fades. Washington Post. www.washingtonpost.com/world/national-security/isiss-propaganda-machine-is-thriving-as-the-physical-caliphate-fades/2017/08/18/4808a9f6-8451-11e7-ab27-1a21a8c006ab_story.html?utm_term=.5886a02d6667

Waseem, M. & Mufti, M. (2009). Religion, Politics and Governance. University of Birmingham Religions and Development Research Programme, Working Paper 27.

Washington Times (2015, January 7). Charlie Hebdo Mocked Islamic State's al-Baghdadi in Last Tweet Before Attack. *Washington Times*. www.washingtontimes.com/news/2015/jan/7/charlie-hebdo-abu-bakr-al-baghdadi-mocked-last-twe/

Watson, K. (2011, June 28). Saudi Women Turn To Social Media For the Right to Drive. BBC News. www.bbc.com/news/business-13928215

Weimann, G. (2014). New Terrorism and New Media. Woodrow Wilson International Center for Scholars. www.wilsoncenter.org/publication/new-terrorism-and-new-media

Weisenthal, J. (2012, September 19). France Plans to Close 20 Embassies After Magazine Publishes Satirical Mohammed Cartoon. Business Insider. www.businessinsider.com/france-plans-to-close-20-embassies-after-charlie-hebdo-publishes-mohammed-cartoon-2012-9?IR=T

Weiss, M. L. (2009). Edging Toward a New Politics in Malaysia: Civil Society at the Gate? *Asian Survey* 49(5): 753–54.

Welsh, B. (2013, November 21). A New Battlefield for PAS: The Campaign. Din Merican. http://dinmerican.wordpress.com/2013/11/21/a-new-battlefield-for-pas-the-campaign/

Weprin, A. (2012, March 22). Layoffs at CNN as Network Transitions to Acquisition Model for Documentary Programming. TV Newser. www.mediabistro.com/tvnewser/layoffs-at-cnn-as-network-transitions-to-acquisition-model-for-documentary-programming_b117576

Westrop, S. (2013, July 3). UK Funds Terror Connections: Islamic Relief Worldwide. Gatestone Institute. www.gatestoneinstitute.org/3792/islamic-relief-worldwide-terrorism

White House (May 2011). International Strategy for Cyberspace. www.whitehouse.gov/sites/default/files/rss_viewer/international_strategy_for_cyberspace.pdf

Wiktorowicz, Y. (2001). *The Management of Islamic Activism: Salafis, the Muslim Brothehood, and State Power in Jordan.* Albany, NY: Suny Press.

Winter, C. & Clarke, C.P. (2017). Is Isis Breaking Apart? *Foreign Affairs.* https://www.foreignaffairs.com/articles/2017-01-31/isis-breaking-apart

Wintrobe, R. (2006). Extremism, Suicide Terror, and Authoritarianism. *Public Choice* 128(1–2): 169–95.

World Bank (2015). Mobile Cellular Subscriptions (Per 100 People). World Bank. http://data.worldbank.org/indicator/IT.CEL.SETS.P2

World Bank (2017). Mobile Cellular Subscriptions (per 100 People). World Bank. http://data.worldbank.org/indicator/IT.CEL.SETS

World Post (2012, September, 14). Sudan Embassies Attack: Protesters Target British, German Embassy in Khartoum. www.huffingtonpost.com/2012/09/14/sudan-embassies-attack_n_1883749.html

Yaqub, A. (2013, October 3). Middle East Smartphone Usage Trends. *Arabian Gazette.* www.arabiangazette.com/middle-east-smartphone-usage-trends-infographic-2013100/

Young, A. (2012, December 25). Saudi Arabia's Own "Salman Rushdie" Arrested for Mohammad Tweets. *International Business Times.* www.ibtimes.com/saudi-arabias-own-salman-rushdie-arrested-mohammad-tweets-968536.

YouTube (2015). Statistics. www.youtube.com/yt/press/statistics.html

Zanini, M. & Edwards, S. (2001). The Networking of Terror in the Information Age. In J. Arquilla & D. Ronfeldt (eds), *Networks and Netwars.* Santa Monica, CA: Rand. www.prgs.edu/content/dam/rand/pubs/monograph_reports/MR1382/MR1382.ch2.pdf

Zelin, A. (2013, December 4). New Statement from the Global Islamic Media Front: "Warning About The Use Of The Program 'Asrār Al-Ghurabā'." Jihadology. http://jihadology.net/2013/12/04/new-statement-from-the-global-islamic-media-front-warning-about-the-use-of-the-program-asrar-al-ghuraba/

Zennie, M. (2014, September 4). The American Computer Wiz Running Brutally Effective ISIS Social Media Campaign. www.dailymail.co.uk/news/article-2743737/The-American-computer-wiz-running-ISIS-brutally-effective-social-media-campaign-College-educated-son-Boston-doctor-FBI-Most-Wanted-list.html

INDEX

ILLUSTRATION CREDITS

1 YouTube, uploaded by "TheTunisietunisia," 2010.

2 PEN.

3 Vimeo, "Power to You, Vodafone Egypt," Ninja Marketing, 2012.

4 Twitter, "Salafai_Jihadi" account, 2014.

5 Twitter, "Sami Shah" account, 2013.

6 BBC, ISIS image posted to Arabic video game social media accounts, 2014.

7 Bryan Denton.

8 Sahar Richa Khan.

9 Facebook, "Imran Khan (official)" page, 2013.

10 Twitter, "Jama 'ud' Da'wah" account, 2012.

11 Fathiyah/VOA.

12 Twitter, "The Associated Press" account, 2013.